WITHDRAWN

CONTEMPORARY SOCIAL THOUGHT

CONTEMPORARY SOCIAL THOUGHT

Contributors and Trends

M. C. ELMER

UNIVERSITY OF PITTSBURGH PRESS

Library of Congress Catalog Number: 56-12214

CONTENTS

Preface

Recently a statement was made that during the past sixty years greater changes have taken place in social thinking than have occurred in the natural sciences. It is not possible to separate one area of knowledge from the other. Their growth and change have been interdependent and co-existent. The difference is found largely in ideas of the experts of each field of thought. Because of the rapidity of change which has taken place, the persons working in one area tend to be far behind in their understanding of the other. This gives rise to mutual accusations of inadequacy.

The purpose of this book is to indicate the part contributions of sociologists during the past seventy-five years have played in developing concepts which have become basic in the ideas, ideals, attitudes, and practices of America.

This volume on contributions to sociological thought has not developed suddenly. It is not limited to a summary of the published statements of contributors to the various areas. Rather, it contains, in addition to such published statements, the background of many of the chief contributors. It includes personal statements to the author from over two hundred sociologists, many of them now dead, regarding what they considered to be their chief contributions and objectives. Sometimes the contribution which is considered of greatest significance by a sociologist may be relatively unknown to others within the field. This may be due to the vagaries of publication or to a phrase which is easily grasped. An example is the "consciousness of kind" concept of Giddings, which he considered of rather minor significance among his contributions, but which is used again and again by writers who discuss his contribution to sociology. Throughout the entire period covered there has been steady growth and development. While many of the major concepts were recognized for centuries, their development and application vary with the changes and growth of new social situations. Likewise, the interpretation and application made by different sociologists have been largely influenced by the social experiences of each. An attempt has been made to bring together many aspects of the development of sociology which, in addition to what is found in other books and articles, are the result of contact and personal knowledge of these contributors since 1909 when the first of such contacts was made with Lester F. Ward. The last decade is discussed only as "in process," including mere touches of what is familiar to all, and what is included in the sense of highlights of the passing panorama. What will be the actual highlights of the last half of the twentieth century cannot be determined. This, however, is apparent: where the basic social concepts were recognized by a few score individuals sixty years ago, today they have become the basis for everyday thinking and acting of untold millions. Ideas which were debated by a small group of scholars have become incorporated into the life and living processes of people throughout the world. This has been made possible through the growth of mass communication, by which means sociological principles have become a part of everyday thinking.

Manuel C. Elmer
University of Pittsburgh
June, 1956

I

Social Trends and Trends in Sociology

SOCIOLOGICAL thought usually follows social trends, but social thought, at the same time, lays the basis for social action by giving impetus to new approaches. Sociology as a discipline follows certain particular lines of thought; the emphasis, however, is determined by the trends of interest in society. The average person pays no attention to systems of thought. He works day by day, and is moved by the stream of life about him. Every idea is the result of centuries of experience which some person puts into a definite statement. Sociology is concerned with human relations and with group activities and their interrelationship.

The results of sociological study may manifest themselves in a wide variety of forms. To some extent they represent a varied social philosophy, and to some extent they depend upon a particular, often temporary, status of social structure, of social processes, of social organization, of social conditions, or of social activities. An event may occur in society which will focalize the attention of the general public upon a situation, and give rise to a demand for information and for data. Sometimes a small group of sociologists in the van of some major social event comes to represent a dominant line of thought activity, but represents no more a permanent and basic line of thought than a small creek which because of a cloudburst becomes a torrent. Shifts of interest in human affairs gives rise to emphasis on new topics dealing with human affairs. At any period of time, different writers represent a wide variation in their interests. Their contributions lead out in many directions. Then, due to a combination of social situations, public interest tends to determine the direction of social thought and inquiry. In such a manner a relatively minor aspect of general sociology may become dominant for a period of time.

No exact date can be given for the beginning of contemporary social thought. In fact, aspects of practically any group relationship may be found in the writings of ancients. The period of 800 to 500 B.C. contains expressions of many of the principles which today we think of as contemporary social thought. In the remnants of the writings and pronouncements by Confucius, Laotze, The Vedic Laws, Buddha, Zoroaster, the minor prophets of the Hebrews, Hammurabi, and the ancient Egyptians and Greeks, we may find many principles which form the basis for contemporary sociological thinking. Many of these principles were assembled by a group of men who were known to persons still active in the field of sociology. When Albion W. Small, Lester F. Ward, William Graham Sumner, Franklin H. Giddings, and others got together in 1895, it was the actual functional beginning of the development of sociological thought in America.

The rapid specialization which soon began to take place caused Albion W. Small to say: "Sociologists are specializing so minutely on particular types of human groupings that they are in danger of losing sight of human society as a whole." That situation is true in any area of thinking which is concerned with social action, hence, in order to maintain an even keel it is well to trace the development of thinking toward the accepted principles. It shall, also, be our plan to present incidents and experiences of some of the leaders of social thought which may, in part, help us to understand the conclusions they reached. Long ago someone said, "If we knew everything about everybody, we wouldn't blame anybody for anything." If we knew more about the apparently insignificant things of a man's life, we might have some explanation of why certain things are emphasized over and against other apparently more important matters.

In much of our history of the past, as found in the literature, there is the expression of individual thinking. This may have been of a high type, and may, at certain times, have shown peaks of development which have reached far above the general plateau of social thinking represented in life today. Consequently, many persons will select ideal-istic writings of the past, and conclude that the people of another age excelled our generation in social thinking. Comparison, however, is being made between the heights obtained by an individual genius and the general level of the multitude. It is this general level which we must consider in discussing social thought, and when we speak of a leader in social thinking, we are merely concentrating on the person who has put into concrete form the unexpressed thoughts of the group.

During the last half of the nineteenth century, many previously undeveloped forms of group association were taking form. These added to the older social groupings which had developed through the ages gave rise to a variety of new situations for which there were no established accepted procedures. Under the general designation of "sociologists," individuals interested in human relationships began to attempt to apply rules of knowledge to the subject matter in particular fields. They began to assemble facts about human association under the widely divergent areas of interest developed by Charles R. Henderson, Mayo-Smith, Veblen, Ida Tarbell, Upton Sinclair, Jacob Riis, Jane Addams, Graham Taylor, Robert Hunter, and Amos Warner. This created the need for a conceptional approach. It was needed, not only to present the facts about human association, but to discern repetitious similarities which could be crystalized into a single, inclusive, understandable, logical relationship. The problem of organizing meanings and explana- tions of various aspects of group relationships into a clear pattern was difficult since available knowledge has often been little more than scattered observations. Because of the lack of exact information there had been a tendency to interpolate explanations which were frequently unwarranted and which caused confusion because of the lack of accepted conceptual agreement and understanding. Individual sociologists some- times used terms which to them very nearly explained a combination of circumstances, but these terms gave rise to different meanings to other persons. The development of accepted concepts, consequently, became one of the first problems for this group of early sociologists whom we intend to consider.

A start had been made by European scholars. Two apparently divergent lines of thought were taking form. One was based upon philosophical concepts, the other emphasized objective measurement. We will, first, consider the approach stressed by the social philosophers since the second group did not begin to exert much influence in America until some later years, even though recognized by a few individuals like Mayo-Smith and Giddings.

European Sociologists
of the Nineteenth Century

Sociological thinking in Europe did much to focalize the develop- ment of social thought in America, and may be briefly indicated by certain representative sociologists. Any difference of opinion with the selection made merely emphasizes the sociological contention that an individual is a product of a period in human experience, rather than the character of a period being the result of an individual's contribution.

We have selected three European sociologists to serve as examples of the phase of sociology considered in this period; Auguste Comte, Herbert Spencer, and Ludwig Gumplowicz. In later chapters where other phases are discussed, mention will be made of other men.

About 1830-1840 sociological interest was represented by Comte.[1] The main sociological positions of Auguste Comte were derived from St. Simon's *Conceptions of Science Politique*. St. Simon, in turn, had based his treatise upon the principles and works of others preceding him. Comte brought together the opinions of Turgot, Condorcet, Kant,

---

[1] Isidore Auguste Marie Francois Xavier Comte, 1798-1857, was born at Mont- pellier, France, of middle class parents who were devout Catholics and Royalists.

Herder, Hume, Montesquieu, and many others. Like any writer who brings together the more or less scattered thinking of his period, Comte's major contribution was in systematizing and integrating the social thinking of his time. We may thus state that while, on the one hand, Comte is spoken of as the founder of sociology, it is not because of the new principles which he expounded, but rather because he pulled together points of view and principles already known. From this basis a new type of structure was developed. In the first quarter of the nineteenth century there were dynamic efforts to systematize the thinking of the past. Comte appeared on the scene and gave a name and made a positive attempt to organize social thought. While his purpose was to formulate the basic principles of a science of society, he found it necessary first to develop a philosophy of the sciences. As sociologists, we are not inclined to attribute an idea, a principle, or a system of thought to any one individual, but rather we hold that the individual, appearing at a particular time, becomes the magnet which focalizes the various elements into a system which would have occurred even if the person with whom the origin of the structure is associated had not existed.

Comte suggested that political and social institutions must be studied in a setting of their entire configuration. They are not based upon a logical plan, but rather the result of social needs and historical development. Consequently, they must be studied on the basis of sociological principles and not the natural laws proclaimed by some of the earlier philosophers. The function of social control, which later became an important line of thought with sociologists of the early twentieth century, was recognized by Comte, and so was a recognition of the social processes involved in social trends. Comte has played a lesser part in sociology since his day than one might have expected. This resulted, in part, because of the pressure of specific problem phenomena and because of the emphasis upon isolated situational analyses. It may be that sociology was not yet ready for a comprehensive reorganization of the social order.

Auguste Comte was apparently the first man to use the term sociology. His chief contribution, *Positive Philosophy,* (1835), held that all fields of study are directly related to each other and grow out of each other. This idea resulted in a hierarchy of the sciences, i.e., mathematics, astronomy, chemistry, physics, biology, social sciences, and finally sociology. He, also, presented the three stages in the development of thinking: theological, philosophical, and scientific. Comte did much to consolidate thinking up to the middle of the nineteenth century. He helped to bring together the diverse emphases on social thinking found among historians before the time of Eichhorn, Neibuhr, and Savigny. After the writings of these men, and probably influenced by the Comte

interpretation, historians began to include more emphasis on social interpretations. Statisticians like Conring, Petty, Graunt, Sussmilch, Achenwall, Halley, Jean Baptiste Fourier, and Quetelet were attempting to
explain social phenomena largely with objective data. A new school of
philosophers was being heard, and the political economic programs of
Robert Owen, St. Simon as well as Voltaire, Rousseau, Kant, Adam
Smith, Fichte, and Herder were beginning to be noted. Some of the
interest was diverted into the channels emphasized by Karl Marx,
Proudhon, Engels, and others.

Auguste Comte began an ambitious plan of sixty-two lectures to
be delivered to the French leaders of thought which would combine the
scientific and the philosophical approaches based upon objective information and critical analysis. These were carefully prepared, but before
he delivered the second lecture, he became violently insane and was confined in the Esquirol Insane Asylum. While there, in periods of lucidity,
he completed his six volumes on *The Course of Positive Philosophy*. He
would think out a book completely from cover to cover without the aid
of references or written notes. Then, page after page of the manuscript
would appear, written from memory.

Comte held that it is sociology which will bring together and utilize
the results of preliminary sciences which affect human relations, but
that it will be necessary to make use of the results of other sciences.
Comte considered it necessary in the demonstration of sociology to check
induction by deduction. He found that in order to demonstrate sociology,
we need both a knowledge of human nature and conclusions reached
from a study of human history, and that both induction and deduction
must play a part in scientific procedure. This approach is the keynote
of positive philosophy.

Auguste Comte did not make any new discovery. He simply gave
general direction and focalized the interest of philosophers and of
scientists to the connection or association between group life and logical
thinking. Comte marked a stage in the development of sociological
thinking where fact and observation began to be recognized, although
it still remained largely a mixture of social philosophy, philosophy of
history, and pseudo-science.

Comte was interested in positive philosophy about the same time
that Adolphe Quetelet was attempting to explain social phenomena in
terms of statistical measurement, Robert Owen was emphasizing group
interest in human welfare and in industrial reform, and Darwin, A. R.
Wallace, and others were calling attention to biological inheritance.
Even Goethe antidated Darwin and Wallace with his study of the
inferior and superior maxillary bone of the sheep. The general social
trend of thought emphasizing biology became so dominant that it in-

fluenced the trend of sociology. For the next two decades sociological thinking was typified by Lillienfield and by Schaeffle in his "Bau und Leben des Sozialen Korpers." In 1859 Treitschke brought forth his "Gersellschaft und Wissenschaft" which was concerned with an attempt to treat the data of human association scientifically. Although he considered the prospect of a scientific approach to the study of sociology unsound, he actually stated some of the principles which sociologists have since developed.

While Comte directed the attention of some social philosophers toward sociology, Herbert Spencer aroused the interest of natural scientists, and in fact most of the English speaking and writing leaders.

Herbert Spencer was born in 1820 and died in 1903. Young Herbert was taught by his father chiefly in mathematics and the physical sciences, and until he was twenty-two, when he designed an airplane, he devoted himself largely to those fields. In 1837 he was chief engineer of the London and Birmingham Railroad, and retained that position until 1848. However, his father, who was considered somewhat radical in social views, directed his son's attention toward social problems. Herbert Spencer shifted from his interest in engineering and concentrated on a somewhat biologic and economic interpretation of society. Young Spencer began to write articles in The Non-Conformist, criticizing the extension of government control over the lives of the people and advocating the limitation of governmental activities to the preservation of the social order. By the time he was twenty-eight he was giving up the idea of becoming an engineer and was devoting his time entirely to writing. He became associate editor of the Economist. In his early thirties Spencer had shifted from his discussion of the function of the state and had begun to write in the field of social philosophy. He presented his idea in a paper on the development hypothesis. The paper dealt with the general theory of evolution. During the years from 1855 to 1860 Spencer's ideas had been presented in his Principles of Psychology and the beginning of his work on Synthetic Philosophy. This work was undertaken because Spencer feared that Darwin's Origin of the Species, published in 1859, would divert the recognition which was developing in his favor. In 1873 he had prepared a monograph on the Study of Sociology which is thought by some to be his best book. This was several years before his first volume on Principles of Sociology appeared in 1876. His interest then was turned to ethics for several years so that it was not until 1896 that his third volume on Principles of Sociology appeared. During this period in the development of Spencer's writing, there also appeared his eight volumes on Descriptive Sociology to which he chiefly gave direction and inspiration, but the work was done almost exclusively by his secretaries. Spencer's health

SOCIAL TRENDS, EUROPEAN					7

was never very good. Even as a young man his poor health was largely responsible for his failure to attend Cambridge University. Probably his health had as much to do with the matter as the fact that Cambridge University did not offer much engineering work. The story is told of Spencer that in his more mature years he was unable to work consistently for more than fifteen or twenty minutes at a time. Because of this he had wooden pegs prepared which fitted in his ears. If he was not feeling well, he did not object to talking with visitors, but if an idea came into his mind that he wanted to write, he would ignore his visitors, would put his pegs in his ears, and would work until he was fatigued. It is almost impossible for us to appreciate how Spencer's extensive writing was accomplished under such handicaps. However, his large secretarial staff made it possible. Unmarried, Spencer lived a rather isolated life, and he was, at times, hard pressed for finances.

Spencer popularized sociology to the English speaking world, but not until 1873, when Spencer wrote his *Study of Sociology* and included it as a part of his synthetic philosophy, was sociology considered of importance to the scientific world. Although Spencer never acknowledged his indebtedness to Auguste Comte, many of his principles were stimulated by Comte. But, as we stated when mentioning Auguste Comte, Herbert Spencer might have developed many of his principles as he did without Comte, or someone else would have done so to some extent. Spencer's method of writing was very largely in the form of presenting an hypothesis or a speculation and bolstering this projection by extensive illustrations. This is, at times, so effective that the reader is carried along and is nearly convinced, stopping only when Spencer comes in direct conflict with certain other established points of view.

Spencer was the product of a variety of concepts, principles, and fields of study. He sometimes mingled the ideas of fatalism, of biological survival, of social psychology, and of an enlightened philosophy. As a result, Spencer was the center of many of the conflicting whirlwinds of opinion which appeared during his life time. Sometimes these gave rise to a new approach to an understanding of society as was the case in the controversy which arose between Spencer and Lester F. Ward.

Herbert Spencer was not a reformer; he was a social philosopher, and as he stated in his autobiography: "Thus while admitting that for the fanatic some wild anticipation is needful as a stimulus . . . the men of the higher type must be content with greatly moderated expectations, while he perseveres with undiminished efforts. He has to see how comparatively little can be done, and yet find it worth-while to do that little: so uniting philanthropic energy with philosophic calm."[2] Spencer be-

---

[2] *Autobiography*, II, p. 403.

lieved that the slower the rate of integration occuring among the complex evolutionary processes in society, the more satisfactory results
would be obtained. Spencer was in every respect a social philosopher to
whom the immediate solution of an apparent problem was of significance only if it fitted into the larger, long time, broad viewpoint of
sociology. He lacked any reliable method of investigation which was
definitely a weakness as was his gloomy laissez-faire conclusions so
vigorously challenged by Lester F. Ward. Spencer was popular with a
group of persons who were fearful of any planned objective, although
the publication of his *Study of Sociology,* beginning in 1872, and the
growth of his *Principles of Sociology,* 1874-1885, give sociology permanent recognition in English speaking countries.

As an example of a third type of thinking which appeared in
Europe and which had a marked effect on American social thought, we
have selected Gumplowicz. Ludwig Gumplowicz (1829-1909) represents
a growing crystallization of social thought in the beginning of the
period with which we are concerned. On the one hand, he brought
together the thinking of European sociologists, but on the other hand,
in later life he was greatly influenced by Americans, particularly Lester
F. Ward with whom he had considerable contact. Gumplowicz was born
in Cracow of Jewish parents. After studying in Cracow and Vienna,
he entered the practice of law. He became docent at the University of
Grag in 1875 and in 1882 an associate professor of law. His family
life was filled with many hardships, including the unfortunate death
of his son, his wife's blindness for several years, and his own affliction
of cancer. He and his wife both committed suicide in 1909. Much of
this gives a reason for his particular emphasis on conflict. While already
interested in race and the state in 1875, it was in 1883 that he wrote
what he considered his outstanding contribution, *Der Rassenkampf.*
Some sociologists consider his *Grundriss der Soziologie* (1885), translated by F. W. Moore in 1899 as *Outlines of Sociology,* of more importance. Gumplowicz may be classed among German sociologists in
somewhat the same position as Spencer was among the English and as
Comte was among the French. He recognized the contributions of
Comte, Quetelet, Spencer, Bastian, Lippert, Ward, and others. Probably influenced by his legal background and his materialistic concept,
he placed no importance on value judgments and the origin of groups.
He felt that men are governed in their relations to one another by
rigid inflexible laws; he gave no importance to individual volition or
free will. Rather than accepting the point of view that man thinks, he
felt that the community thinks, that mind and thoughts are the
product of the social medium, and that since social phenomena are the
operations of one group upon another, the tendency is for each group

to exploit others. While his work was somewhat one-sided, he aided the concentration of our attention upon the phenomena of conflict.

The main propositions of Gumplowicz were:

1. Social phenomena are subject to the general law of causation.
2. Human acts, whether individual or social, are the product of natural forces.
3. Society is not simply an organism analogous to, but as high above, man as man is above other organisms in nature. The social group is an organism different from any other; it is unlike any of its parts; system begins with social elements; man is a product of these in mind and body.
4. Every political organization and every developing civilization begins at the moment when one group permanently subjects another.

Gumplowicz played an important part in paving the way toward specific social processes which led to the study of various phenomena and concepts as his own work did to conflict theories.

With the background which was represented by Comte, Spencer, and Gumplowicz, we find sociological thinking emerging in America. There were less restrictive patterns and no established points of view to modify the contributions of the early American sociologists. This provided a fertile field for the growth and development of thought dealing with social processes found in the study of group activities and their interrelationships.

II

Emerging Sociology in America

THE MEANDERING of social thinking over the years is often the result of numerous personal factors. Some minor event, which seemed of such insignificance that it was never recorded, may have been the influence which determined the direction of social thinking. Likewise, advanced social thinking was sometimes lost to society because there was a lack of sufficient intelligent understanding among those to whom it was presented or because there was the absence of an understanding and appreciative audience.

These observations are evident in much of what is presented in the following pages. We have included the statements of what early leaders of social thought in America considered their contributions. These, in many cases, did not agree with what their contemporaries considered their contributions to be. Present day sociologists might explain many things in the publications of their contemporaries which could not be known to future sociologists. Without this explanation or interpretation by men who have had personal contact or personal knowledge of the writers, the actual significance of their studies might never be fully understood. In 1916 Albion W. Small said that one impression he had received from his years of study of the social scientists of the preceding four centuries was the lack of detailed and personal data. "Nearly every one of these writers might have done more for the instruction of subsequent generations if each had left on record certain testimony from his personal knowledge which he probably regarded as trifling and which his contemporaries would probably have pronounced impertinent, than they did by writing much of a more pretentious nature which they actually transmitted."[1] An attempt to provide some of this interpretative material from my own personal contact with most of the men who will be discussed will be one of the purposes of this book.

While there were several men who were active in the period of emerging sociology, we have included in this section Lester F. Ward, Franklin H. Giddings, William Graham Summer, and Albion W. Small. This group worked closely together in setting up the scope and general principles of sociology, and while differing to a very marked degree,

---

[1] Small, Albion W., "Fifty Years of Sociology in the United States, 1865 to 1915," *American Journal of Sociology,* Vol. 21, May, 1916, pp. 721-22.

they were working toward the same particular end. Other men whose contributions were somewhat more specialized are discussed in what follows.

Lester F. Ward, the youngest of ten children, was born near Joliet, Illinois, in 1841. His father, a member of a sturdy New England family, was a mechanic whose tendency to drift from place to place was not particularly annoying to his wife, who was the daughter of a clergyman named Loomis. When Ward was sixteen his father died, and he went to Pennsylvania to live with a brother. Here he worked on a farm and in a sawmill for his board and room. In his spare time he made wagon hubs which were traded for books, articles of clothing, and other things he needed. He picked up a scattered education which was largely un-directed; however, he became rather proficient in French, German, Greek, and Latin. For one year he attended an academy at Towanda, Pennsylvania. In 1862 he joined the army but was married before leav-ing for service. He was wounded in 1864 at Chancellorsville.

From 1865 to 1905 he was in government service, first as a clerk, then as librarian for the United States Bureau of Statistics, and finally the U. S. Geological Survey. In 1892 he became chief paleontologist. His work with the government enabled him to continue his academic studies and he received the A.B. in 1869, the LL.B. in 1872, the M.A. in 1872, and the LL.D. in 1897 from Georgetown University. Ward resigned from his work with the government in 1906 and went to teach sociology at Brown University where he remained for seven years until his death. He had accomplished a full lifetime of outstanding work in botany, geology, and paleontology by the time he was sixty-five, when he became the leading sociologist of America.

In the summer of 1909 a University of Wisconsin announcement stated that Lester F. Ward was giving a series of lectures there. I en-rolled for the six weeks at the University in a course given by Lester F. Ward of Brown University. Many prominent persons were at the University that summer attending special institutes. Among them were leaders of the Ethical Culture movement, such as Anna Garland Spencer and Henry Newman. Also present and attending Ward's lectures were Walter Rauschenbauch, who was working on "Christianity and the Social Crises," Ellen Gates Starr of Hull House, and Edward T. Divine who was giving New York and the East the same kind of leadership in applied sociology that C. R. Henderson was giving Chicago and the Middle West.

The first morning when he entered the room the class noted a tall man with square shoulders, side whiskers, and black heavy eyebrows over his well placed gray eyes. In a voice that was softer and higher pitched than his appearance would indicate, he announced that most of what he was going to cover in his lectures could be found by reading his *Dynamic Sociology* and his more recent volume on *The Psychic Factors of Civilization*. Further, that the keynote of what he had to say and what he would cover might be expressed in the statement that Mother Nature was cruel and harsh, and that she had left a path of destruction behind her where only the exceptional unit was able to survive. Ward felt that the real progress which the human race had made was based upon an understanding and application of the findings and discoveries of men. He startled the group by stating that "the artificial is superior to the natural." By artificial he meant the application of discovered techniques and procedures being applied to the course of nature. Directing our attention to his disagreement with Spencer, he stated that because of this he held that social progress depended upon a *planned objective*. Ward reached into his pocket and pulled out two peach stones. He threw one of them out of the window and said: "That peach stone may fall upon responsive soil and may grow into a peach tree. This other peach stone will be planted in soil which has been discovered to be suitable for peach trees. The young seedling will be grafted upon a sturdy root stock. It will be protected from disease, San Jose scale, and insect pests. As all the established knowledge of peach culture will be applied to aid the growth and protection of this tree, we are more certain of having a satisfactory peach tree." Ward then concluded his remarks by telling us that those who understood what he had said already knew all that would be presented to the group. Those who wished further discussion of it might find some profit in remaining in the class. He warned us to be accurate in repeating another person's ideas and stated, "My greatest problem regarding what I say at length is usually not a quotation of what I have said, but a misquotation."

In 1946 at a Convention in Chicago I met a nationally known geologist. He made a facetious remark about the sociology meeting and the geology meeting both being held in the Stevens Hotel, stating that the two fields represented extremes of interest. When asked if he had ever heard of Lester Frank Ward, he said, "Do you mean my old chief from the Geological Survey?" and was surprised to learn that he had also been "our chief."

Lester F. Ward, paleontologist, becoming interested in Spencer's inadequate interpretation, led out by 1885 with his monumental idea of dynamic sociology which is still significant. He emphasized what he called "*social telesis*" which he defined as a planned society where man's intelligent use of the products of nature are superior to the results of nature alone. However, the interest in that field would not have satisfied present day publishers. He stated that during the first ten years after his book was published only five hundred copies had been sold.

Ward's publications in his various fields of interest totaled nearly six hundred books, monographs, and articles. His principal writings in sociology were his great two volumes on *Dynamic Sociology,* which really contained his basic social philosophy, and his *Outlines of Sociology, The Psychic Factors of Civilization,* and *Applied Sociology.* There were, of course, many papers and articles which emphasized certain aspects of these subjects as well as his shorter volume prepared for a textbook and the extensive compilation of his papers and writings entitled *Glimpses of the Cosmos.*

As was stated earlier, sociology received an impetus when Herbert Spencer included sociology in his series on synthetic philosophy. Scientists in other fields took note. Lester F. Ward became interested, but questioned Spencer's emphasis upon natural selection. His point of difference was that human society as presently constituted is not the product of passive and unconscious forces. He felt that the mind of man is an important factor in shaping society into a useful instrument for man. Thus several years before psychological sociology began to be recognized Ward was a proponent of the importance of the psychic factors in civilization. He emphasized the difference between biological evolution and social evolution. Ward recognized and stressed the need for greater mass education and the equalization of knowledge. He foresaw the development of state control and urged a realistic social education. He feared that unless the rank and file of the population was lifted to a much higher plane of understanding that when exploiters of society are cast out in one form, they will simply appear in another. He once stated, "We are still in the Stone Age of Politics." While not a social reformer, he considered the value of sociology with its laws and principles to be of use to society in serving to reduce wasteful methods of social change and social evolution.

The influence of Lester F. Ward on contemporary social thought cannot be measured in terms of the number of contemporary sociologists who have read his works, nor by the reaction of a young professor who commented that Ward's ideas are of no importance since he died in 1913. Small said regarding Ward's concept of "Social Forces": "This concept played an important role in changing the current of American sociological thinking from the course which English theory had followed as a rule up to the present time—it amounted to the first impressive challenge of the fatalist's implications of Herbert Spencer's rendering of the evolutionary theory."[2]

He was independent in thought. In reading Lester F. Ward's diary, one observes that it was very early in the development of his

[2] *Ibid.,* p. 755.

social thinking that he found a point of disagreement with Herbert Spencer. Spencer believed in natural and social evolution, but based his belief largely on the principle of survival. However, Spencer placed little value on change within the individual unit of society. Ward felt that there was a certain distinction between natural development and artificial development. This he finally put into definite form in his *Dynamic Sociology*.[3] This early edition of his *Dynamic Sociology* also carried the subtitle "Applied Social Science as Based Upon Statistical Sociology and the Less Complex Sciences." Ward held that human selection deserved an appropriate term for its distinct expression, and proposed using the term teleology, which when applied to the action of man and to the plans and measures of man in society he qualified as Anthropo-teleology.

He states further, "The kind of social progress which is needed is teleological progress." This he felt should supersede the "slow and imperceptible genetic progress which society has thus far made,"—and which has barely kept pace with the increase of population. He held that natural forces always exist and that they operate according to fixed and invariable laws, but that while they can neither be created nor destroyed, they can be controlled. And hence, that many an individual by planned action based on what is known may succeed in harmonizing the lines of least resistance with those of greatest advantage to humanity.

Ward believed that the word 'teleology' expressed the general idea of the group of thinkers who may be represented as doing while those who hold the point of view that everything is being done are not represented by a comparable term. In Volume II of his *Dynamic Sociology* he stated that "psychic phenomena are always teleological and that while psychic phenomena are in a sense genetic, they are not the result of physical causes." There are, hence, two principle classes of phenomena, those produced genetically and those produced teleologically.

Ward suggests that teleological phenomena may be both direct and indirect or, as a secondary approach, natural and artificial. "The natural phenomena take place according to uniform laws, obey the mechanical axioms, are impelled by true natural forces."

The artificial phenomena are the teleological phenomena. Ward thus summarized the classification of phenomena:

"Genetic; physical; unconscious: producing change through infinitesimal increments.
Inorganic: the result of physical, or mechanical forces.
Organic: the result of vital, or biological forces.

[3] Appleton and Company, 1883, p. 28, 29, 34, 80, 105, 106.

Teleological; psychical; conscious; proceeding from volition and in-
volving purpose.
Direct: proceeding according to the direct method of conation.
Indirect: proceeding according to the indirect method of conation.
Zoological: as manifested by creatures below man.
Natural: taking place according to uniform laws, and produced by true
natural forces; capable of prediction and modification.
Anthropological: as manifested by man. Domain of the social forces.
Artificial: natural phenomena modified by the inventive faculty."

Individual planned effort, Ward held, was the principal kind employed at present, collective effort being still largely theoretical. Most
social progress, thus far, has been dependent upon individuals, the
operations of society being the result of the combined activities of individual members. This in spite of the fact that group consciousness is
more than the sum total of the individual consciousness. Ward concluded his discussion with the following statement: "The so-called over-
production takes place while men are starving, and while thousands
desire, want, and even need the very products whose production must
be abandoned . . . It is the natural result of individual telesis active
under the law of nature so far as society at large is concerned. It checks
production by choking circulation."

Ward considered collective effort to be the keynote of sociology.
"Sociology, as I understand it, differs in no essential respect from other
sciences except that it deals with the social forces." He held that individual planning did not involve the control of the social forces, and
that in general social progress had dealt chiefly with situations in which
the individual could act with some degree of effectiveness.

The general art of scientific control of the social forces by the
collective mind he summarized as follows:

"1. Individualism has created artificial inequalities.
2. Socialism seeks to create artificial equalities.
3. Sociocracy recognizes natural inequalities and aims to abolish
artificial inequalities.
4. Individualism confers benefits on those only who have the
ability to obtain them, by superior power, cunning, intelligence,
or accident of position.
5. Socialism would confer the same benefits on all alike, and aims
to secure equality of fruition.
6. Sociocracy would confer benefits in strict proportion to merit,
but insists on equality of opportunity as the only means of
determining the degree of merit."

The gist of Ward's sociology was in his own preface to the first
edition of *Dynamic Sociology*.

"1. The law of Aggregation as distinguished from Evolution proper.
2. The theory of Social Forces, and the fundamental antithesis which they imply between Feeling and Function.
3. The Contrast between these two Social Forces and the guiding influence of the intellect, embodying the application of the Indirect method of Conation, and the essential nature of Invention, of Art, and of Dynamic Action.
4. The superiority of Artificial, or Teleological, processes over natural or genetic processes.
5. The recognition and demonstration of the paramount necessity for the equal and universal distribution of the extant knowledge.

While there certainly have been adumbrations of many of these truths, it is believed that thus far no one of them has been systematically formulated or distinctly recognized."

In addition to giving Ward's opinion of his own contributions, the above statements give us a picture of his vigorous feeling of sufficiency when once his statements had been formulated. His years of effective work as a scientist may be reflected, in part, in his attitude of finality. Ward was profoundly impressed with his own conclusions and was outspoken in his rejection of other points of view. In 1912 I repeated to Edward Cary Hayes a statement heard in a lecture by L. F. Ward. Hayes smiled and responded, "It appears to me that Ward's conclusions are not correct. However, I may not be a competent critic since Ward has stated that because of my different point of view, I am not a sociologist."

Franklin H. Giddings has often been grouped with Ward, Sumner, and Small as one of the four outstanding pioneers in American sociology. Above all, Professor Giddings was a great teacher, endowed, as one of his students, Howard W. Odum, has said, ". . . with a charming style, keen analysis, inimitable humor and satire, logical thinking, lucid presentation."[4]

What are the real contributions of a man? Sometimes an unrecorded contact gives one the key to unknown "rooms of the house in which a man lives." Visualize a young teacher in a small western community who has a local study reported in the small town paper. He receives some local criticism and a little local publicity about his work. One morning in his mail there is a letter from Columbia University, and on opening it, he finds a letter written in longhand by Franklin H. Giddings, congratulating him on his work, urging him to continue the study, adding some advice about what he should do or should not do toward its publication, and suggesting ideas for future studies.

[4] Odum, Howard W., *Civilization and Society,* New York, Henry Holt and Company, 1932, p. v, (introductory note).

For several years whenever I published anything, Giddings would write to me and give advice and suggestions. I did not meet him in person until ten years after he had first written to me. He took the time to help and advise me after many other men who had been my teachers had long lost any interest in what I was doing.[5]

Franklin H. Giddings was born on March 23, 1855, in Sherman, Connecticut. His ancestry was rigid and Puritan. His father was a Congregational minister; one of his grandfathers had been a farmer, and his other grandfather, a tanner. Giddings felt that the religious practices of his home were boresome and depressing, and he always attempted, therefore, to deal with the practical aspects of life. His effectiveness as a teacher, as a leader, and as a propagandist for scientific methods and research in the field of sociology may have been modified, however, by his early life and training in the home and as a member of a Congregational preacher's family.

At Schenectady, New York, Giddings entered Union College and selected courses which would prepare him to become a civil engineer. Because he was not very much interested in his studies or in college life, he quit after two years. He then taught school in Massachusetts and Connecticut. In 1877, however, he received the degree of Bachelor of Arts from Union College, and then went into newspaper work. During a period of ten years he wrote for the *Winsted Connecticut Herald,* the *Springfield Republic,* and the *Springfield Union.* While connected with these newspapers, he learned much about the events of the world and about people which undoubtedly helped to prepare him

[5] While Giddings went out of his way to help a young unknown person who was teaching in a small college in Fargo, North Dakota, he did not hesitate to uncover and deflate individuals whom he thought needed it. In 1917 great interest was found in some circles with anything concerning Russia. In New York a noted bibliophile, Gustave Simonson, liked to give the impression of familiarity with all published books, including author, title, and dates. One evening it is reported that two writers, Richardson Wright and William George Jordan, asked Simonson whether he had ever seen a copy of *Vyvodne* by Feodor Vladimir Larrovitch, a famous Russian author. A number of people who were in on the joke got the Author's Club to sponsor a formal dinner in the memory of Larrovitch. A page from the "original manuscript" of his novel *Crasny Barba,* photographs, and other mementos were exhibited.

In 1918 Jordan and Wright edited a book under the title *Feodor Vladimir Larrovitch* — an appreciation of his life and work, including letters and an essay called "A Prolegomenon to Larrovitch" by Professor Franklin H. Giddings. *The Boston Transcript* "P6 J1 17 1918" seriously reviewed the book. *The Tribune* raised doubts as to its authenticity, and *The Nation* defended the book and criticized *The Tribune* and others who questioned his authenticity. It was not until after Giddings' death that the joke was uncovered.

[See "The Irisman in Larrovitch," *The Nation*, November 30, 1918, and Dennis, Joseph, "How Big Can a Joke Be," *Cosmopolitan*, September, 1949.]

for his future work in sociology. Also, at this time, Giddings read articles and books in the field of sociology, and wrote for the *Political Science Quarterly,* then being published at Columbia University, and for the Massachusetts Bureau of Statistics of Labor. These articles dealt chiefly with social aspects of economic problems and economic theory. When Woodrow Wilson went to Wellesley in 1888, Giddings was invited to Bryn Mawr to take Wilson's place as lecturer on politics, but he soon became professor of politics. He taught four subjects: (1) Development of Political Institutions, (2) Political Economy, including Economic Theory and Economic History, (3) Methods and Principles of Administration, and (4) Methods and Principles of Charity and Correction.

Giddings attributes his early interest in sociology to his accidentally reading a copy of the *Popular Science Monthly* and the first chapter of Spencer's *The Study of Sociology.* Some men form their social philosophies in their early years of maturity, but Giddings developed his slowly and continuously throughout his entire life. As early as 1885 he read a paper on "Sociology" in which he attempted to show that social activity is not the same as the sum total of the activities of the persons making the social group. He did not agree with Comte that sociology was the final science in "the hierarchy of the sciences," nor with Spencer that it was a science resulting from social subsciences synthesized into a general theory of society. Neither did he agree with Ward's view of sociology being a scientific compound rather than a synthesis created by other social sciences. Sociology, according to Giddings' view, was a distinct and independent science developed along with the entire field of all the social sciences.

We may begin to consider Giddings a sociologist in 1888 when he wrote a paper on the "Sociological Character of Politicial Economy." He now placed particular emphasis on social relationships in his writings on economic and political problems. He was actively interested in founding the *Annals of the American Academy of Political and Social Science.* In 1890 in Volume I, No. 1, of that publication, he wrote on "The Province of Sociology." For this article he drew upon Ward's *Dynamic Sociology,* Spencer's *Principles of Sociology,* Schaffle's *Bau und Leben,* deGreef's *Introduction a la Sociologie,* Gumplowicz's *Race Conflict,* and others. This was significant, not only in developing Giddings' thinking, but in helping to crystallize the field of sociology at that early date. Here he first stated his concept of sociology which asserted that sociology is a general science like biology, that it must serve as the foundation for special study in all departments of social science, and that it must be clearly differentiated from psychology.

Psychology is concerned with the associations and dis-associations of the elements of conscious personality. How sensations are associated and disassociated in perception; how perceptions are associated and disassociated in imagination and in the marvelous composite, the individual personality—are problems for psychology to state and, if it can, to solve. But the phenomena of conscious associations do not end with the appearance of the individual personality. They are then only engendered. Individual personalities as units become the elements of that vastly more extensive and intricate association of man with man and group with group which creates the varied relations of social life. A society is, therefore, on its conscious side a super-physical product just as on its physical side it is superorganic and a product of tertiary aggregation.

In 1891 Giddings gave lectures on sociology at Columbia University in the absence of Professor Mayo-Smith, but he continued his teaching at Bryn Mawr. He became professor of sociology at Columbia in 1894. He wrote an article "Sociology as a University Study" in 1891 when there was a general controversy found among the college faculties about the place of sociology in the curriculum. During this period sociology in colleges and universities was limited to an occasional course, and only a few men, such as F. W. Blackmar at the University of Kansas and Albion W. Small at Colby College, were giving courses in sociology. It was at this time that Giddings stated, "The object of sociology is to learn all that can be learned about the creation of social man."[9] He emphasized social structure and growth, volitional association, and social progress.

In the July, 1894, *Annals of the American Academy of Political and Social Science* (Supplement), he wrote a monograph on "The Theory of Sociology." It contained a clear-cut statement of the ideas that had been growing for the previous ten or fifteen years. The first six chapters were these: (1) The Sociological Idea, (2) The Province of Sociology, (3) The Problems of Sociology, (4) The Primary Problem: Social Growth and Structure, (5) The Secondary: Social Process, Law and Cause, (6) The Method of Sociology. These chapters include practically all of his later sociological theories which were further developed in 1896 in his *Principles of Sociology*.

A leading thought of his was that society exists for the purpose of creating a social personality. He held that society tends to become

[8] Giddings, Franklin H., "The Province of Sociology," *Annals of the American Academy of Political and Social Science,* Vol. I, No. 1, 1890, pp. 66-70.
[9] Giddings, Franklin H., "Sociology as a University Study," *Political Science Quarterly,* Vol. 6, No. 4, December, 1891, pp. 642-643.

something which to an increasing extent is the product of conscious planning. Here he is in agreement with Lester F. Ward. In his monograph he stated:

> The sociologist has three main quests. First, he must try to discover the conditions that determine mere aggregation and concourse. Secondly, he must try to discover the law that governs social choices. Thirdly, he must try to discover the law that governs the natural selection and survival of choices.[10] [Giddings' final theory—namely, the consciousness of kind—was beginning to take form.]

Inductive Sociology, which Giddings wrote in 1901, was a syllabus of methods, analyses and classifications, and provisionally formulated laws. Here we see the influence of Mayo-Smith's *Sociology of Statistics* upon Giddings. The first few chapters of Giddings' book laid the foundation for much of his later social research development and his emphasis upon it in his teaching.

In his *Study in the Theory of Human Society* in 1922, Giddings brought together some of his ideas for the scheme of sociology.

1. A situation or stimulus is reacted to by more than one individual; there is pluralistic as well as singularistic behavior. Pluralistic behavior develops into rivalries, competitions, and conflicts, and also into agreements, contracts, and collective enterprises. Therefore, social phenomena are products of two variables, namely situation (in the psychologist's definition of the word) and pluralistic behavior.

2. When the individuals who participate in pluralistic behavior have become differentiated into behavioristic kinds or types, a consciousness of kind, liking and disliking, approving or disapproving one kind after another, converts gregariousness into a consciously discriminative association, herd habit into society; and society, by a social pressure which sometimes is conscious but more often, perhaps, is unconscious, makes life relatively hard for kinds of character and conduct that are disapproved.

3. Society organizes itself for collective behavior and achievement, if fundamental similarities of behavior and an awareness of them are extensive enough to maintain social cohesion, while differences of behavior and awareness of them in matters of detail are sufficient to create a division of labor.

---

[10] Giddings, F. H., "The Theory of Sociology," *Annals of the American Academy of Political and Social Science,* Supplement, July, 1894. See Theodore Abel's "The Significance of the Concept of Consciousness of Kind," *Social Forces,* IX, October, 1930, pp. 1-10.

4. In the long run, organized society, by its approvals and disapprovals, its pressures and achievements, selects and perpetuates the types of mind and character that are relatively intelligent, tolerant, and helpful, that exhibit initiative, that bear their share of responsibility, and that effectively play their part in collective enterprise. It selects and perpetuates the adequate.[11]

Throughout his professional career Giddings advocated the use of scientific methods and techniques in the study of social phenomena and social situations. Sociology includes social statistics, Franklin Giddings states, and so much of history as may truthfully be said to repeat itself; i.e., those constant facts of cooperation, institutional life, and social welfare which recur in all communities and in all ages. The method of sociology is inductive. Its chief dependence is upon comparative historical studies and upon statistics.

He encouraged many of his students to make use of scientific methods and statistical techniques. Among his students were: John L. Gillin, Howard Odum, F. Stuart Chapin, Newell D. Sims, Howard B. Woolston, W. F. Ogburn, Frank Hankins, J. P. Lichtenberger. This is only a small and incomplete list of Giddings' well known students who have been instrumental in developing scientific sociology.

Robert E. L. Faris is unquestionably right when he credits Giddings with having provided a significant part of the process which made American sociology what it is. Giddings evolved an original and somewhat systematic conceptual system. He stimulated the development and application of research methods, particularly statistical methods. Giddings was a pioneer in a trend which made impressive progress in the application of statistics to sociology, and the future of sociology may show far more development of techniques of measurement than we have yet seen.

Giddings felt that some of his most important work was given less credit than it merited, and some of his less important work was given too much credit. In my last conversation with him in 1930 he stated that he considered his work in Inductive Sociology to be his most important contribution to sociology.

Influenced by the ideas which took form in the writings of St. Simon and Fourier in France, in England of Robert Oliver, Ruskin, Kingsley as well as Bentham and Mills, the so-called "social scientist" philanthropist and reformer in the United States, William Graham Sumner (1840-1910), was one of the first teachers of sociology in America. He was never quite accepted by Small, Ward, or Giddings

---

[11] Giddings, Franklin H., *Study in the Theory of Human Society*, New York, The Macmillan Co., 1922, pp. 291-292.

as a sociologist, but neither did Sumner accept them. Small frankly expressed surprise when Sumner was elected president of the American Sociological Society. "It came to me consequently as a surprise and a shock that he was thought of as second president of the American Sociological Society. At that time (1907) he was not within my field of vision as even nominally a sociologist."[12]

Sumner had intended to become a minister and had gone to Germany and to Oxford, England, to study theology, but he returned when he was twenty-six years old, and became a tutor at Yale in mathematics and Greek. However, he was ordained, and from 1870 to 1872 was a rector in the Episcopal Church at Morristown, New Jersey.

In 1872 he went back to Yale as a professor of political science, and as a teacher of economics and sociology. He offered the first course in sociology at Yale in 1874. Sumner was one of the most vigorous proponents of the laissez-faire point of view. In fact, he was in accord with Herbert Spencer, and at first he used Spencer's *Study of Sociology* as a textbook. This caused some disputation, for Spencer was considered an atheist. Because of the do-good implications associated with the term sociology, Sumner preferred to use the term "science of society." He was very cautious about the use of words that contained any taint of altruism, and although in 1882 he wrote a book entitled *What Social Classes Owe to Each Other,* the purpose of this book was to demonstrate the philosophy of laissez-faire.

Sumner always claimed to be completely emancipated from his religious bias, and he once stated with regard to his religious beliefs: "It is as if I had put my beliefs in a drawer and when I opened it, there was nothing there at all . . ." However, to the end of his life, he maintained his priesthood in the Episcopal Church and regularly made his reports as a priest. One is inclined to wonder whether his pronouncements in this line were also in part mental exercise. The humor of Sumner is shown by his succinct statements, for example, "The type and formula of most schemes of philanthropy—or humanitarianism is this: A and B put their heads together to decide what C shall be made to do for D." Sumner collected an almost incredible amount of material in support of his point of view which is expressed by him as follows: "It is vain to imagine that a scientific man can divest himself of prejudice and put himself in an attitude of neutral independence toward the mores. He might as well try to get out of gravity or the pressure of the atmosphere."[13]

The shaping of Sumner's thoughts was due in part to the influence of Julius Lippert's *Kulturgeschict* and of Gumplowicz's *Der Rassen-*

[12] Small, Albion W., *American Journal of Sociology,* Vol. 21, 1916, pp. 732-33.
[13] Sumner, William B., *Folkways,* Boston, Ginn and Company, 1906, p. 98.

kampf. Sumner was in many respects an independent thinker, consciously avoiding any tendency to follow the course set by any of his
colleagues or contemporaries. He encouraged his students to avoid too
much contact with related fields, such as psychology. He quite generally
ignored Comte, Ward, Giddings, and William James. His most positive
attempt was to separate sociology from any connection with social
reform or social reorganization; consequently, Ward's idea of social
telesis did not appeal to him. However, he admitted that young men
learn by imitation, tradition, and authority, and that "when conviction
as to the relation to welfare is added to the folkways, they are converted
into mores and by the virtue of the philosophical and ethical element
added to them, they win utility and importance and become the source
of the science and art of living." And in regard to the mores, he said:
"They coerce and restrict the newborn generation. They do not stimulate to thought, but the contrary. The thinking is already done and is
embodied in the mores. They never contain any provision for their own
amendment. They are not questions, but answers to the problems of
life. They present themselves as final and unchangeable, because they
present answers which are offered as 'the truth'." And further he
states: "The mores are the folkways, including the philosophical and
ethical generalizations as to societal welfare which are suggested by
them, and inherent in them as they grow."[14] Here are some typical
Sumner statements:

> Education in the critical faculty is the only education of which
> it can be truly said that it makes good citizens.
> Every student during his academic period ought to get up one bit
> of history thoroughly from the ultimate sources, in order to
> convince himself what history is not.
> The folkways are unconscious, spontaneous, uncoordinated. It is
> never known who led in devising them.
> There is no class which can be trusted to rule society with due
> justice to all, not abusing its power for its own interest.
> Great crises come when great new forces are at work changing
> fundamental conditions, while powerful institutions and traditions
> still hold old systems intact.
> Every group, in every age, has had its "ideals" for which it has
> striven, as if men had blown bubbles into the air, and then,
> entranced by their beautiful colors, had leaped to catch them.
> Men begin with acts, not with thoughts.

Sumner enjoyed vigorous controversy, whether it was defense of
academic freedom, laissez-faire, or political and economic controversies.

---

[14] *Ibid.*, pp. 30-31.

As might be expected, he was an ardent advocate of free trade, and on this subject, he and Franklin H. Giddings enjoyed many arguments which were undoubtedly mental relaxation for both of them.

The fourth man in this famous quartette was Albion Woodbury Small. The influence of Small upon American sociology made an impression in a threefold manner: first, through his writings in the *American Journal of Sociology* and other publications; second, through his work as editor of the *American Journal of Sociology,* where he played a very major part in selecting and directing the type of research and discussion followed by American sociologists; third, through his work as head of the department of sociology at the University of Chicago, his classroom teaching, and his personal direction of students.

As a teacher he always worked on the assumption that any of his students might discover something or make an interpretation which would not only be of basic value but which might supersede anything that had been done up to that time. Annie Marion MacLean stated, ". . . he always treated the humblest auditor with intelligent respect. By giving courteous attention to puny opinions, he fostered confidence in the timid. While he could flay with vitriolic words, he knew how to temper words with justice."[15] An illustration which shows Small's method of handling an enthusiastic but immature student is shown in the story of a young man who had done some graduate work at two other mid-Western universities, and had gone to the University of Chicago in order to carry on research on a project dealing with attempts to standardize an aspect of social research. This student first went to W. I. Thomas on the advice of his previous major advisor. After explaining what he wanted, he was told that his type of problem was not of interest to sociology, but would fall more nearly in the field of economic statistics. The student then discussed the matter with Charles R. Henderson. Henderson, while sympathetic, told the student that if he hoped to become a sociologist, he would need a more definite human interest, or as Henderson put it, "more of the milk of human kindness." As a last resort, the student went to Albion W. Small. Small's reaction was as follows: "Young man, I believe you are on the wrong track. I believe that you will find your search for research methods leading you into a blind alley. That, however, is perfectly satisfactory. Do your job so well that no one need ever waste any time on that project again. I spent three years of hard work on a study of the Cameralists. I think it was largely futile. But I covered the ground completely enough that no one needs to go over it again. Therefore, I consider it three years well spent."

[15] MacLean, Annie Marion, "Albion Woodbury Small—An Appreciation," *American Journal of Sociology,* XXXII, July, 1926, pp. 45-48.

Albion W. Small's lectures were occasionally very monotonous. Sometimes his students organized to break up the monotony of them. In a certain class E. E. Eubank was given the task of interrupting his lecture on Tuesday with pertinent questions, Clarence E. Blachley on Wednesday, M. C. Elmer on Thursday, and Roderick D. McKenzie on Friday. When these interruptions took place, Dr. Small would lay down his sheaf of papers, step forward, and give the class an exciting discussion of the point concerning which he had rather ponderously written in preparation for that lecture.

Small wrote extensively in the *American Journal of Sociology*. His books were not among the best sellers. He once remarked about the lack of acceptance of his books, and said he had decided to write a book in "novel form." This book, *Between Eras—From Capitalism to Democracy,* consisted of dialogues among leaders in different fields of thought who were Small's contemporaries. He tried to present the point of view of leading social workers, clergymen, politicians, capitalists, manufacturers, labor leaders, and university professors. He had his graduate students read the book and in some cases told them whom he wanted a character to represent. This added to their interest in the thoughts expressed, but, unfortunately, all of the characters used the long sentences and re-modified verbiage of Albion W. Small.

Small wrote the first article in Volume I of the *American Journal of Sociology,* July 1895. The following statements give us a view of what he thought was ahead. He introduced the subject by stating, "Sociology has a foremost place in the thought of modern men. Approve or deplore the fact at pleasure, we cannot escape it." He continued his discussion in this introductory article by discussing the following:

I. In our age the fact of human association is more obtrusive and relatively more influential than in any previous epoch.

II. The distinguishing mental trait of our age is undisciplined social self-consciousness.

III. The inevitable contact of man with man has produced confident popular philosophies of human association.

IV. Popular social philosophy has its counter part today in a social gravitation or "movement" in the line of certain sympathies and assumptions begotten and fostered by reflection on contemporary societary conditions.

Small presented the contention that "sociology is not primarily a product of the school"— that sociologists are trying to answer *"obtrusive questions about society which the ordinary man is proposing every hour."* "Life," he said, "is so much more real to the people than to the schools that the people are no sooner possessed of some of the tools of thought, and some means of observation, than they proceed to grapple with

more vital questions than the scholars had raised. The doctrines of professional sociologists are attempts to substitute revised second thought
for the hasty first thoughts composing the popular sociologies in which
busy men outside the schools utter their impressions." *"If sociology is
to be of any influence among practical men, it must be able to put its
wisdom about things that interest ordinary men in a form which men
of affairs will see to be true to life."*

Thirty years later Small stated: "A humiliating proportion of the
so-called 'Sociology' of the last thirty years in America . . . has been
simply old fashioned opinionativeness under a new fangled name."[16]
". . . a scientific specialist is constituted not principally by the subject
matter of his interest, but by the peculiarity of his procedure." "Sociology . . . is the application of a distinctive method to a designated
type of problem." Small felt that "Sociology has become the first attempt
to organize a technique of scientific interpretation of human experience
upon the basis of the group hypothesis in contrast with the individual
hypothesis."

Out of the mass of conflicting points of view, he felt that there
was evolving a gradual set of concepts, facts, and problems which
might be expressed as "group process." According to Small, the distinctive function of the sociologists was to discover the "categories of group
structure, and group processes and group behavior, and in applying
these categories to interpretation and control of human situations." He
felt that a man might be a useful citizen, an important public function-
ary, an author of useful books about social facts and yet not be a sociologist. He cited Carroll D. Wright with his volume *Practical Sociology*
as an instructive example. Small felt that in our meanderings from the
discourses of church pattern to sex relations we may find social
phenomena but not necessarily sociology. The descriptions of social
phenomena may merely locate the point at which sociology has "found
its center of equilibrium."

Albion W. Small considered that sociology reached its maturity
in 1883 when Gustav Ratzenhofer (1842-1904) published his *Wesen
und Zweck der Politik*. Small was very much influenced by the writings
of Ratzenhofer. Ratzenhofer felt that "urkraft" or primeval force
originates or is expressed in the form of inherent interest. Ratzenhofer
gave five basic interests which arise as the expression of a need through
the awareness of necessity. This theory of interest was utilized and
developed by Small, and much of Ratzenhofer's work was incorporated
into Small's *General Sociology*. Ratzenhofer's interests became the basis

[16] Small, Albion W., *Origins of Sociology*, University of Chicago Press, 1924,
p. 346-350.

for Small's "health, wealth, sociability, knowledge, beauty and right-ness" interest groups. Ratzenhofer held that society existed only in the social process which in turn was made up of the intersocial relationship between individuals and which was the basic instigator of all social action. He held that the social process was "a moving complex of re-ciprocal relationships" within the group rather than based upon the impact of group upon group as suggested by Gumplowicz.

By 1918 Small considered that sociology had manifested itself in six leading tendencies.[17]

1. Methodology—a criticism of points of view, working presump-tions, attitudes toward divisions of labor and details of opera-tive programs.

2. Group Psychology—here he specifically designated as examples: McDongall, Elwood, Cooley, and E. A. Ross.

3. Social Analysis—he mentions Thomas and Znaniecki's *The Polish Peasant* as the most conspicuous example, and quotes E. W. Burgess "As a distinctive method it involves the detec-tion, description and causal explanation of all the factors enter-ing into the social situation, or determining the behavior of group studies. Social analysis is purely scientific in its interest, and is not concerned with social action. Social laws discovered by social analysis are, however, of value for the determination of fundamental policies of social construction."

4. Social Survey—he stated that social analysis was to social survey as research in physics is to a civil engineer's orientation. "Social survey is so much more immediately available for practical purposes then either of the foregoing tendencies that its biblio-graphy deserves special prominence."

On the methodological side in order of publication:

Gillin, J. L., "Application of the Social Survey to Small Com-munities," American Sociological Society Proceedings, 1911.

Riley, Thomas, "Sociology and Social Surveys," *American Journal of Sociology,* Vol. VII, May, 1911.

Kellogg, Paul, Shelby Harrison, and others, "Social Surveys," Russell Sage Foundation, 1912.

Elmer, M. C., "Social Surveys of Urban Communities," 1914.

Park, Robert E., "The City, Suggestions for the Investigation of Human Behavior in the City Environments," *American Journal of Sociology,* Vol. XX, March 1915.

Gillin, J. L., "Social Survey and Its Further Development," *American Statistical Association Publications,* September, 1915.

[17] *Encyclopedia Americana,* 1918.

Burgess, E. W., "The Social Survey: A Field for Constructive Service," *American Journal of Sociology,* Vol. XXI, January 1916.

McKenzie, R. D., "Neighborhood," 1923.

Harrison, Shelby, "Community Action Through Social Surveys," Russell Sage Foundation, 1916.

On the operative side:

Booth, "Life and Labour of the People in London," (nine volumes 1892-1897).

Bowntree, "Poverty: A Study of Town Life," 1902.

Kellogg, Paul, (Director), "The Pittsburgh Survey," (six volumes), The Russell Sage Foundation, 1904-1914.

Burns, (Director), "Cleveland Education Survey," (twenty-five volumes), Cleveland Foundation, 1915.

Harrison, Shelby, (Director), "The Springfield Survey," (three volumes), 1918.

5. Case Method—as a Social Diagnosis.

6. "Concrete programs for amelioration and construction. Charles R. Henderson included all these in the term Social Technology."

Thus we may compare the statement made by Small in the first article of the *American Journal of Sociology* in 1895 with what he considered its status in 1918—twenty-three years later.

Ward, Giddings, Sumner, and Small seemed to differ in their approach so much that their followers were looked upon as representing entirely different schools of sociological thought. As we look back upon their contributions, however, we can see that their thinking represented the angle from which they viewed the same social processes. They worked to develop and to establish sociology as a field of study which was to become of increasing importance for an adequate understanding of social organization, social control, and the social processes of an increasingly complicated society.

III

Changing Emphasis of Sociologists

DURING the time covered in this study, there is no person who has been active in it for the nearly whole period covered except Edward Alsworth Ross. (1866-1952)—it might almost be called the Ross era. There are few men with even a shorter span of activity who have been a part of their period to the extent that was true of Ross. He was a vigorous part of any social situation with which he was associated. Though left an orphan when eight years old, he was an active, interested and happy boy as a member of three different farm families in Iowa. The last, the Beach family, while not blood relatives, supplied the needs of real parents and he considered them in that light. With a "Covenanter" background, a rigid Presbyterian childhood, and a vigorous body he was able to meet the rigors of rugged farm life and profit thereby. "In seventy years of it," he states, "it was a good thing for me that, during my more sensitive years, I was a member of an element that was looked down on; it saved me from the vice of snobbery. I have never cared to look down on anyone." Ross was always recognized as one who would arise to the defense of the less popular side of a controversy. He wanted both sides to be considered on its merits. This resulted sometimes in bringing forth bitter accusations. He was accused of being opposed to religion because he spoke of certain inadequacies of churches. He was accused of being a communist because of his discussions and books about Russia. Ross "called his plays as he saw 'em'." In 1928 he was my guest in Pittsburgh. Fanny Hurst had written a bitter article about a mine strike at nearby Russelton. The whole Pittsburgh district was aroused because of the plight of the miners. We went out to the area. The conditions were tragic. Ross spoke to a union leader—asking how many men were on strike; then how many men the mines employed when working at full capacity. The figures did not jibe. Ross took the leader to task on the spot for having nearly twice as many men on strike at those mines as it was possible to employ at full capacity. The labor leader accused Ross of being a capitalist sympathizer. Irrespective where criticism fell, it was dealt out when the situation warranted it in his opinion. This attitude brought forth criticism of his own work, when conditions changed and new evidence appeared. As he stated, "In the thirty-five years since the book left my anvil, I have scrutinized society in many countries and the society which 'controls' does not look so global to me now as it did in 1900." . . . "I doubt if 'lessons from history' will have much to do with shaping humanity's future. Basic conditions are changing so rapidly that most of the old techniques of control are junk" . . . "Science and invention—together with applied psychology open vistas into a wondrous new age with its own problems of control, in which control devices will be employed that the past never heard of."[1]

In speaking of his book on *Principles of Sociology,* 1920, he stated that when he put it out he thought it was sound, but "even then sensed that certain parts were labored and foggy." He stated that almost every month fresh shortcomings had appeared, and that if by 1960 it would be 40 to 50 parts sound, he would be content. How different from the mediocre person who produces a poor product and feels he must devote his life to defending his 'half-baked,' crippled brain child! Ross considered the social processes to be the real subject matter of sociology. Since a process cannot be a hold-over from a by-gone stage nor a borrowed culture item, it represents the *"actual life* of society."

Ross' nearly thirty volumes represent three periods of writing:

1. Books of a specific approach, like *Social Control, Social Psychology, Sin and Society.*
2. Books with a popular appeal, such as: *The Changing Chinese, Changing America, Across the Rio Grande, Standing Room Only.*
3. *Principles of Sociology, The First Seventy Years and New Age Sociology.*

The following is a personal statement by Ross: "Here is my look-back over my sociological past."

"In my postgraduate study in the universities of Berlin and John Hopkins, 1888-1891, I took courses in philosophy and economics, but nothing in sociology, for nothing was offered. As soon as I held a university chair (1891), however, I began teaching sociology for it had a fascination for me. While preparing the series of papers that became *Social Control* (1901), it was borne in upon me how unsettled everything was about the new would-be science, and for at least eight years I gave my spare time to such studies as 'The Scope and Task of Sociology,' 'Social Laws,' 'The Unit of Investigation in Sociology,' 'The Properties of Group-Units,' 'The Social Forces,' 'The Factors of Social Change,' and 'Recent Tendencies in Sociology.' These and other like papers were brought out in 1905 under the title, *The Foundations of Sociology.*

"These years of critical examination of sociological writings left me

---

[1] *Seventy Years of It,* D. Appleton-Century, 1936, N. Y., p. 96.

exceedingly dissatisfied with the way in which the development of sociology so far had been affected by reigning religious, ethical, or philosophical ideas. I realized that I needed a much broader knowledge of society than I had. In those days no funds were available for social research, but I found that by teaching two summer sessions without pay I could, once in every three years, have a summer and a semester *with* pay for social exploration. I saw now the possibility of educating myself into a real sociologist by studying different societies 'on the spot,' and I sized it.

"In 1910, I spent six months going about in China in mule litter and sedan chair, filling notebooks with my observations and queries and later seeking of Chinese scholars or Christian missionaries the meaning of what I had observed. The result was a series of articles in the *Century Magazine*, which in 1911 were brought out under the title *The Changing Chinese*.

"I profited so greatly from my China study that in 1913, having limbered up my college Spanish, I devoted half a year to observing and prying into the societies of South America. The result was a series of magazine articles which in 1915 were brought out under the title *South of Panama*. Being able to read and speak the language, I got deeper into Latin-American society than I had into Chinese society. I was able to discern how certain social classes dominated and exploited the ignorant, superstitious, toiling masses. Thenceforth, I never studied a society without keeping a sharp lookout for signs and evidences of institutionalized exploitation.

"In 1917, thanks to the public spirit of the late Charles R. Crane, I was able to visit Russia in order to study and report upon its revolution. The outcome of this was *Russia in Upheaval*, 1918; *The Russian Bolshevik Revolution*, 1921; *The Russian Soviet Republic*, 1923. After several visits to Mexico, I dedicated the summer of 1922 to a concluding study which enabled in 1923 *The Social Revolution in Mexico*.

"In the summer of 1924, at the request of the temporary Slavery Commission of the League Nations, I made a field investigation which resulted in my 'Reports Upon the Employment of Native Labour in Portuguese Africa.' In the winter of 1924-1925 I spent some months studying India, which resulted in my papers 'Sociological Observations in India' and 'The United States of India.'

"Among the effects upon me of these and other studies (not recorded here) carried on through twenty years were:

1. I saw that sociology must go forward on its own, not as a mere offshoot of some other science.
2. I lost confidence in the value of analogies between social processes and other processes.

3. I ceased to trust the hypothesis that there is one *dominant trend* in the development of *all* societies, whatever their geographic environment, make-up, or history.
4. I rejected the idea that there is a single underlying pattern for each class of social process and each order of social institution.
5. I arrived at the conviction that the actual character of a given society is best revealed in the two or three score of major *social processes* that go on within it. These *processes,* the *factors* determining each of them as well as the *products*—institutions, groupings, and interactions—to which they gave rise, are the principal things the sociologist has to study and set forth.

"As I review the course taken by sociological thinking and research in the fifty-seven years since I began to teach the subject, I am well contented. Less and less is arm-chair thinking relied on; stronger and stronger is the demand for honest-to-goodness *social research.* There is great difference of opinion as to the best techniques of research, but never have I met with a suspicion that the methods followed are 'rigged' in advance in order to insure the emergence of certain desired results.

"I *do* feel, however, that our sociological treatises and journals are far more optimistic than they are justified in being. They take little notice of the fact that natural selection has been almost put out of business insofar as it pertains to human beings, and that in scores of ways the hereditarily inferior, the constitutionally less fit, are being helped to survive and multiply. Unless more attention is given to the significance of biology for human beings, it is easy to foresee the plight of our posterity after three or four centuries!

"Again, sociologists are ceasing to hold the complete confidence of the higher intellectual circles by their neglect of what is happening in the field of population growth and population pressure. Owing to science's astounding conquests over disease and to the certainty that many of the means of combatting disease and maintaining health will be socialized in the near future on the part of the more advanced societies, the general death rate will be lowered to undreamt-of figures, while birth rates will hover at about two-thirds of their historic figure. The result will be an extremely rapid growth of numbers in most parts of the world. The few areas in which the general standard of living is high run the risk of having their standards trampled into the mud by the flooding in of immigrants from the more crowded and backward nations. In case something like a world-state is organized in order to assure international peace, it is quite possible that the component states will not be allowed to restrict international migration to the extent they desire; so we may see all the marvelous discoveries of medical science resulting, not in the bulk of humanity living a far more beautiful and desirable life than they do now, but in the population of the globe rising to five billions instead of the present two billions, with their plane of living not much higher than it is now!"

No sociologist has had as extensive contacts with leaders in all fields of social thinking as Ross. His writings always were on the border- line of a university professor and the lay reader seeking a further development of his point of view. In 1936 Ross estimated that 300,000 of his books had been sold. At the time of his death the estimate was over 1,000,000. This cannot be compared with the tremendous sales of certain elementary textbooks. Most of Ross' books were of a type pur- chased and read in order to secure his point of view rather than for the purpose of general information. His hundreds of magazine articles were more widely distributed than those of most sociological writers. Hence, while some critics may contend that he did not leave a great systematic sociology, it was actually interwoven in the idea, ideals, attitudes, and practices of people of America and to a large extent of the leaders of the world.

Sitting in a hotel lobby in Washington, D. C. was a group of young sociologists. They were discussing techniques and methods of research. Someone brought up the subject of Ross and asked whether they felt what Ross did could be classified as research. At that moment Ross came across the lobby and joined the group. One of the young men spoke up and told Ross that they had just been discussing methods of research and the question had arisen "What methods of research you follow." Ross chuckled and said, "I'm not a research man, I just write what I think best explains a process or a situation. For example, a num- ber of years ago I decided to spend some time in China. I told everybody I was going to China and asked if they knew anybody there. By the time I left for China I had three thousand names and addresses of people: Chinese officials, Chinese scholars, coolie brothers of laundry men, beach combers, missionaries, teachers, relatives. I made up a list of five things I would like to know about changes taking place in China. I contacted, wherever possible, as many of the names I had and countless others. When I talked with them at first our general conversation might lead to the person expressing himself on one or more of these five questions. If the answer did not come up naturally, I asked him questions. After the interview I would sit down on the side of the road on a stone or back in my room and write up, as nearly as possible, an exact account of what had been said to me. I returned to Wisconsin with many boxes full of notes and with the aid of some intelligent assistants classified these notes and put them in the form of a little book,

The Changing Chinese. Nothing scientific about it, it was just what I had gathered from hundreds of sources." Some of the young men in the group smiled cynically and nodded knowingly at each other. Later in that week I ran across a man by the name of Adolph Zucker whom I had known many years before. He was teaching at the University of Maryland. He told me that he had seen in the newspapers that E. A. Ross from Wisconsin was in Washington and he hoped to meet him. As we were speaking, Ross rounded a corner and went into a drugstore. He let himself down on one of the stools. Dr. Zucker and I went in and climbed up on the stools beside him. I introduced Zucker and said that he had mentioned his desire to meet Ross. "For a number of years," said Zucker, "I have been in China working for the Rockefeller Foundation in the location of hospitals and clinics. It is very difficult to secure reliable information. I have found that government reports, official documents, and even the information secured by American and European businessmen, missionaries and others have limited value, but during my years there, there was one book that I always found reliable within the field with which it dealt. That was *Changing Chinese* by E. A. Ross." Ross laughed, turned to me, and with a gentle tap that almost knocked me off the stool said, "Pat, you go and tell that bunch of young men who have been razzing me what Dr. Zucker says about the reliability of my work."

Among the many contemporaries of Ross, there were few who made more of an impact on the thinking of his period than Ellwood. His books, written in a clear and uncomplicated manner, were easily understood and readily translated.

Charles Abram Ellwood (1873-1946) was respected and appreciated by more people interested in education generally and criticized more specifically by certain groups within his own professional group than any other leading sociologist. A farm in northern New York, Cornell University, University of Chicago, University of Berlin—were his sources as a student. A secretaryship with a social agency in Nebraska, the University of Missouri, and Duke University were the range of his occupational itinerary. On the way he made contact with E. A. Ross, W. F. Wilcox, J. W. Jenks at Cornell; A. W. Small, C. R. Henderson, George E. Vincent, W. I. Thomas, George H. Mead, and John Dewey, and James R. Angell at Chicago; in Germany, Schmoller, Simmel, and Paulsen; and later in London, L. T. Hobhouse and R. R. Marett. It is not difficult to account for the nature and effectiveness of his contribu-tions. In turn, we find among his students, E. B. Reuter, H. Blumer, Carle Zimmerman, L. L. Bernard, C. C. Taylor, and scores of others who moved on, developing the germ of enthusiasm into work which specifically went far beyond the areas covered by their early teacher.

While Ellwood wrote on "Some Prolegomena to Social Psychology" as early as 1899, and in 1912, *Sociology in its Psychological Aspects,* he did not reach his best presentation of this aspect of his thinking until the final revision of this work in 1925 under the title of *The Psychology of Human Society.* Here he was much influenced by C. H. Cooley's *Social Process.* Elwood's style was clear and uncomplicated and his writings were easily translated into other languages. This was particu- larly true of his book on The Social Problem. Here he contacted a wider audience than with his writings on social psychology, and it was the forerunner for several books dealing with social aspects and needs for religion. While particular studies have given more recognition to some of Ellwood's contemporaries, he was singularly successful in presenting systematic sociology with its psychological implications. Ellwood's work was not particularly new nor was it presented in any startlingly brilliant style. It was, however, written in such a clear, logical style that it was readily understood, easily translated, and each step built logically on what had preceded.

In 1933, Ellwood turned his efforts toward methods in sociology, where he vigorously criticized the tendency to over-emphasize objective and statistical methods and techniques in sociological research. This caused a great flurry of protest, but did much to revive interest in non-statistical procedures. Even some of his most bitter critics suddenly discovered procedures which were more in line with Ellwood's appraisal than their own previous claims would have indicated.

One of the last articles by Ellwood contained the following:

"Indeed, in one sense the whole mission of sociology as a science is to bring about a transition from arbitrary and emotional traditions to scientific traditions in guiding social behavior. There need be no fear that the real values in past social traditions will be destroyed by scientific examination and criticism. They may be, to be sure, if social scientists are not aware of the facts of history and the lessons which those facts teach. But, at bottom science is not an attempt to destroy anything; it is an attempt to understand, to control, and to use for human advantage. A sociology which understands its human mission will undertake this task.

"But the continuity of civilization and of civilizing values is, after all, not the main practical problem of scientific students of human relations. What we call civilization has been filled with too many errors, too many value-judgments not based upon all the facts of experience, for sociologists to be over-zealous about the continuity of human cultures. Inevitable questions of intelligent rational changes in human relations will arise. If the social sciences are worth anything, they should afford guidance in the bringing about of rational social changes. The advocates of the use of force in bringing to pass social changes have not only so far won out that they wish to suppress criticism of the institutions of certain groups, but some even talk openly of a war after the present one to settle the relations between classes.

"Science is, after all, at bottom, faith in human intelligence, in its capacity to solve problems, if the right method of approach is used. Its faith is in patient study, in the diffusion of knowledge, and in the establishment of reasoned social values based upon the solid facts of human experience. This is as true of the social sciences as it is of the natural sciences; and some of us cannot help but feel that it is something of a disgrace that the students of the social sciences have not seen that this is their work. There is, of course, the excuse that the social sciences have been so neglected, so pushed aside, that they have had no opportunity to make their contribution to a world-wide civilization based upon valid judgments of human experience and recognizing the interdependence of all mankind. But if this war leaves any worthwhile sociology surviving, it is surely time that sociologists should recognize the inadequacies of their past efforts and formulate a new program for the future."[2]

Perhaps there were no two sociologists who differed more than Ross and Cooley in general appearance, personality, attitude toward their work or in amount and type of what they wrote. They were similar, however, in the part they played in developing sociology and effecting the thinking of their time. Charles Horton Cooley (1864-1929) spent seven years as an undergraduate student in Michigan University because of ill health. How much effect his ill health, and the influence of his able jurist father, Thomas M. Cooley, may have had on his quiet, effective thinking and writing, we do not know. At any rate, he did not bounce into print whenever he discovered a set of new facts, or felt he had found a new procedure or principle. Most of his work was not so much uncovering additional or new facts as digesting the writings of others and interpreting them and applying the conclusions to life about him. He was not a reformer, a propagandist, nor an egoist who felt he was called upon to create a new system of sociology. His approach to sociology, while centered around certain social psychological aspects, was based upon the interaction and interrelationship of the individual and society in all aspects and situations. As we find with many sociologists, they are remembered most frequently because of some striking or succinct phrase or idea—Giddings for his "consciousness of kind," rather than his contribution to inductive sociology. Cooley for

---

[2] Ellwood, C. A., "What's the Matter with Sociology," *American Sociologist* Feb. 1943.

his "primary groups," rather than his idea of society as an organic whole, and that the individual is a social product resulting from primary group experiences. Cooley's writing and thinking center around the ideas that the individual is a result of the social order, and the social process by which the social order becomes unified.

Charles Horton Cooley made a distinctive shift in emphasis of sociologists. He gave impetus to the consideration of life about us, as a source laboratory for sociological analysis. There had been a tendency to emphasize the more distant, the unique, the unusual. Instead of emphasizing distressed elements of our population, negative forces in government, general philosophical principles, or political and religious concepts, he called the attention of sociologists to the behavior patterns of the groups with which all of us are associated from infancy. The face-to-face, or primary groups, with their less inhibited relationships, and the larger community groups within which the individual functions for a specific purpose or because of a derived interest. The configuration of the child's developing personality is molded by his primary group relations. These primary group contacts continue in different forms throughout life, but with less obvious effects.

Cooley indicated that what is considered progress is always in reference to some social value that is recognized as having importance to some organization, to a belief or a principle, to a group, a person, or some objective the attainment of which is considered to have value. Our measure of progress is determined by various units, comparative indices, and measures of achievement included in such valuation. This valuation Cooley considered a social process which is measured in terms of values placed upon alternatives. The social process "takes place through the medium of psychical communication, the vehicle being language, in the widest sense of the word, including writing, printing, and every means for the transmission of thought."

The instinctive life is no longer a mere mechanism, but a plastic thing with a mind to guide it. Human intelligence is able to develop and organize its control. In this we see Cooley agreeing with Ward on the one hand, and with L. L. Bernard on the other. He gives his approach to social organization by stating: "The unity of the social mind consists not in agreement but in organization, in the fact of reciprocal influence or causation among its parts, by virtue of which everything that takes place in it is connected with everything else, and so is an outcome of the whole."[3]

[3] With a minimum of display Cooley's interest in individuals often took a very effective turn.

In 1915 the income of a sociology teacher in a college with one hundred and twenty students enrolled was not exorbitant. The idea of taking a trip to the annual meetings from Fargo, North Dakota to Washington, was not in line

The trend toward applying principles of sociology to existing situations was particularly in emphasis after the beginning of the twentieth century. The writings of men and women began to call attention to the various types of social maladjustment. Sociology was beginning to have an established place in colleges and universities. While the general student was not concerned about the more specific variations in the interpretation of sociological concepts, he was interested in an explanation of the social processes occurring about him, and proposals for the analysis of causes as well as procedures of social control. This increasing demand for information and guidance as a member of society was met by scores of teachers throughout the country. Most of them have been forgotten, like the pebble dropped into the pool, even though the waves set in motion continue to vibrate long afterwards. Many of the men who have contributed to the development of social thought are still living when this is being written. What a man is recognized for may be limited to certain of his writings which happened to attract the attention of a particular influential commentator, was used as a basis for other studies, or happened to be written at a time when its particular emphasis was significant. Sometimes an apt phrase becomes a key word and superficial writers and speakers will re-quote such a phrase to the neglect of other significant writings. This was mentioned in connection with Giddings who considered what he had done in inductive sociology was of more lasting significance than his oft quoted "consciousness of kind."

Another sociologist who played a distinctive role in changing the emphasis of sociology was W. I. Thomas. While his publications were significant, his particular contribution was in the influence he exerted upon his students. They not only learned about sociology, they

with the income received. One morning, a few days before the meeting, an envelope was on the breakfast table with $125 in it. My wife had borrowed it and told me that I was to go to the meetings. When I returned, she asked me if I thought it was worth $125. I told her it was, that I had met an old man (he was fifty-one and I was much younger) named Cooley, from the University of Michigan. There had been an evening smoker. When the gathering had been going on for about an hour, this man walked up to me and said he noticed I was not smoking, and asked whether I would care to step outside where we could talk. That was my first contact with Charles Horton Cooley. It was worth far more than the price of going to the National Convention. He remained a friend of mine to the time of his death. He gave me suggestions and showed an interest in whatever I was doing. This was of particular value to me since my field of interest and writings were rather far removed from the personal interests of Cooley. Two of my major moves to university positions were directly related to suggestions Cooley made to university authorities inquiring for possible teachers. I cite these instances merely to show how the interests of Cooley extended beyond his immediate circle of students and colleagues.

developed an understanding about it. William Isaacs Thomas (1863-1947) had a tremendous influence upon the social thinking of his students. He did not fit into a fixed pattern and as a result, stood out among the sociologists of his day. His childhood life—roaming the hills of Tennessee alone—was typical of much of his later life. He tended to express his thoughts even if not in line with accepted procedure. If the chimes of Mandel Hall interrupted a discussion he was conducting, he might express himself vigorously regarding the chapel service being proclaimed.

While scores of his former students admit his influence on their thinking, he did not admit any similar influence on his thinking. He denied having received any explanation of reality from philosophy. He felt no influence by any of his teachers of sociology, tending to scoff at Small's historical and methodological approach and at C. R. Henderson's remedial and correctional interests. Perhaps influenced by them more than he thought, he was still an independent and original thinking Tennessee boy with his squirrel rifle. His teachers of sociology understood him better than he may have known. Several times I heard Henderson defending his outbursts against the clergy in 1913, and several years later with tears running down his cheeks, Small defended Thomas to E. A. Ross and me against widespread newspaper statements. He spoke of Thomas as one of his boys, whom people misunderstood, because Thomas refused to defend himself against gossip.

While my contact with Thomas lasted for many years, I never had the fortune of being in his classes. Because my interests were in objective research, while a graduate student in Chicago, he rather bluntly told me there was nothing in his courses for me. In 1932, however, he talked with me at length on this subject, and indicated a very considerable change in his point of view regarding quantitative investigation.

The general content of Thomas' books does not give his contribution to social thought. Instead, it is the approach and the principles which indicate the extension of individual psychology to the situations of group behavior. The particular occurrences in the experiences of the social group which will carry over to its social organization and modify its culture—contacts with other groups and the resulting phenomena; the inherent and acquired variations in the mental reaction of races and social groups; the relation of educational systems and social change—are some of the principles which are developed in the works of Thomas.

In his *Source Book for Social Origins,* dealing with the life of primitive man, 1909, and *Primitive Behavior,* 1936, he developed the sociological concepts of social control, social customs and habits, and crises with resulting response in the form of social organization and modification in the culture. His methodological concepts are found in many of his works.[4] However, this is largely presented in the methodological note of Thomas and Florian Znaniecki's great work, *The Polish Peasant*: "This report can be concluded with a listing of some of the more important contributions which have made *The Polish Peasant* meritorious and which explain the profound influence which it has had on sociology and social psychology."

1. A demonstration of the need of studying the subjective factor in social life.
2. The proposing of human documents as source materials, particularly the life record, thus introducing what is known as the life history technique.
3. A statement of social theory which outlines the framework of a social psychology and the features of a sociology. The view of social psychology as the subjective aspect of culture has been particularly influential.
4. A statement of scientific method which has stimulated and reinforced the interest in making sociology a scientific discipline.
5. A number of important theories, such as that of personality, that of social control, that of disorganization, and that of the four wishes.
6. A variety of concepts which have gained wide acceptance, such as attitude, value, life organization, definition of situation and the four wishes.
7. A rich content of insights, provocative generalizations, and shrewd observations.
8. An illuminating and telling characterization of the Polish peasant society.

"What is perhaps of chief importance is the marked stimulation which it has given to actual social research."[5]

There were many persons who have become associated with schools of thought who were contemporaries of the men mentioned. In some cases they made a significant contribution to the trend of their period which sometimes rose to a considerable amount of recognition for a while. As an example we might mention the theories of Pareto, while never accepted or of basic importance by any considerable number of sociologists of the twentieth century, were found in the political and

---

[4] *The Unconscious, 1927—Proceedings of the Second Colloquium on Personality Investigation, 1930—Essays on Research in the Social Sciences, Brookings Institution, 1931—Critique of Research in the Social Sciences, 1939.*

[5] Blumer, Herbert, *Critiques of Research in the Social Sciences*: (1) An Appraisal of Thomas and Znaniecki's *The Polish Peasant in Europe and America*, 1939.

social thinking of a large part of the population of the Western world, and were an active factor in the world events of the period of 1900 to 1950. Since they played such a large part in the social thinking of the Western world, he is mentioned here. His contributions may to some extent have been direct. Often, however, the effect was indirect, in that they gave rise to expressions of thought, the purpose of which were to counteract his ideas.

Vilfredo Pareto was born in Paris in 1848 and died in 1923. His father was an exiled republican of Genoa. His mother was French. Since the family was permitted to return to Italy in 1858, young Vilfredo was able to complete his education there and graduated from the Institute Polytechnic in Turin when he was twenty-two years old. He followed the profession of engineering until he was forty-two years old, working in the fields of transportation and in metallurgy. However, his actual interests extended into social and economic questions. In view of his family background, this was a natural field of interest. In 1893, he was offered the chair of political economy at the University of Lausanne, through the efforts of his friend, Professor Walras, whom he succeeded in that position. While working within the field of political economy, he began his work in sociology. This culminated in 1917-19 with his *Traite'de Sociologia Generale*. His point of view was looked upon most favorably by leaders of fascism and he was considered to be an authoritative spokesman for that group. He was not impressed by their recognition, realizing that he was used as "window dressing" for a group which hoped to gain by the prestige he contributed.

Pareto was a mathematician of the first rank. He applied principles of mathematics to political economy, stating that mathematics—

1. Is useful in the examination of concrete facts
2. Can be used in the solution of particular problems, and
3. Can be used to express the relation of mutual dependence of the different aspects of economics to the whole.

In this respect his thinking may be grouped with those who emphasize objective measurement of social phenomena.

Pareto did not develop any system of sociology. He worked rather on specific social institutions, basing his approach upon his theory of *residues*. This is carried in the concept that society is not homogeneous, but is made up of individuals who differ both physically and mentally. That they are not equally capable of holding any position of responsibility. In all branches of society, this is the case. Only a small elite part of the population possesses the necessary qualifications in the greatest degree, and hence, Pareto contends that even where democracy and equality apparently exist, an elite group will dominate the remainder of the population. He contended that thus control is concentrated in the elements containing the qualities which enable some to rise to positions of control. It is in this approach that Pareto includes his concept of *residues*. He considered society to be organized like a truncated pyramid with the upper strata dominating and controlling everything.

Another person of this period whose work was of importance was Michael Davis. He represents a considerable group of young sociologists who were moving beyond the area set by the early group in America.

In 1906 Michael M. Davis prepared a monograph on Tarde's theories of imitation and in 1909 he enlarged this to *Psychological Interpretations of Society*. Some of his statements give us the status of social psychology during the first decade of the twentieth century.

"We may study any dynamic phenomenon in two ways: first in that of function—how it works; second, in that of genesis—how it came to be. Between these two aspects a general relation may be expressed."

"In any group of inter-acting phenomena, function, although often related with genesis, is not dependent upon it."

"This very general statement can, for practical purposes, be best put as two more specific derivative principles:

1. The genetic relations of the parts of a group of inter-acting phenomena do not govern their functional relations. Briefly, genetic order is not necessarily significant for causual order. (p. 205)

The psychological basis of the principle can be stated as follows:

a. At any given moment, all parts of the mental content function in mutual interdependence.

b. To any given stimulus, the observed response is the net result of the reaction of the entire mental state or content, not of any separate portion alone.

c. While it is true that all ideas or sentiments establish at least temporarily, certain lines of association connected with the circumstances of their origin;

d. Yet, the reaction to any given stimulus is primarily determined by the reaction to any given stimulus is primarily determined by the relation (association) of each portion of the effective mental content to the new stimulus directly, rather than by its habitually or temporarily established inner associations. (p. 206)

"This analysis opens the way to the second principle:

2. Ideas or sentiments, and also social institutions, when once in existence, become thereafter psychic or social factors in all future reactions in essential independence of their origin or their original associations. (p. 207)

3. All parts of an evolving organic aggregate are mutually inter-influencing, and the nature of the aggregate, and of its

alterations, is determined by the interactions of all its parts with each other and with their environment. (p. 208)

"The fourth principle is an attempt to formulate certain large aspects of organic progress and may be approached through a series of propositions:

    a. Changes in an aggregate take place either through the produc' tion of new units or through selection among existing units.

    b. Selection involves either the elimination of certain units or their segregation and regrouping.

    c. The impulses, ideas, and other elements of a mental content, the traditions, institutions and group elements of a social state, function as mutually selective criteria for each other. Individual development from childhood, and social progress, may largely be interpreted in terms of a selective process.

    d. Human influence over both psychical and social change can be exerted less by control of the productive processes than by control of the selective; and we can in fact, affect the former, but little except through the latter. (p. 209)

    4. Psychic and social progress takes place through productive and also through selective processes. Control over progress is at' tained primarily through comprehension and control of psychic and social selective criteria." (p. 211)[6]

The changing emphasis in sociology was particularly brought forth by the work of Ross, Cooley, Ellwood, and Thomas. This is shown not only in their published works, but in their activities and contacts with their students and the life of their times. Emphasis was placed upon a change from emotional to scientific traditions in human behavior. In summarizing the scattered considerations regarding human behavior, there was a more clearly defined understanding of the factors in social control, social organization, and psychic aspects of sociology. The great step was being taken which moved sociology from a realm in which the philosophical basis of a new discipline was of chief consideration to the understanding and explanation of human relations in the current social structure.

---

[6] Davis, Michael M., *Psychological Interpretations of Society*, N. Y., Columbia University, Longmans, Green and Co., Agents, 1909, pp. 205, 206, 207, 208, 209, 211.

IV

Early Teachers of Sociology

DURING the last decade of the nineteenth century, much interest was becoming evident in various aspects of group relations. While some of this was focalized in the writings of men such as Spencer, Lester F. Ward, and others, much more found its way into general writing, lectures, sermons, and classroom teaching in fields related to sociology. For example, a professor of philosophy at Wittenberg College, John Henry Wilburn Stuckenberg (1835-1903), wrote a book in 1880 entitled *Christian Sociology*. In this field he may be recognized as the definite forerunner of Charles R. Henderson, Walter Rauschenbush, and at a later date Charles A. Ellwood. In 1897 Stuckenberg in his volume *The Social Problem* presented one of the first books of this era, emphasizing the sociological approach to various aspects of social maladjustment which one might expect to find in a Christian society. This followed in 1898 with an *Introduction to the Study of Sociology* and his two volume work in 1908 on *Sociology: The Science of Human Society*. Stuckenberg in 1898 started a chain of events, or rather of books on the scope, province, relationship, and methodology of sociology which, with relatively little improvement, has been reiterated even down to the present time.

Stuckenberg considered his contribution to sociological ethics as the most important of his writings. There is no doubt that in this he was definitely a leader. Many of his contentions were further developed by Edward Cary Hayes, *Sociology and Ethics,* published in 1921. Stuckenberg's attempt to deal with ethics from a social point of view rather than metaphysics or a priori philosophy, caused a shock in 1895 which we can hardly appreciate today. Many of the accepted ideas and procedures of today were startling when first suggested. Likewise, change in the acceptance of principles caused by social change and social progress was a seed planted by Stuckenberg and developed later in the writings of Ogburn and Simms. Both Stuckenberg and Ward felt that the state should play an important part in the search of a socially desirable phase. Stuckenberg definitely may be considered as one who added a balanced point of view to the disassociated jumble of pseudo-sociological ideas and thoughts that were being ricocheted into the arena of developing social thought.

Stuckenberg was born in 1835 near the old German city of Osna-

bruck. The family came to the United States in 1839, living in Pittsburgh, Cincinnati, and Indiana. Stuckenberg received his preliminary
training at Wittenberg College and later continued his studies in Halle,
Germany, where he went for the first time in 1857. At the beginning
of the Civil War he returned to the United States and was commis-
sioned a major in the Federal Army, and served as Chaplain with the
145th Pennsylvania Volunteers. After the war he returned to Germany
and continued his studies at Gottingen, Tubingen, and Berlin. In 1873
he went to Wittenberg College as professor of theology where he remained until 1880; then he returned to Berlin and served as pastor to
the "British American Union Services," later called the "American
Church." This period also saw the publication of a number of his books.
In 1894 he returned to America and resided in Cambridge, Massachusetts, where he remained during the last period of his life. Most of
his sociological writings were published during this time. He was in
London at the time of his death in 1903.

An Introduction to the Study of Sociology is just what the title
implies, an introduction to, not a study of, sociology. As the author
says, "It leads up to but not into sociology." Perhaps as a result of his
German training, Stuckenberg felt that a long preparation and elaborate
clearing of the way was necessary for the beginning of a study of any
science. Another reason for this is probably the fact that Stuckenberg's
primary interest had been philosophy, and his wide reading in that and
related fields made this elaborate preparation seem necessary to him.
The book was reviewed by A. W. Small in the May, 1898 issue of the
American Journal of Sociology. Small declared himself in sympathy
with the general point of view of the book, but criticized it severely for
what he called "too much of this getting ready to commence to begin
business." The book dealt with the subjects which were found in most
of the earlier works, such as the special social sciences, methodology,
sociology as a science, and social ethics. It showed a wide acquaintance
with sociological literature from German, French, and English sources.
The author laid considerable stress on his concept "sociation" which he
considered more or less a new idea. The term was used to clarify the
relation between the individual and society.

Stuckenberg's last work on social theory was his "*Sociology*" published by Putmans in 1903. This book represents, perhaps, the culmination of his work in sociology and contains his whole sociological system.
It is undoubtedly his most important contribution to sociology. After
two introductory chapters in which he deals with practically the same
thing discussed in the book previously mentioned, he divides his sociological system into three divisions; the first deals with the nature of
society, the second with social evolution, and the third with social ethics.

He rejects Comte's division into social statics and dynamics because they seem to imply too much of physics, natural science, and materialism, but he practically adopts the same concepts in his divisions: the nature of society and social evolution. In the first division, the nature of society, he seeks to trace the physical and biological bases for society and to describe the psychic nature of society or "psychic interaction," as the essence of the social. Next, he deals with the relation between the in- dividual and society, and finally he describes the nature and types of social forces. These he classified into fundamental, constitutional, and cultural. In the second division of the work he deals with the nature, causes, and general characteristics of social evolution. He sees three stages in the process; the consanguine, the political, and the interna- tional. In the last part of the work he deals with social ethics, the social ideal, social reality, and means of changing reality into the ideal.

One of the influences which possibly directed Stuckenberg's in- terests in the direction of social problems may have been the social characteristics of the community in Germany from which his people came. It is not possible to show that there was a direct connection since the family left Germany when he was only four years of age. It is possible, however, that this influence may have survived in the family tradition, and we do know that he was familiar with the history of Westphalia, through his contact with it while in Gottingen as a student, and with some of the scholars which the community produced.

Because Stuckenberg was not associated with any of our great American universities, his sociological influence has often been over- looked even though his ideas have long since become a part of the struc- ture of sociological thinking in America.

A discussion of the place of teachers in establishing sociological thinking in America must give a most prominent place to Frank Wilson Blackmar. His teaching was not limited to his work at the University of Kansas, but to the people of his state and to the part he played as an advisor and consultant to administrators and legislators in Topeka. F. W. Blackmar (1854-1931) was not by any means the first teacher of sociology in American universities, but the Department of Sociology at the University of Kansas was the first university department under that name. Blackmar was once asked how this came about, and he told the following yarn which it is probably not possible to verify.

In 1889 Jerry Simpson was United States Congressman from Kan- sas. He was a practical, colorful character who liked to boast that he was of the common people, not given to fancy haberdashery. He was known as "Sockless Jerry Simpson." The trustees of the new university asked him to look around while he was in the East and find men to take charge of certain departments. He quite readily obtained someone to teach mathematics, ancient languages, and literature, but rather took it upon himself to add something further. He wondered why the people of Kansas were Populists; Missourians, Democrats; and Nebraskans, Republicans. He felt that someone at the University should attempt to explain these social variations. He went to see Herbert Baxter Adams at Johns Hopkins. Professor Adams said he thought he had a young man who would meet the requirements. He had a young instructor by the name of Thomas Woodrow Wilson, who was working on a study of Constitutions and minority representations, but Simpson thought Wilson would be more suited to work in an Eastern school.

Richard T. Ely was presented by Professor Adams. Ely told Congressman Simpson that he was interested in greater socialization of the consumption and distribution of wealth. Simpson responded that that was no problem in Kansas, since for the past two years, Kansas had been living on "toasted grasshoppers and hay tea."

Albion W. Small was next introduced. Small was very much impressed with the idea that Congressman Simpson had in mind and indicated that he was likewise attempting to understand society on the basis of their various group interests; that the group interests as indicated by their health, wealth, beauty, rightness, knowledge, and sociability interests might explain certain regional variations. Simpson hesitated, but finally indicated that since the boys and girls who would come to the University of Kansas were farm boys and girls who, in turn, would go back to their own communities, probably Small's discussion might be too abstract.

Frank Wilson Blackmar was then called in. Simpson cut the discussion short by bluntly asking: "Have you ever heard of Kansas?" Blackmar told him yes, he had crossed Kansas twice. Blackmar was born in Pennsylvania, attended an academy but left school to work in Philadelphia. Blackmar was not successful in getting a job but his companion George C. Blickensdorfer secured a position as cash boy at Wanamakers where he developed an automatic cash carrier and later a simple little machine for copying columns of figures (Blickensdorfer typewriter). Blackmar signed up to drive a wagon to California. Because he did not find gold in California, Blackmar moved on to Mexico, where he ended up stomping wool in great bags on a sheep ranch at a peso a day. He finally got back to the College of the Pacific, graduated, and drove a wagon back east to continue graduate work at Johns Hopkins. These facts satisfied Simpson, and after telling Blackmar what he wanted taught, he asked, "What shall we call this new department?" Blackmar, who had written a monograph on the Spanish Institutions in the South West, suggested "History and Politics." Simpson said, "Hell, no, we can't have politics in a state university." Then Blackmar, who had just completed reading Lester F. Ward's *Dynamic Sociology,* suggested the Department of Sociology and History. And thus, according to the tale related by Blackmar, the department was established.

Blackmar's leading publications were: *The Story of Human Progress* —1896; *Elements of Sociology*—1905; *Outlines of Sociology,* with J. L. Gillen—1914; *Justifiable Individualism*—1922; and *History of Human Society*—1926. Blackmar's publications, while significant, do not begin to indicate the influence he had as a teacher and as a guide to young teachers. Perhaps the following incident may give an additional picture.

In the fall of 1915 I went to the University of Kansas to teach. Blackmar looked at me for perhaps a minute then said, "Young man, what do you know about the people of Kansas?" Correctly, I admitted my ignorance. "You can't teach young people without knowing some-thing about their background." He tossed me a *Kansas City Star.* I looked at it for a few minutes. "Do you see anything about Kansas that interests you?" "Yes, I see the name of a city, Beloit. I lived not far from Beloit, Wisconsin as a boy." "All right," he responded, "I have arranged for a fund of $900.00. You will teach five hours a week this first semes-ter. Next week, you go to Beloit, spend a couple of days there, talk with anyone and everyone till you have an idea of what people around Beloit do and think." The next week I went to Pittsburgh, then to Marysville, Clay Center, Wichita, Council Grove. Once he reprimanded me for "scrimping too much" on my expense account, insisting that I should not try to save money on meals, hotel room, and physical neces-sities. "Remember, when people meet you, you are the University of Kansas to them." These contacts helped establish rapport with students, and later were the basis for several community surveys. It is regrettable that some of the methods and techniques of great teachers of sociology are not recorded along with the writings or statements of research methods.

Blackmar was as typically a pioneer in his sociology as he was in seeking new experience as a young man. Beginning in the field of history with *The Study of History and Sociology* in 1890 and *History of Human Society* in 1896, he was approaching both history and sociology from viewpoints that did not find an enthusiastic audience. What was appearing as sociology was more influenced by a philosophical back-ground, and historians had not yet begun to interpret their field from the sociological point of view. Greater works have appeared than Black-mar's, but the interest shown by young people in his work encouraged others to work along the same line. An outstanding characteristic of Blackmar was to enter new fields. When a new man came to his depart-ment, Blackmar was actually pleased if the newcomer indicated that he would like to teach a course which Blackmar had been teaching. Examples of such a shift occurred in the case of V. E. Helleberg, Walter Bodenhafer, Maurice Parmallee, M. C. Elmer and others. It gave Black-mar a chance to explore a new area. The result in his case was that he did not make as deep an impression in any one field as would have been the case if he had not shifted. However, he was always at the vanguard. Social theory, social problems, human geography, cultural anthropology, and ethnology, social research, the community survey, educational soci-ology and social mobility demanded his attention. At the time he gave his presidential address before the American Sociological Society in 1919, he spoke of a working democracy and pleaded for a realistic ap-proach toward our form of social life. Because he demanded that "America must take stock of what is happening in the world or pass out of existence", one of the most prominent of the younger sociologists contended that Blackmar had become a "doddering thinker". Both Blackmar and the young man were speaking 30 years too soon. Such had always been Blackmar's experience. By 1914 sociology had made extensive strides in becoming established as a university and college subject. Its stages of development are excellently brought out by the following summary. The progress made in developing social thought during the period since 1895 was largely the result of the enthusiastic teachers of that period who brought together the best thinking of the preceding century and began presenting the results to thousands of students in America.

Reasonable Department of Sociology for Colleges and Universities[1]

"The division of social sciences into departments in universities is largely for pedagogical reasons. It would be possible to put them all under one head with different lines of work, such as economics, sociology, history, politics, ethics, and anthropology; for they have a correlated interest and the courses of study in each could be made to fit into a general plan of instruction. But the trend in recent years has been to differentiate these main lines, and to some extent divorce them from the close relationship which their nature and purpose imply.

"Sociology, the last of these main divisions to be developed, like the others, has a central idea of its own, yet bears a close relationship to all the others. Yet sociology as a distinct department must be broad enough to include many subjects and lines of work in order to maintain its independence. If it is to be a social philosophy only, it could well be

---

[1] Blackmar, Frank W., "Reasonable Department of Sociology for Colleges and Universities," *The American Journal of Sociology,* September 1914, Vol. XX, No. 2, pp. 261-263. (Misprint of the name on the article. It was spelled Blackman. As a result, it was generally overlooked in bibliographical lists.)

placed in the division of philosophy; if it is to be merely social psychology, it could be included in the department of psychology; if merely the
history of social and political movements, civil government and history
could include it. Even in this case, the central idea of the general forces,
laws, and problems of social generalization would be lacking. Assuming
that sociology has developed a scientific purpose not possible to obtain
under the present organization from the other social sciences, and that
it can and ought to maintain a separate pedagogical department, what
should be the nature and scope of its subjects? There is a chance for
great difference of opinion in the scope of the organized group of
studies in the department of sociology. In the University of Kansas the
department is trying to work out its position in accordance with the
following plan:

DEPARTMENT OF SOCIOLOGY

I. *Bio-social Group*
  *1. General Anthropology
  *2. General Ethnology
  3. Social Evolution
  4. Criminal Anthropology
  5. Race Problems
  *6. Eugenics (graduate)
  *7. American Ethnology (graduate)
  8. Seminar Bio-social Research

II. *Pure or General Sociology Group*
  *1. Elements of Sociology
  *2. Socialization and Social Control
  *3. Psychological Sociology
  4. Geographical Influence on Society
  *5. Development of Sociological Theory
  *6. Seminar of Sociological Research **(graduate)**

III. *Applied or Specialized Sociology Group*
  *1. Principles of Applied Sociology
  *2. Rural Sociology
  *3. Social Pathology
  *4. Remedial and Corrective Agencies
  *5. The Family
  *6. Socialism
  *7. Contemporary Society of the United States
  *8. American and European Charities (graduate)
  *9. Seminar of Social Research (graduate)

IV. *Social Technology and Social Engineering (carried by advanced students and instructors)*

*1. Preparation for Social Service (graduate)
*2. State Work in Connection with the Conference of Charities and Correction
*3. State Work in Connection with State Board of Health
*4. State Work in Relation to the Board of Control
*5. Field Work in Relation to Penal and Reformatory Practice
*6. Field work in Social Surveys of Rural and Urban Communities
 7. Municipal Engineering

*Course given in the University of Kansas or field work done.

The sociologists of the last decade of the nineteenth century were concerned with the scope, provisions, and place of sociology in its rela' tion to other sciences. They were seeking a common ground, or an accepted tool for penetrating the "hard pan" of the established place' ment of social relationship. They believed that by breaking through this crust of accustomed thinking they would reach a stream of purer water in social thinking.

Perhaps one of the most significant results of sociological thought from 1890-1914 was the emergence of the *group concept.* The signifi' cance of the individual was subordinated to the group in an attempt to explain human experience. A monograph in 1890 by Henry C. Adams, *Relation of the State to Industrial Action,* in Johns Hopkins Studies in History and Politics presented basic principles for emphasis on individ' ualistic and collectivistic ideals. Other teachers made it a part of the sociological thinking of the twentieth century.

Albion W. Small became head of the department of sociology, University of Chicago in 1892. During thirty years as editor of the *American Journal of Sociology,* he laid the foundation for sociology as a university study. Small is definitely a link between the first and second stages of the era of sociology as discussed here. With a background of economics and political philosophy, history and theology, he was one of the group which tried to crystalize sociology as a distinct university discipline. He always participated actively in the formulation of the scope, purpose, and general concepts of sociology. Small carried over into a second major phase of the sociological era, as is indicated by his relation to the teaching of sociology.

When the department of sociology was established at the Univer' sity of Chicago, about 1892, President Harper sought out young Albion W. Small at Colby College and asked him to head up the department. Small was not interested in doing so because he was satisfied with his position at Colby, but he was finally persuaded to do so, starting with what was at that time an enormous salary. He was instructed to build up a great department. Small persuaded Charles R. Henderson, who had been a Baptist minister and social worker, to come to Chicago to teach applied problems, or as Henderson called it, "Social Technology." Fredrick Starr headed up anthropology; W. I. Thomas, professor of comparative literature at Oberlin, came to teach social origins. George E. Vincent, who had been managing the program at Chatauqua, New York came to Chicago and soon developed an introductory course in sociology. With these as a nucleus, a great department was built.

George E. Vincent presented the following as "The Province of Sociology, A Syllabus of a course occupying four hours per week during twelve weeks." This was printed in the American Journal of Sociology in January 1896. The scope of this proposal is so significant in the development of teaching sociology that we include it here.

I.   The Nature and Function of Method.
II.   Historical Outline of Social Philosophy.
III.   The System of Auguste Comte.
IV.   The Development of Biology and the Idea of Evolution.
V.   The Application of the Evolutionary Theory to Social Phenomena.
VI.   The Organic Theory of Society.
VII.   Classification and Scientific Distribution of Social Phenomena.
VIII.   Demands for a New Department of Social Science.

With the progress of knowledge about society certain needs or demands have arisen. These may be, in general, grouped under four divisions.

1. Demands for the coordination and integration of all kinds of knowledge about society into a coherent system, i.e., the combination of abstractions into a concrete account of reality.
   a) Insight into the contemporary order or historical *regimes.*
   b) Explanation of the process of change by which past regimes have succeeded each other and produced the present.
2. Demands for the scientific investigation of certain social phenomena that are not specifically or adequately dealt with by other sciences.
3. Demands for the construction, on the basis of scientific observation, of social ideals to which the nature of men and society may be gradually readjusted.
4. Demands for the utilization of knowledge about society,

i.e., the practical application of social forces in such a way as to give development at least a tendency toward an ideal.

IX. The Relation of Sociology to These Demands.
X. Three Divisions of Sociology.
  1. Descriptive.
  2. Statical Sociology.
  3. Social Dynamics.
XI. Criticisms of the Above Scheme.

Belfour: *Essays and Addresses*, Edinburg, 1893. "Doubts about Progress."

Sumner: *The Absurd Effort to Make the World Over.* Forum, March, 1894.

Moses: *The Nature of Sociology,* Journal of Political Economy, December 1894.

De Lestrade: *Elements de Sociologis.* Introduction.

1. Criticisms of the divisions outlined under XI come less from difference of opinion as to the tasks themselves than from the disagreement about names for the tasks. It would be strange if there were a consensus, and at this stage in the development of social study, it ills becomes anyone to be dogmatic. Doubtless with longer experience and clearer insight, a definite division of labor will take place according to individual points of view. Some such tendency is already evident. The main point of contention is as to the extension of the term sociology to include more than the general laws of social structure and evolution. The chief objections to such extension are:

  (a) It is too large a field for effective work.
  (b) Social ideals can never be scientifically constructed; speculation is sure to be involved.
  (c) Social control is an art and not a science.
  (d) Social control is Utopian and cannot be exercised in a large measure or in the interest of a remote aim.

2. In reply to these objections it may be said:
  (a) That the preliminary task is to outline the whole field. If it proves too large for one scholar, it will quickly be subdivided.
  (b) Ideals are the only spur to progress; they are universally present; they are effective in direct proportion to their harmony with the possible; it may well

be a scientific aim to eliminate the speculative element from the ideals which society is constantly
constructing.

(c) As to the extent to which social forces can be modified, there is room for wide differences of opinion,
but so long as even a slight margin of possible change
is admitted, the obligation to take the wisest advantage of the opportunity remains.

(d) Again it may be reiterated that the tasks are more
important than the name. Let the former be clearly
grasped, and nomenclature will adjust itself to the
facts.

3. Conclusion: From the relation which the tasks sustain to
each other, it is clear:

(a) That chief emphasis must be laid at present upon the
fundamental importance of *Descriptive Sociology,*
i.e., the general facts and laws of association as in-
duced from the data of the special social sciences,
and properly related in a synthetic view of society,
and of those divisions of *Statical and Dynamic
Sociology* which deal with the present and the past.

(b) It is, however, necessary to put such knowledge as
is already available, at the service of society in the
most effective way. Therefore, it is important to
develop a method to accomplish this result. Ideo-
statics and the dynamics of active progress undertake this task. With the development of the fundamental pursuits these subsequent departments will
increase in efficiency.

Albion W. Small states that George E. Vincent attempted to
"infuse some human interests" into Small's interpretation of Shaeffle's
social anatomy and physiology. At the St. Louis Exposition Congress of
Arts and Sciences in 1906, he discussed the development of sociology
and in part made the following comment: "Sociology began by being a
social philosophy, a philosophy of history, and such it has been until
very recently. To put social philosophy into the language of a natural
science is not a science. As a philosophy it has rendered important
service. It has preserved the unity of social theory, a unity constantly
menaced by specialization which has abstracted different groups of
phenomena. It has afforded a point of view by which all the social
sciences have been unconsciously, or consciously influenced.

"Of late sociology has given less heed to vague general consideration of society as a whole, and has come into closer question with certain definite phenomena of association. Group struggle as molded by conflict has received attention. Mental unity and processes of the group have been studied. The theory of the relation of the individual to society has been reviewed and greatly modified. Environment is thought of as exercising a complex and indirect influence on society. Finally, soci- ology is seeking to add to its science as a philosophy the contribution of a science which shall formulate valid laws as to the universal prin- ciples that underlie the phenomena of association."

Another important influence on the teaching of sociology in America was the contribution of Gustave Ratzenhofer who was dis- cussed in Chapter II. His work was specifically associated with social thinking in Austria. He, along with Gumplowicz, represented the group which believed that in the process of conflict, a cross-fertilization of cultures took place which resulted in a rapid evolution of their re- spective social structures. Ratzenhofer's influence was directly brought to America in 1904 and his contributions made a definite part of the teaching literature for the next ten years. Hence, his inclusion in this discussion.

Ratzenhofer felt that with the growth of greater recognition of sociology, many bulky works would begin to appear in which sociology would be "applied to the most incongruous fields of thought."

There were many individuals who are not generally remembered whose contribution to the development of social thinking was of im- portance. These men and women made their greatest contribution as teachers, not only in training other persons to teach sociology, but creating a germ of enthusiasm for a socialized approach to old and new situations. They interpreted old and new concepts for young men and women who became the fathers and mothers of the next generation as well as the professional, industrial and technical backbone of America.

An example of one who helped establish sociology by teaching, even more than by writing, was Edward Cary Hayes (1868-1928) who was born in Lewistown, Maine. His father was professor in Bates Col- lege. At the age of six he spent a year in Germany and later on, two different years in German universities. His training consisted of work in sociology with Small at Chicago; in etchics with Mead, Dewey, Tufts, Schmoller, Wagner, and Simmel. Ordained as a minister in 1893 he was for three years a pastor at Augusta, Maine. Hayes was Dean of Keuka College, New York, from 1896 to 1899. He received the Doctor of Philosophy degree from Chicago in 1902. Then for five years he taught at Miami University, Oxford, Ohio. From 1907 until his death he was at the University of Illinois.

His work at Chicago was largely in philosophy, but Small told him: "I believe you are one of the men who can help create the science of sociology." He then spent an additional year in Germany and came back to Chicago for his degree in 1902.

Hayes began to see the significance and effect of religion and ethics upon sociology very early in his work. He made a definite impression and was cited by Small and credited with this particular emphasis. This was later considered by Max Weber and Talcott Parsons. He followed the line of thought of Ward—through Small—that sociology is concerned with social changes and the conditions of change. Perhaps the key contribution of Hayes is found in his discussion of the classification of social phenomena. The theme is the social process. Hence, his concern was with social activities rather than the social group or institution, which serve only as the vehicle for social activities.

Social phenomena, according to Hayes, consist of:

I. Conditioning

II. Problem phenomena

The conditioning phenomena, which give direction and effect the nature of activities, are:

A. Natural physical conditions, including climate, topography, and natural resources.

B. Artificial physical conditions: as, roads, cities, buildings, and other man determined conditions.

C. Psycho-physical conditions, including conditions resulting from density and distribution of population, such as cross-fertilization and general distribution of culture, which thus becomes a part of the conditioning phenomena. The psychic factors which condition the activities included such influences as suggestion, imitation, sympathy, inducement, deterrance, domination, emulation, competition, conflict, and cooperation.

II. Problem phenomena. This included what Hayes considered the principle objective of sociological study. The various activities— economic, political, religious, educational, recreational, domestic, ameliorative, and corrective—as well as vice and crime, were included. The resultant phenomena are the outgrowth of the interrelation and interaction of these specific activities, and constitutes the Social Process.

These general concepts of Hayes have to a considerable extent become a part of our sociological thinking. This is true, notwithstanding the fact that the bulk of our books on sociology are filled with information, data, and discussion of the conditioning phenomena. In our concern to have the conditions adequately presented, we sometimes fail to get much below the surface of a problem. On the other hand, we ignore the conditions and present a solution for the inadequate performance of the activity. Like Comte and Ward, Hayes believed that social activity must be dynamic and must proceed from a sympathetic understanding of all available knowledge concerning the problem under consideration. Hayes presents as five leading social values in his book on Sociology and Ethics.

1. Physical satisfaction.
2. Esthetic pleasures.
3. Intellectual satisfaction, leading to that rational contemplation which Aristotle eulogized.
4. Social contacts and experiences.
5. Self-contemplation and personal idealism, emerging in a well rounded individuality.

There is an obvious influence of Small's "Health, Wealth, Beauty, Rightness, Knowledge, and Sociability" interests traceable in Hayes' basic values.

Hayes was a brilliant classroom teacher. In fact, his students sometimes missed the kernel of his discussion because of their intense interest in his fascinating expression of ideas, his illustrations, and general presentation. Hayes' classes were the ones to which students liked to bring their parents, or out-of-town guests. Even though the visitor did not get all of the points of discussion, he left with a glow of having listened to an interesting and enjoyable lecture. There was always a refined dignity about Hayes, which showed the cultural background of a man with the widest educational and social opportunities. It came almost as a shock when one learned that one of his hands was permanently injured while he was a member of the boxing team at the University of Chicago. Students felt free to go to his home, and when they left, it was with a feeling of having stepped up another rung on the ladder to a better life, and toward a goal of ultimate achievement. Hayes was the embodiment of sympathetic understanding.

Hayes was not interested in social research in the sense of doing specific work in any particular field. He did, however, consider it of great importance. When I suggested that Dr. Henry Neuman of City College had called my attention to the rising interest in social surveys, Hayes said that for several years he had hoped a student would show interest in doing some actual field research, but that he had hesitated even to suggest it because he knew nothing whatever about it, and did not know where to start. In fact, he suggested that I take Who's Who in America, read the citation of men listed as sociologists, and where anything was stated indicative that they had done some field work, follow the suggestion through.

Hayes defined *social realities* as social activities which constitute social life including in their simplest form social ideas, sentiments and practices, and in their compound form, customs and institutions. He considered in *social realities* the inclusion of the social order "with its societies, castes, sects, parties, functional groups—and organizations, as well as individual members of such groups, and the social traits which become ingrained in their psycho-physical organisms." He states further: "The essential unity of society consists in common, correlated, mutually conditioning activities," recalling that "activities" include ideas and sentiments. This aspect is emphasized by stating: "Indeed, we shall think of society most truly if we put the activities rather than the people foremost in our attention."

During the first ten or fifteen years of the twentieth century, many important contributions to sociological thought were in teaching, interpreting, and encouraging young people to spend time and effort on sociological thought and procedures. Unless such contributors had a special spokesman, the real effectiveness of their work was forgotten. A good example of this kind of a contributor was James Quayle Dealey, who was born in Manchester, England, in 1862 and died in 1937. He came to the United States when a child and did all of his academic work at Brown University. After retiring from Brown at the age of 65, he served until the time of his death as editor-in-chief of the *Dallas Morning News,* Dallas, Texas. Dealey was one of the early sociologists, who by teaching, helped develop new ideas. In the field of sociology, he wrote a textbook with Lester F. Ward in 1905, another in 1909, and *Sociology: Its Development and Applications,* in 1921. Most of his other writings dealt with the social, ethical, religious, local, and international applications of social concepts to the state and government, with the exception of a small book on the family in 1912, which incidentally was one of the earliest books on the family written by an American sociologist.

Another great teacher who became a sociologist after he had reached maturity and recognition in history was George Elliott Howard. He was born in Saratoga, N. Y. in 1849, died in 1928. Many persons' concept of Howard is limited to the ponderous three volume work on the *History of Matrimonial Institutions;* however, his contribution to the actual development of sociology was of a much different nature. He was a most effective teacher. He was far ahead of many of his contemporaries in his point of view and was one of the three great teachers of sociology—Blackmar, Ellwood, and Howard—who played such a great part in inspiring and establishing recognition of sociology in the states of Kansas, Missouri, and Nebraska.

Howard's characteristics are shown in many of his overt reactions, varying all the way from his resignation from Leland Stanford as a protest against the dismissal of E. A. Ross to his advocating the teaching of problems relating to the family, at a time when only a few individuals such as Charles R. Henderson considered such topics to be of academic worth.

In 1907 George Elliott Howard prepared an eighty-six page outline on the subject of general sociology for which he said he was indebted to Professor E. A. Ross. The approach included first, the general characteristics of society with particular reference to the use of investigation in which he contended that the unit of society was the "socius" which consisted not of the individual, but an individual with one or more associates; hence, the associates or the social group is the unit of society. He next dealt with the elements of society, the social population followed by an analysis of social forces which lie back of social phenomena. His final emphasis was upon the social processes which give rise to potential socialization and are manifested in association, domination, exploitation, forcible assimilation, opposition, and stratification. He thus established his place as one of the earlier sociologists who were able to foresee the trend of sociological thinking.

When he was president of the American Sociological Society (1917) he presented a paper on the "Ideals as a Factor in the Future Control of International Society." His interpretation of social control was social consciousness. He felt that nationalisms have been overdeveloped at the expense of needed internationalism, and further that a false idea which society needs to get rid of is the concept of the function of war and militarism, "Every race deems itself superior to every other race, and every race is mistaken." He recognized dangers as well as advantages in education, since people could be educated to admire autocracy.

A summary paragraph from an article in the Vol. 1, No. 4 Journal of Applied Sociology gives us an idea of his changing emphasis from institutional sociology:

"The idealist is the inspired social architect, who dreams a plan for the sanitary or moral cleansing of a great city; the campaign for purging politics of graft; a law for saving little children from the tigerish man of the factory or the sweatshop; a referendum for banishing from the commonwealth the saloon, that chief breeder of pauperism, sin, and crime; a conference for the rescuing from the hands of predacious greed, for the use of the whole people, of the remnant of our country's natural wealth. The idealist is the statesman — the head of a nation — who dreams a scheme for safeguarding democracy and guaranteeing peace throughout the world."

Among the teachers of sociology a new approach to the subject was developing. This new approach directed attention toward the conviction that social psychology was to become "the most practical, the most fruitful division of sociological science." Howard stated that social psychology is applied sociology at its best. The appearance of Ross' social psychology, Michael Davis' psychological interpretations, Mc-Dougall's social psychology and Cooley's social organization caused George Elliott Howard to prepare an Analytical Syllabus on Social Psychology. Except for the title, Ross and McDougall had little in common. Michael Davis, however, contributed the historical background. While the contribution to social thought, particularly of Ross, Cooley, and Davis, were presented under changing emphasis of sociologists, it is noteworthy that one of the outstanding teachers at this early period combined these diverse views into a teaching syllabus for social psychology.

This syllabus presented the "characteristics of social psychology, including its historical development." The first section dealt with the rise of psychological sociology: the conception of social unity. The fore-runners of the idea of social psychic unity were given as Auguste Comte's psychological law of the three states or stages in the history of the human mind; the conception of psychology in his hierarchy of the sciences; the relations of sociology to psychology, recognition of the affective faculty, the feeling as the prime motives of the mind and finally, social unity. Herbert Spencer called attention to the need of a knowledge of psychology in social life and the part played by mind and environment. He correlates social type with mental type, but rarely psychic process with social process. George Henry Lewes presented the first clear conception of a "general mind" in his *Problems of Life and Mind;* but E. DeRoberty held that the most important basis of psy-chology is sociological. Folkes' psychology and the collective mind was one of the earliest clear conceptions of the science of a collective mind. The idea of a "volksgeist" was developed by Moritz Lazarus and H. Steinhal in 1860 in *Zeitschrift fur Volker-Psychologie. III.*

The modern builders of systematic psychological sociology, accord-ing to Howard, were headed by Lester Frank Ward and his powerful influence in freeing sociology from the biological "organicist" theory. However, Ward recognized biological and physical, as well as psychic phenomena, with consideration of social forces or desires, of feelings as the dynamic agent, and of the intellect as the directive agent in social achievement. Franklin H. Giddings placed strong accent on psychic forces, concluding that like response to the same given stimulus produces organic and reflective sympathy, which in turn results in consciousness of kind and produces concerted volition. Howard felt that Durkheim laid too much stress on the social mind as a dynamic agent, neglecting the influence of "one on the many." While Albion W. Small's view could be summarized in this area "the final terms in the social process are the psychic factors which occur in the individuals that carry on the process."

The third segment listed as descriptive social psychology is presented as the various interpretations in Folkes' psychology or national psychic unity. This largely limited to such writings such as Charles Dickens' *American Notes* in 1842, Alexis Docqueville's *Democracy in America* in 1835, James Bryce's *American Commonwealth* 1888, Alfred Fouillee in his *Psychology of the People of France,* 1898 and the *Psychology of the People of Europe,* 1903. Emile Boutmy in his *Essays on the Psy-chology of English People,* and the *Psychology of Americans,* 1902, and finally Hugo Munsterberg, *The Americans,* 1904. While these are largely descriptive reactions, they fall within the area indicated.

The conception of social personality developed gradually through the general sociological results of child studies, physical and mental, the study of self by genetic psychologists, and the results of study of per-sonality by social psychologists. In this latter group, we have E. A. Ross and his concept of the stages of collective individuality, Charles H. Cooley and the development of the social person and the general idea that sociology must concern itself especially with man-to-man relations or associations and with the idea that the social person is a psychic fact and that the "social self is simply an idea, or system of ideas drawn from communicative life, that the mind cherishes as its own" . . . Much emphasis was placed upon the psychological interpretations of society by Michael M. Davis and his analysis of the development of social units.

The problems of a social mind with consideration given to "social consciousness," "public opinion," "general will," "social will," and "general mind," are presented. With the contributions of George W. Vincent relating to social mind and education, Howard included Charles A. Ellwood. Ellwood held that society is a psychic unity, that there is a social mind—a social consciousness. Within this group of contributors to the rise of social psychology before 1910 Howard included W. I. Thomas regarding whom he thought of as having excellent equipment and originality. From 1895 to 1904, Thomas had made contributions on the scope and method of Folkes' psychology; psychology of race pre-judice; and the province of social psychology, and E. A. Ross had written between 1901 and 1904 *Social Control, Foundations of Soci-ology, Sin* and *Society and Recent Problems of Social Psychology.* The scope of social psychology by 1910 was beginning to take accepted form and may be best expressed by proposed definitions of social psychology:

1. Thomas: The "Study of the individual mental processes in so far as they are conditioned by states of consciousness". Its pro-vince is the "examination of the interaction of individual con-

sciousness and society, and the effect of the interaction on individual consciousness on the one hand and on society on the other" (A.J.S., X 445-46; or the same in Congress of Arts and Science, V. 860-61):

   a. Hence, social psychology may "make either the individual or society the object of attention at a given moment."

   b. It is an "extension of individual psychology to the phenomena of 'collective life' ."

2. Kulp: The "science which treats of the mental phenomena dependent upon a community of individuals" (Outlines of Psychology, 7; cf. Ellwood, in A.J.S., IV, 656).

3. Ellwood: An examination of the form or mechanism of "group psychical processes"; the "psychical phenomena pertaining to group life as such"; an "interpretation of the psychical processes manifested in the growth and functioning of a group as a unity." (A.J.S., IV, 456-57, V, 105-109).

   a. Implies the existence of "inter-individual psychical processes," for example, the phenomena of revolution, mob-action, group-action, etc.

   b. It does not offer a complete interpretation of society; but it offers the subjective as opposed to the objective interpretation.

   c. Sociology is the "synthesis of the objective with the subjective or psychological philosophy of history?" (See Ellwood in A.J.S., IV, 658-60).

   d. The "fundamental fact" in social psychology is therefore, "Social co-ordination" or group-functioning (action). This is not to be confused with mere "co-operation" (Ellwood in A.J.S., IV, 807-22; compare Giddings, Elements, 77-78).

     (1) Social or group habit; custom, organization, institution, social product.

     (2) Crisis, transition, adaptation or accommodation.

   e. Theories of "social selection" (Ellwood, A.J.S., IV, 820-22; Baldwin, Social and Ethical Interpretations 183-85, 492 ff.).

4. Davis: "We may regard the physical and biological conditions of this co-operative action (i.e., the "concerted action" of individuals in society); we may investigate the forms of institutions through which it passes; or we may look inwardly to the feelings, thoughts, brainstates and impulses which accompany, illuminate, and - - - guide the action. In the first case our sociology is biological or ethnological; in the second, historical and analytic; in the third, psychological." (Psychological Interpretations, 9-10).

5. Ross: "Social psychology . . . studies the psychic planes and currents that come into existence among men in consequence of their association. It seeks to understand and account for those uniformities in feeling, belief, or volition, and hence, into action—which are due to the interaction of human beings, i.e., to *social* causes . . . Social psychology differs from sociology proper in that the former considers planes and currents, the latter groups and structures." Ross distinguished between mob or crowd psychology and normal group psychology. Accordingly, social psychology deals primarily with psychic parallelisms due to the action of mind upon mind; and secondly, with psychic uniformities arising in non-psychic parallelisms. Examples:

   a. Mental uniformities due to the action of epidemic or famine, flood or earthquake, are excluded.

   b. Uniformities due to the action of common physical environment or similar conditions of life are likewise excluded.

Howard is usually mentioned in connection with his specific contributions as contained in his principle publications. He has been included here among the great teachers of sociology who helped bring together the contributions of the earlier American and European sociologists and present this material to the growing number of students of sociology.

When a new species of a plant or of an animal is developed by scientific or accidental selection, it is carefully nurtured and checked, cross-bred and tested to determine its qualities and to establish its reliability. The early efforts to determine the scope and value of basic principles in sociology was largely the concern of a few men who examined these principles and critically evaluated their reliability on the basis of history, philosophy, and logic. When the field became accepted in at least a general way, sociology began to be introduced, not merely as an additional facet in the explanation of human activities and processes, but as a distinctive discipline with its own body of factual knowledge, as well as principles for further analysis of society. Thus the teaching of sociology became an increasingly important field of study. Teachers of sociology began to add the study of social psychology, social control, social organization, and social reform to the established field of history, economics, and geography. The subject took hold with an effective influence on education, which might be compared to the spread of the use of hybred corn, or the crossing of Brahmin cattle with native stocks. It is perhaps a fact that is overlooked that the first half of the twentieth century made greater changes in social relations and social understanding than in any other field—

notwithstanding the more obvious mechanical and industrial changes which were made possible because social changes made their introduction possible. This is the direct result of the thousands of contributions made by teachers of sociology. Hundreds of thousands of students during the half century were developing a point of view which was seemingly as fantastic fifty years ago as a flight to the moon.

V

Background for Sociological Research

SOCIAL research develops slowly and often irregularly. An important factor in the apparently slow progress of sound social research has been the failure to build upon the work already done. Each social situation that attracts enough attention to be considered worthy of a research project is found in a social setting which, because of its variation from other situations and settings, appears to be distinc- tive and unique. Research projects frequently are limited to a description of something new or unique. The organization or individuals concerned with the attempt take the front of the stage and their perpetuation becomes the main objective, rather than the research projects or the effort to meet the situation giving rise to the inquiry. Too frequently a research project is undertaken without adequate knowledge of similar studies or without making use of the experience of others. This results in retarding sound social research and progressive development.

By what men have done we learn what men can do. This is specially true in the area of social research. Techniques, methods, procedures are not the result of a sudden inspiration. Many procedures have been effectively used to aid in forward steps and then found inadequate as better techniques have developed or a change of emphasis has taken place. Even when discontinued, every attempt has been of value for the future, even though the results have indicated that the project was concerned with a barren field. During my first contact with Albion W. Small in 1913, at which time I told him what I wished to work on, he said: "Young man, I think you are on the wrong track. But my advice is, go to it. Do a good job. You will, I think, find that you have covered a blind alley. But do it so well that no one need ever go over that ground again."

The background for social research might cover a variety of aspects, but for this discussion it will be divided into three stages:

1. The long-time development of techniques for objective and mathematical study of mass data, in which the mechanics of statistics has reached an effective level of reliability.
2. The relatively recent emergence of a sociological approach and recognition of the need for application of research methods to social phenomena.

3. The establishing and selecting of definite procedures and fields of research, the attempt to break down causal factors to determine units of measure, and the beginning of the study of more minute and specific aspects of social situations.

Some of our present-day attempts to measure social situations may be compared with attempts made during the last 600 years. The reason many of these attempts did not become a part of established procedures was that they were limited in their explanation of causal relationships. No single approach to explain the factors in a situation can be sufficient.

Students of social phenomena have long attempted to predict or to calculate probability. Accuracy, however, has been of slow and gradual development, and sometimes very unpopular. Ramon Lull (1235-1315), who attempted to classify ideas objectively, was stoned to death. In 1267 Roger Bacon considered the application of principles of mathematics to observation, the only correct method by which to understand phenomena of all kinds. His reasoning frightened his contemporaries. They tried to excommunicate him, but Pope Gregory IV saw the importance of his work. Bacon's ideas were typical of what leaders of that period were beginning to emphasize. The introduction of the use of the Hindu notation, transmitted to Europe by the Arabs, made the study of mass data easier. The nine numerals plus the zero and the simple system of tens, hundreds, thousands, and millions simplified certain aspects of mathematical calculation and changed it from drudgery to recreation.

A few references will illustrate the gradual growth of the use of increasingly exact methods of research, without over-emphasis on details. An example of an early extensive study is *The White Book of the City of London* by John Carpenter, 1419, 14 volumes: translated in 1862 by H. T. Riley from the original Latin and Anglo-Norman.

Attempts to explain social phenomena and social relationship objectively have a long history. The following list gives a few of the more outstanding contributors in the development of the use of objective methods in the study of social phenomena. The list indicates the early growth of statistical research.

Lulle, Ramon (1235-1315)—Scientific method.
Bacon, Roger (1214-1294)—Scientific method.
Muenster, Sebastian (1489-1552)—*Cosmographia,* 1536-1544.
Sansovino, Francesco (1521-1585)—Laws and Customs of People, 1562.
Bodin, Jean (1530-1596)—*Les Six Livres,* 1577.
Conring, Hermann (1606-1681)—*Staatsmerkwurdigkeiten,* 1660.
Graunt, John (1624-1674)—Natural and Political Observations Upon Bills of Mortality.

Neuman, Kasper (1648-1715)—The danger to health as certain years.

Huygens, Christian (1629-1695)—*De rationiniis in ludo aleae,* 1658.

Pascal, Blaise (1623-1662)—Posthumous pub. 1665.

Fermat, Pierre de (1590-1665)—Posthumous pub. 1679.

Petty, Sir William (1623-1685)—*Essay on Political Arithmetic,* 1682.

Leibnitz, Gottfried Wilhelm (1646-1716)—*De Arte Cominatoria,* 1666.

de Witt, Jan (1625-1672)—*Mortality Tables and Purchase Price of Annuities,* pub. 1671.

Halley, Edmond (1656-1742)—Life tables, 1695.

King, Gregory (1648-1712)—Population Estimates and Conclusions upon the State and Condition of England, 1696.

Wallis, J. (1616-1703)—*Population Changes,* 1684.

Craig, J. (1680-1718)—Calculation of the Credibility of Human Testimony (Anon.) 1699.

Bernoulli, Jacques (first of the name) (1654-1705)—*Arts conjectandi,* Posth. 1713.

Bernoulli, Jean (1667-1748)—Theses, prob. 1713.

Bernoulli, Nicholas (1687-1759)—Nephew of two brothers, Jacques and Jean—Published posthumous works of Jacques.

Bernoulli, Daniel (1700-1782)—Son of Jean. *Essai d'une nouvelle analyse de la mortalite cause par la petite Verole, et des advantages de l'Inoculation pour la prevenir,* 1766.

Van Hudden (1640-1705)—Pub. 1671.

Sauveur, J. (1653-1716)—Pub. 1679.

Prestet, (le Pere) S. J. (1648-1690)—

de Montmort, P. Remond (1679-1719)—*Essai d'Analyse sur les Jeux de Hazards,* pub. 1708-1713.

de Moivre, Abraham (1667-1745)—*Doctrine of Chances,* 1718; *De Mensura Sortis,* 1711.

Vauban, Marechal (1633-1707)—Recommended centralization of official Statistics of France. 1699-1707.

Davenant, Sir Charles (1656-1714)—Discourses on Public Revenues, 1698.

Elvius, Pehr (1710-1749)—Classification of deaths of Swedish population according to age, sex, and cause of death.

Runeberg, E. F. (1722-1770—Published Population Statistics of Sweden and Finland, 1764-1765.

Wargentin, Pehr (1717-1783)—"Our nyttan af Fortechningar po fodda och doda" 1754-1755. Mortality tables for Sweden, 1766.

Sussmilch, Johan Peter (1707-1767)—*Reflections on the Divine Order,* 1740.

Franklin, Benjamin (1706-1790)—*Moral Algebra,* 1772. Sent to Joseph Priestley, Sept. 19, 1772.

Achenwall, Gottfried (1719-1790)—*Abriss der Staatswissenschaft der heutigen vornehursten eurapaischen Reiche und Republikin: 1749.*
Condorcet, Marie Jean Antoine (1743-1794)—*Tableau general . . . l'application du calcul aux sciences politiques et morales, 1795.*
Lavoisier, Antoine Laurent (1743-1794)—Recommended Department of Statistics for France, 1784.
Fourier, Jean Baptiste Joseph (1768-1830)—Variation in Population Profile of Stationary Population, 1817. (Not to be confused with Francois Marie Charles Fourier 1772-1828).
Laplace, Pierre Simon (1749-1827)—Theory of Probability, 1812.
de Champneuf, Guerry (1788-1852)—Criminal Statistics of France, 1827.
Guerry, Andre Michel (1802-1866)—*Essay on the Moral Statistics of France, 1833* (Data and charts of Guerry de Champneuf); *Moral Statistics of England and France, 1857.*
Quetelet, Lambert Adolphe (1796-1874)—*Sur l'Homme et le Developpement de ses Faculties, 1835.*

This marked the beginning of modern scientific statistics and the development of our present type of private research, official statistics, and private and public investigations and research bureaus.

The interest in an approach to "regional sociology" was indicated by Sebastian Munster (1489-1552) at Heidelburg in his attempt to explain the varying activities of different people on the basis of history, state organization, laws, customs, and manners. He lacked present-day developments of psychology and sociology for adequate interpretation of his data, but he did recognize some aspects of the problem. This was a far cry from the present-day regionalism in the study and analysis of social problems, but there was the beginning of recognition of situations which had to await further techniques, for the analyses of Odum, Mumford, Pannunzio, Ogburn, and others.

The cultural approach to the study of certain Mediterranean countries was indicated in the work of Francesco Sansovino (1521-85). His attempts to study and explain the laws and customs of these groups were decidedly of more importance to present-day research in sociology than many of the social philosophies of the nineteenth century which are frequently cited.

The early contributors to social research were not chiefly concerned with social phenomena; they were concerned with determining probability. Yet, Pascal (1659) emphasized the effect of climate upon social phenomena, and Fermat (1679), Brossin (1685), and Huygens (1858) began to apply calculations of probability to matters of public interest.

We need only be reminded of Jean Bodin's demand (1577) for exact data as a basis for controlling social disorder, and of John Graunt, who in 1661 began to show causal relationship in the data assembled by the "Bills of Mortality" *(Natural and Political Observations . . . made upon the Bills of Mortality, with reference to the government, religion, trade, growth, aim, diseases, etc . . . of the City of London).* Graunt attempted to show that there was some relationship between the frequency of suicides and other data and the section of the country, seasons, occupations, and business conditions. Graunt went a step further than Sansovina. The term *human ecology* had not been formulated.

About the same time (1660) Herman Conring at the University of Helmstedt gave lectures on *Universitatswissenschaftlichestaatmerkwur-digkeiten* (universal scientific facts pertaining to outstanding peculiarities of the state), using the data collected by Bolero and De Thou, he tried to find the causal connection. A few years later, Jan de Witt (1671) discussed the value of life annuities (Waardige van Lyfrenten naar proportie van Losrenten). Interested primarily in establishing distribution of mortality rates, he also attempted to apply calculations to political questions. Sir William Petty (1682) was confronted by the need for more correct nomenclature whenever he attempted to measure social phenomena statistically. He criticized the use of terms such as *larger, much larger, many, more,* and *less* and attempted to eliminate individual opinion, individual bias, and to establish the use of objective standards. This was 200 years before Mayo-Smith's *Sociology and Statistics* and Giddings' *Inductive Sociology.*

It is not necessary to give details on the well-known efforts of Casper Neuman, Leibnitz, Vauban; but by the last quarter of the eighteenth century great steps forward had been taken. Sweden, particularly with Pehr Elvius, Wargentin, Runeberg, and others, had developed population data and had succeeded in applying this knowledge to social problems. Practical objectives were made the basis for social statistics. As early as 1766 Daniel Bernoulli, who, with other members of his family, is still recognized in connection with their work on thermo-dynamics, made a careful study on a new analysis of death carried by smallpox and the advantage of inoculation for its prevention. Jacques Bernoulli (1654-1705), the first of that name, is credited with writing the first book devoted entirely to statistics. It has taken many years for sociologists to recognize such work as of sociological significance, on the same basis as Kant's essay, "Critique of Pure Reason."

There are certain highlights which we need to recognize in the development of background for social research. Some of these seem of no importance to the young researcher, so that he may even scoff at his predecessors concerning their inadequacies.

Emphasis on research relating to social phenomena first dealt very largely with the more observable facts of population—births, deaths, propagation—and the profile of population based upon age and sex. This naturally led to such studies as Sussmilch's population theories (*Betrachtungen uber die Gottliche Ordnung in den Veranderungen des menschlichen Geschlechts aus der Geburt, dem Tode und der Fortpflanzung derselben erwiesen*) and the studies of the Bernoullis and Achenwall. Even Benjamin Franklin wrote, in 1772, concerning moral algebra, that is, the attempt to predict the direction and probable existence of social reactions on the basis of mathematical formulae. After the death of Condorcet, there was published in 1795 a monograph by him, in which the principles of calculation were applied to politics and social relations.

In 1821-27, Guerry de Champneuf, director of Criminal Affairs, prepared his studies on criminal statistics of France. Jean Baptiste Joseph Fourier aided him in the preparation of the five volumes, *Recherches statistiques sur la vie de Paris et la Department de la Seine.* Some of these data and charts were compiled into an essay in 1833 by a young man, Andre Michel Guerry. Guerry de Champneuf was sent into exile because of his studies, and most of the materials were destroyed by the new government in 1830. His exile terminated about twenty years later, at which time Andre Michel Guerry recompiled his study on moral statistics of England and France (1857) and received the Grand Prix of the French Academy. But this material was again destroyed by the French government about ten years later. Three copies of this are known to exist. They contain many excellent maps and charts showing the relation of various crimes to specified areas in England and France and the correlation of these data with population density, age, and education. There were some attempts to develop an interest in social statistics among scholars of different nations. Among these Quetelet was the leader.

Adolphe Quetelet (1796-1874), like Halley, was an astronomer and built upon Laplace's application of the theory of probability to social phenomena. This marked the beginning of modern scientific statistics and the development of our present type of private research, official statistics, private and public investigation, and research bureaus.

Statistical development took the form of:

1. Enumeration of quaint, curious, useful facts.
2. Generalization—particularly at the end of the eighteenth century.
3. Learning possibilities of obtaining various types of results from data (Galton called attention to correlation which we have seen was recognized earlier. Pearson presented a more simplified method of working out the coefficient of correla-

tion.)

4. Use of statistics for measurement and analysis of social activities and the determination of more refined units of measure, sampling, and scoring of social phenomena.

Along with the development of more refined statistical procedures, a new approach to the study of sociology became apparent. Francis Lieber, in *Proposals for a Work in the Statistics of the United States* (1836), suggested the use of statistical data covering the country, inhabitants, social interrelationship, standards of comfort; data concerning religion, education, the arts, and publications; the political state, industry, and commerce; criminal statistics, medical statistics, as well as the usual data concerning the agencies of protection—all this to be summarized as a basis for analysis. It is of passing interest that nearly one hundred years later we find many of his ideas developed in that monumental contemporary study *Social Trends*.

Lieber also saw statistics from a more generalized point of view than had the earlier writers. He stated:

"Statistics consist, in a great degree, in the collection and classification of a number of isolated facts, which thus isolated have little value for human experience, or lead not infrequently to views entirely erroneous. If they are patiently and faithfully collected, judiciously arranged and applied, and wisely digested, they lead to a more positive knowledge of the real state of things, with regard to all subjects of which we are able to collect statistics, than any other mode of inquiry. They often exhibit errors, though cherished for centuries, in their real light, unveil errors never suspected before, or show their roots where they were never expected to be found, thus enabling us to choose the most or the only efficient means of counteracting them. They are, therefore, of the greatest use to the legislator, and to everyone whose duty it is to frame general measures for this community, on whatever branch."

Very few of the social philosophers in 1836 know what Lieber was talking about—so his ideas were seldom mentioned—and those of us who limited our study of the middle nineteenth century to the better-known writers of that time quite naturally never heard of him.

Many good ideas in research were lost because of their association with lagging concepts. Thus in 1875 R. J. Wright observed that classified groups in society are primitive and derivative groups. He foresaw forms of urban growth which were not generally understood until much later. He emphasized the need for observation and experimentation and showed that they were necessary steps in the improvement of society.

This has been mentioned merely to show that there is frequently a recognition of what is necessary and the method of attaining a goal long before circumstances, conditions, and techniques are available, and before there is a receptive audience. An idea takes form, but because of the many obstacles it becomes lost and is not rediscovered until some of these obstacles have been overcome.

While it is largely due to the writings of Adolphe Quetelet, 1796-1874, the Belgian astronomer and statistician, and others like him that we may trace the beginnings of present day concepts of sociology as a field for statistical study, the earliest contribution in the period covered here was made by Richmond Mayo-Smith. He represented a fusion of Quetelet, LePlay, and Durkheim and presented the statistical approach with an understanding of its shortcomings as well as its major functions. Perhaps, other than reference to his statistics and sociology, the best view of Mayo-Smith's contribution is two statements from the catalogue of Columbia University 1893-1894 in which he suggests many topics which men not born at that time have "discovered."

From the Catalogue of Columbia University 1893 and 1894 we cite:

Statistics and Social Science
1. Statistical science: methods and results—This course is intended to furnish a basis for social science by supplementing the historical, legal, and economic knowledge already gained by such a knowledge of social phenomena as can be gained only by statistical observation. Under the head of statistics of population are considered: race and ethnological distinctions, national density, city and country, sex, age, occupation, religion, education, births, deaths, marriages, mortality, tables, emigra-tion, etc. Under economic statistics: land, production of food, raw material, labor wages, capital, means of transportation, shipping, prices, etc. Under the head of moral statistics are considered: statistics of sui-cide, vice, crime of all kinds, causes of crime, conditioning of criminals, repression of crime, penalties and effect of penalties, etc. Finally are considered the method of statistical observations, the value of the results obtained, the doctrine of free will, and the possibility of discovering social laws. Two hours a week—Professor Mayo-Smith.
2. Communistic and socialistic theories—"The present organization of society is attacked by socialistic writers, who demand many changes, especially in the institution of private property and the system of free competition. It is the objective of this course to describe what these attacks are, what changes are proposed and how far these changes seem desirable or possible. At the same time an account is given of actual socialistic movements, such as the international, social democracy, etc. Advantage is taken of these discussions to make the course really one of social science, by describing modern social institutions, such as private property in their historical origin and development, and their present

justification" 1893-94. Two hours a week—Professor Mayo-Smith.

The preceding excerpts from the catalogue of the Columbia University describing the courses of Mayo-Smith are of significance in showing how early this aspect of sociology was recognized in the universities.

Public interest in the last quarter of the nineteenth century was directed toward the questions: What is happening in society? What should be done? What is being done?

About the time that Mayo-Smith was offering these courses at Columbia University, three trends in sociological research began to appear in American sociological thinking.

1. The formulation of methods and procedures for conducting social research which for a time was concerned chiefly with general as well as specific surveys of community life. This trend developed side by side, if not actually a part of the development of the group concept which began to be formulated in the early years of the twentieth century.

2. The application of theory, principles, and methods to actual studies which varied from such specific problems as sanitation, health, industry, child labor to comprehensive historical and contemporary community studies.

3. The third, which was often combined with the two mentioned, was the statistical analysis which took the form not only in development of social statistics beyond what had been done up to this date, but laid the foundation for more objective social research than was generally considered possible. A Catechism for Social Observation and Analysis of Social Phenomena was prepared in 1894 by Charles Richmond Henderson. It was a booklet which indicated the general coverage of a community survey. By including a modification of this in a text book on sociology Small and Vincent directed the attention of students of sociology toward community surveys. In 1897 Franklin H. Giddings prepared a syllabus entitled "The Theory of Socialization" which grew into his Inductive Sociology in 1901. This later volume was subtitled "A Syllabus of Methods, Analyses, and Classifications, and Provisionally Formulated Laws". Under the encouragement and direction of Giddings, Warren H. Wilson made a study of Quaker Hill (1910); and the evolution of the county, community (1912); Newell Simms, The Hoosier Village (1912); Howard B. Woolston, Manhattenville (1909); Thomas Jesse Jones, The Sociology of a City Block (1904); to mention a few typical cases which research students of the

latter half of the twentieth century could profitably study and thus avoid presenting some of the half developed sociological principles found in much later community studies which were made without an understanding of the principles which had developed through the years and had been crystalized in the writings of Mayo-Smith, Henderson, and Giddings.

The purpose of this study does not go back to all of the early attempts of social research, but places its chief emphasis upon development since 1890. However, Charles Booth, in 1887, began the monumental survey of *Life and Living Conditions of the People in London* which inspired comparable studies in this country.

Probably the most extensive studies of this kind were made by the survey associates of the City of Pittsburgh, and published from 1907 to 1914 in six major volumes and several minor reports under the editorship of Paul Underwood Kellogg.

1. Women and the Trades (1907-1908)
2. Work Accidents and the Law, Eastman
3. The Steel Workers, J. A. Fitch (1910)
4. Homestead—The Household of a Mill Town, Margaret F. Byington (1909)
5. The Pittsburgh District Civic Front (1910)
6. Wage Earning Pittsburgh (1914)

In 1912 Carol Aronovici prepared a pamphlet entitled "Knowing One's Own Community" with suggestions for a social survey of small cities or towns. He followed this with a series of community surveys for the American Unitarian Association similar to the studies that were being made by Warren H. Wilson for the Presbyterian Church. Charles J. Galpin who was associated with the extension division of the University of Wisconsin described a method for making a social survey of a rural community in 1912. In 1914 Manuel C. Elmer prepared a study on "Social Surveys of Urban Communities" followed three years later by his first edition, 1917, *Technique of Social Surveys*. Margaret F. Byington, 1915, prepared a very useful outline which did much to clarify problems of social workers entitled "What Social Workers Should Know About Their Own Community." Following the first world war the social survey movement received special impetus from many national organizations as well as individuals. Carl C. Taylor in 1919 wrote the *Social Survey, Its History and Methods;* F. S. Chapin, 1920, *Field Work and Social Research:* Emory S. Bogarduc, 1926, *The New Social Research.* The extent to which social surveys developed is indicated by the bibliographies prepared by Shelby Harrison in 1926

and 1931. In the 1926 bibliography of *Social Surveys* over three thousand titles are recorded.

The community surveys began to take on widely diversified forms.
Some of the particular aspects were expressed as educational surveys;
health and sanitation surveys; recreation surveys; and crime surveys. At
first these were largely enumerative, indicating the extent and location
of the problem under consideration. These were followed by more analytical studies indicating specific factors, as for example in 1916 M. C.
Elmer and Donald Paterson made a study of Council Grove, Kansas
which focalized on the mental variations of members of the community;
in 1918 a study by M. C. Elmer and E. Swanson dealt with primary
groups, and interest centers around Agenda, Kansas; J. H. Kolb made
a similar study, 1921, in S. Dane County, Wisconsin. Reaching into
other fields we find "Women in Industry in St. Paul," 1923-24 and,
Juvenile Delinquency in St. Paul in 1924, which was an analysis of
delinquency areas. These studies were made by groups from the University of Minnesota, M. C. Elmer, director. Thus the social survey
which began as a general community inventory took on specific aspects.
Such specific aspects of community studies began to appear at the
University of Chicago. These for a time showed the ecological approach.

The concept of human ecology was further presented in the
American Sociological Society in 1926 *The Urban Community and The
City* by a number of writers on the subject.

The concepts which sociologists recognize as a minimum equipment
for carrying on their work, may sometimes include an approach to a
subject as well as an acceptable statement of what it involves. Such
a concept and approach may be included in the term *ecological*. While
the term has been extensively used relating to the plant and animal life,
and to the factors which make up their environment, and the basis for
the origin, development, complexity, or extinction of plant and animal
life, it has become increasingly used in regard to human relationships.
In 1913 a young Canadian, Roderick D. McKenzie, enrolled for grad-
ate work at the University of Chicago. I was interested in directing
some dramatic work at the Chicago Commons on Chicago's West Side.
McKenzie was very much interested in the city of Chicago. He used to
go with me to those meetings and after rehearsals we would walk from
Sangamo and Robie Streets down Halstead. Sometimes we walked the
entire distance to the University of Chicago at 58th and Ellis. We would
take different routes on different evenings. McKenzie wanted to do this
because life in Chicago was so different from life on the Canadian
prairies. The beginning of his interest in human ecology began to manifest itself. The patterns which took shape due to the spatial relationship of human beings, their formal and informal group organizations,

and their struggle for existence aroused his interest. Sometimes we would
sit on the shore of Lake Michigan and he would attempt to formulate
this hazy picture which was beginning to take form in the overlapping
series and conflicting group organizations, through which we passed in
our walks. Neil McIntyre, E. E. Eubank, and I used to try to get him
nailed down to some concrete subject for his thesis. But after hours of
haranguing he would end up by disagreeing with what we had felt we
had convincingly told him, and he would say, "I'm not satisfied to work
on that. It is too limited. I would like to find out what factors are
present, what processes contribute in the development of mutual cooperation, competition, or even the development of human parasites such
as we see functioning on our trips from the West Side down to the
University." He would continue, "It cannot be attributed to heredity, or
to a whole life of experience because it seems to indicate something
which will accommodate itself relatively quickly to changes in transportation, in housing, in occupations and various other factors." When
we read McKenzie's later writings which began to take form in the
development of his doctorial dissertation, there comes to mind many of
the early experiences he had when he came from Manitoba to the city
of Chicago with its unique population and setting. This he later put
into a concrete statement, "Human Ecology is the science which deals
with the changing spatial relationships of human beings and human
institutions", and further, "The fact that man is a cultural animal
makes his ecological organization more dynamic and unpredictable, but
at the same time more interesting and important, than that of the pre-
cultural organisms.—The ecologist is concerned with the processes of
human distribution as they operate under different conditions of culture and mobility."

McKenzie outlines the scope of human ecology as consisting of:
1. Ecological Distribution meaning the spatial distribution of
   human beings and human activities resulting from the interplay
   of forces which affect the more or less conscious, or at any rate
   dynamic and vital relationship among the units comprising the
   aggregation.
2. Ecological Unit, any ecological distribution—which has a unitary
   character sufficient to differentiate it from surrounding distribution.
3. Mobility and Fluidity, an ecological organization is in process
   of constant change.
4. Distance, ecological distance is a measure of fluidity. It is a
   time-cost concept rather than a unit of space.
5. Ecological Factors, the changing spatial relations of human

beings are the result of the interplay of a number of different forces. These may be classified as geographical, economic, cultural and technical, and political and administrative.

6. Ecological Processes, by ecological process is meant the tendency in time toward special forms of spatial and sustenance groupings of the units comprising an ecological distribution.
7. Regional Concentration, is a tendency of increasing number of persons to settle in a given area or region.
8. Regional Specialization, no description.
9. Dispersion, no description.
10. Centralization, no description.
11. Specialization and Centralization, types of centers.
12. Decentralization and Re-centralization.
13. Segregation.
14. Invasion.
15. Succession, and finally;
16. Structure, where ecological processes operate within a more or less rigid structural base.

The development of the concept of Human Ecology was expressed by James A. Quinn in the *American Journal of Sociology,* September, 1940, in his discussion of "Topical Summary of Current Literature in Human Ecology." Even at that time the concept was taking form but it had not attained the status reached at the time of Quinn's book on ecology published ten years later. Quinn indicated that there seemed to be an increase in the strength and the degree of emphasis upon the ecological field, but that the field of human ecology was variously defined with no clearcut outline of topics which were unanimously accepted. However, he used the outline followed by McKenzie in his readings in Human Ecology 1934. This outline was based on five principle headings:

a. "The Nature of Human Ecology"
b. "Ecological Organization and Dominance"
c. "Interpretations of Spatial Distribution"
d. "Migration and Mobility"
e. "Succession"

Much of the research in the field of human ecology has been focalized toward particularized aspects of human relations in particular environments. This was developed and illustrated by many of the Chicago series of studies.

One of the most obvious contributions of human ecology has been its methodological approach. Taking advantage of every type of material it re-emphasizes the need of considering every possible factor which may have any influence in determining social activities and attitudes. A positive contribution, which is perhaps more effective than becoming a distinctive area of a discipline, is an exploratory attitude, with some more emphasis on spatial relations than is sometimes recognized. It is an added procedure in the evaluation of the social order and social processes.

McKenzie in defining human ecology stated that 'Human Ecology is fundamentally interested in the effect of *position*, in both time and space, upon human institutions and human behavior'; and further defined it, 'as a study of the spatial and temporal relations of human beings as affected by the selective, distributive, and accommodative forces of the environment.' He classified the subject matter of human ecology into three divisions: the spatial arrangement of population and institutions; the dynamic or functional aspect of spatial relationships; and the temporal changes in the community, or ecological succession.

A study of human ecology means much more than the manner, distribution of people, activities, agencies, interest groupings in their spatial relations. In order to understand the ecology of a community, it is necessary to understand the factors in the development and growth of that community, it is necessary to understand how certain conditions appeared. It is necessary to understand the historical background of the factors which are bringing about modification and change. The entire historical and cultural background is necessary to understand and to explain ecological situations. Some of the more obvious ecological groupings may be based upon a common culture, language, race, nationality, or occupational interest, but underneath these obvious groupings are additional elements which are much more subtle, and, while less usually observed, of the greatest significance. The more obvious factors are readily determined. For example, it is a rather simple matter to collect the material and make base maps upon which will be indicated the concentration of juvenile delinquencies, of homicides, of suicides, of variations in the divorce rate, of variations in the age, sex, or occupations of people. The factors, however, which motivate them, the attitudes, found in special concentrated areas, the basis for the development of special attitudes, the control and modification of those attitudes, the resultant social processes, are really the key to the situation. The obvious data may merely be the resultant phenomena and give us no key as to the causative factors in the situation.

An ecological approach to the study of a social situation is more than a cross-section of a particular area at a given time. It is not limited to a descriptive determination of the variation in intensity and existence of the phenomena under consideration in a particular cross-section. As Charles C. Adams summarized this, "Cross-sections have their value, but the past and the future must receive attention in dealing with life relations, and provision should be made for this phase in the surveys or it will be lacking in the results. This means that specific efforts should be made to determine just what *processes, pressures,* and *trends* are at work in any given condition or community."

The ecological approach to the study of various special population groups, or the spatial distribution of particular interest groupings, tends to indicate waves of succession, the mobility of population, and the gradual growth of areas of influence. An attempt was made by Guerry de Champneuf to divide France into five regional areas for a study of crime and education in the early part of the nineteenth century. The present-day development of ecological research techniques has been largely perfected by the significant series of studies at the University of Chicago. These studies serve as models in this field of research and should be carefully considered in this connection.

Shortly after 1900 there developed a widespread desire to understand social conditions and activities. In almost every city of any importance investigations were carried on in some field or other. The organization carrying on the survey may have been a church or affiliated religious organization making a study of its particular community; a civic league making an investigation of the local industrial situation; a charitable organization investigating the poor quarters of the city; a department of health making a sanitary survey; a special committee appointed by the state or city studying the efficiency of some public institution; or it may be an intensive survey of the industries and living conditions, as was carried on in London, Pittsburgh, Birmingham, or Springfield, Illinois. Whatever the source of the particular investigation, the number and variety of surveys that were continually being made throughout the country indicated that there was a general demand to have information in regard to existing conditions.

The findings of a social survey should bear much the same relation to the community's activities as a geological survey would have to the development of the industrial program of a geographical area. It furnished the data which will determine the nature and extent of future developments, as well as the basic data for determining the causal factors in past or current phenomena. Its purpose was not only to help remedy present maladjustments, but also furnish the data for scientifically laying the foundation upon which future generations may build.

In summary then, the objectives of the social survey are:
1. Accurate data scientifically obtained.
2. The securing of data which will be of use in meeting some local situation or temporary program.

3. To serve as a basis for the formulation of a long time program or making some fundamental change in the organization of the community.
4. Making an historical monograph of a community.
5. A pathfinder study, as a preliminary to any kind of intensive research along a specific line.
6. Education of community leaders and establishment of purposeful cooperation between various groups.

A first step is necessary toward measuring social attitudes, ideas, ideals and practices, and for making a scientific analysis and evaluation of group activities, their inter-relationship and the resulting social processes.

This first step to social research made by the general survey was very similar no matter what the specific objective. It gave the overall view of the conditions and activities which existed. During the first quarter of the twentieth century the thousands of general surveys made established the principle of the need for this general background. It is true that very often by the time the general survey was made, the enthusiasm, or the funds available was exhausted and nothing further was done. This brought the general social survey into disrepute. However, the recognition for the need of general information had been established and it was observed that there were similar data required of all research studies. An outgrowth of this was more refined data secured by the census department. Several cities began to subdivide their area into "census tracts" thus making it possible to secure all types of census data on the basis of small areas, or by combining areas, districts which included similar characteristics, but were not absorbed in the general ward data. This step, which had reached a high degree of proficiency by the time of the 1930 census, removed the necessity for a very tedious phase of the general community survey and made it possible to devote that effort to more refined analysis. Harvey W. Zorbaugh stated in 1925—"The natural areas of the city are real units. They can be accurately defined. Facts that have a position and can be plotted serve to characterize them. Within the areas we can study the subtler phases of city life—politics, opinion, cultural conflicts, and all social attitudes. As this data accumulates it becomes possible to compare and check our knowledge. With natural areas defined, with the processes going on within them analyzed, statistics based upon natural areas should prove diagnostic of real situations and processes, indicative of real trends. It is not improbable that statistical ratios might be worked out which would afford a basis for prediction beyond the mere agglomeration of population, making it possible to apply numerical measurement to that collective human behavior in the urban environment which is the growth of the city."

Along about this time there appeared the development of the *Regional Survey*. Some men have contributed to the development of social thought through their general contacts, their teaching and activities in society. Unless these aspects of their lives are recorded much of their actual contribution is forgotten. Others are remembered because they have put into concrete form the unexpressed attitudes of their fellowmen, or have written new interpretations of social thinking and its manifestations. Few men have so effectively contributed in as wide a range of activities and interests as *Howard Odum* (1884-1954). Born in Georgia, trained in psychology at Clarke University, and sociology at Columbia University, he worked in Philadelphia then went into college teaching. There are few persons who have had the insight shown by Odum into folkways and folk culture. His genuine interest in life about him made him a leader in understanding the stories and the songs of the people of the South. His work in research, in community organization and in regionalism did much to effect the attitude of social thinking in this period. Whatever he undertook became an example of the achievement possible. Few sociologists know that in line with his interest in regional development, he was concerned with the economic security of the average person in the Southland. With the equipment possible for almost any small farmer he developed a herd of Jersey dairy cattle and was selected as the master dairy breeder of America. His interest in this was to be of benefit to the social life of the region. In answer to a letter he wrote the following.

"In reply to your inquiry of a few days ago, I too have heard Giddings say that one of the great disappointments of his career was that sociology did not take up his inductive sociology and try it out in the same way in which medicine and other sciences experimented with their premises. I am also sure that sociology would have profited in a big way.

"Now in my own case, naturally, I am glad to have a chance to emphasize the concepts in which I have become interested.

1. The first of these is folk sociology as a general sociology in which, through historical and empirical studies of the folk and of the folk quality, we come to certain theoretical conclusions concerning the continuity of the folk process as the basic societal process.

2. Our studies of regionalism as a science of the relation of component units to the total society and the folk-regional society as the basic unit for the study of all society developed from empirical studies. Regionalism, also, becomes a methodological

approach in the combining of the various social sciences and it becomes, also, a tool for administrative purposes in social planning, especially world planning.

3. The concept of the technic-ways has developed in the same way from the study of the folk culture in contrast to state civilization. The technic-ways are the ways of measuring behavior in response to modern civilization in which the trend is toward a technological order instead of a moral or societal order. The technic-ways are easily defined operationally.

"In the study of these concepts, we have to conclude that an 'achievement lag', as a special aspect of 'cultural lag', is the basis for not only society's local dilemmas but of the impasse which comes from the ideological demands of a super-society which are greater than the practical ways of achieving the desired ends. That is, 'achievement lag' is to 'cultural lag' what civilization itself is to culture in general.

"If I want to designate certain concepts which become the elements for a formula both to understand society and to arrange for the continuity of its survival and evolution, it would be in the following pairs:

1. Folkways and technic-ways.
2. The folk culture and state civilization.
3. Cultural lag and achievement lag."

Odum considered that the application of the social sciences to public welfare by 1930 could be likened to the emergence of "social science" in the 1860's and 1870's, and that where social science became professionalized and departmentalized the current trend was to apply the findings of social science to government and social organization, the demand tending to be technical, applying the results of the findings of social science to the requirements of society, rather than to be limited to philosophy and theory. Odum felt that the emerging needs were: "(1) a more adequate public relief, adapted in principle and methods to meet the demands of social changes . . . (2) the development of a place for social insurance . . . and, (3) social planning which will bring to bear the fullest utilization of social science and social research, and their application through social work and public administration."

We have seen in the preceding pages how the methods of the social survey gradually became standardized. This made possible resurveys and experimental studies for purposes of comparison, and for measurement of social change. We have seen how the survey approach has developed through a number of steps: first, including general descriptive data within political areas; second, the inclusion of somewhat more detailed material, with special consideration of the social pathology of cities; third, attempts in the direction of an intensive analysis of all the social processes within a limited area, or the intensive study of one phase of social life such as, health, recreation, population, or delinquency within a political area. The result of these efforts has been a further approach to the study of *regional areas:* first, along the line of trade and service areas; second, through planned regional areas; third, the natural areas. Finally regional studies have become a combination of all types into a study of regional areas based upon similarity of culture, or of economic, industrial, and social interest.

Robert E. Park called attention to the city as a mosaic of small communities, "strikingly different from one another, but all more or less typical". He directed attention to the "natural areas, which though unplanned, take on a form inherent in urban situations." This idea of the natural areas and the culture area was analyzed further by E. W. Burgess with special reference to the "gradient"—showing the decrease or increase of certain attributes as the distance from the center of concentration varies. In addition to the relatively stratified local communities, there are regional areas within which are certain constant factors; in such cases the regional area becomes the more effective unit for research.

The concentration of population in urban centers took on colossal proportions during the last quarter of the nineteenth century. This gave rise to new types of social problems. At first, efforts were made to relieve the intensity of the resulting situations on a purely local scale: a little playground here, a milk station there, a baby clinic elsewhere. The industrial concentration gave rise to various localized efforts. The garden city movement in England, housing efforts in Berlin, Vienna, and the larger American cities were steps in the direction of recognizing the region beyond municipal boundaries. The study of any social phenomena soon demonstrated the necessity of going beyond the sterotype boundary of ward, township, city, county, or even state lines. The natural area, and the region, have come to be recognized as the correct spatial unit for social research.

The regional survey developed in a logical manner from localized studies. Regional studies, analyzing social phenomena as they exist and function within regional areas, have developed from general descriptive surveys and simple spot maps locating certain centers of conditions or activities, to extensive attempts to synthesize independent studies and to interpret them in accordance with significant social trends. The aim of such descriptive studies is to determine to what extent any region is the focal point for action resulting from and conditioned by the religious organizations, ethnic groups, income groups, educational and recreational organizations; in fact, all the elements and factors built into a configuration of the whole area. This development of the social survey from inaccurate recording of general observation to careful study and planning on the basis of the research on a regional basis has been made possible because of development in all lines of knowledge and of research dealing with regional phenomena.

The understanding of what is meant by regional research is still indefinite. Sometimes it is used to mean a study of the interrelation of phenomena and the causative factors present. Sometimes it is little more than a simple cartograph, base map, or spot map, of the more obvious community and regional material, agencies, or population factors. Rupert B. Vance in writing about the Implications of the Concepts Region and Regionalism stated: "Regionalism is still an indefinite term, albeit one to conjure with. The theory of regionalism has already outrun its practice and there is danger lest the concept come to mean all things to all men. There is the region of the physical geographer, of the political scientist, of the metropolitan and national planner, of the student of culture and of the sociologist. In the region converge the lines of forces from geography, ecology, human biology, economics, and cultural and folk sociology. Indeed it seems but obvious to say that there exists a regional aspect to spatial distribution."

In discussing "Forerunners of Regional Research" Shelby Harrison very adequately summarized the development of this movement.

Fortunately the matter has not ended in mere observations. The local community, city or region, has set to work trying to do something about it. Among the efforts set on foot, two have significance here. The first is the endeavor, dating from about 1905, through the medium of the city or social survey to provide more adequate information on local questions than was previously available. Facts were seen to be a primary requirement as a means of a stimulating concerted action. The recognition of this basic need developed gradually, but between 1910 and 1930 increased to hundreds of different survey projects. The numbers included general social surveys, surveys of urban and rural areas, surveys of public education, of health and sanitation, industrial relations and unemployment, housing conditions, problems of crime and mental hygiene, the work of private social agencies and government services, and many other questions. As the twenty-five or more years of their history moved on, however, there has been a growing trend toward the inclusion of recommendations, invented as measures of social control, toward the setting up of social plans for cities and regions.

The second development toward doing something about local problems has been the rise of the city and regional planning movement. It began in the United States in 1905, the year in which the first plans appeared after the long quiescent period following L'Enfant's plan for Washington. These first three were for Manila, San Francisco, and Columbia, South Carolina; and one of the next important plans to be completed, one which undoubtedly gave great impetus to the early growth of the idea, was that made for Chicago in 1909 under the general guidance of Daniel H. Burnham.

But the really great sweep of the city planning movement followed the large increase in the use of the automobile which began about 1910. The movement has grown, until in 1930, of the 93 cities of over 100,000 population, 77 had issued fairly comprehensive planning reports. Of about 1,700 remaining cities ranging between 5,000 and 100,000 in population, something over 250 have issued such reports. Thus the movement has enlisted the effects of about 335 or one-sixth of the cities of 5,000 people or more in this country.

City planning and its accompanying local studies have broadened in scope in two other directions as Shelby M. Harrison said:

1. Geographically, they have spread from city, to county, to metro-politan area, to region—even to whole states and the nation; and
2. In subject matter they have added to architecture and engineer-ing the consideration of legal, economic, and sociological aspects of city and regional life.

The scope of the plan for a regional survey, which was projected during the period following 1932, was summarized by L. L. Bernard in the following statement:

"Consequently it shall be our endeavor to determine such socio-graphic matters as the size of families, marital conditions, divorce and marriage rates, income, planes and standards of living, education and other cultural traits and facilities, travel, home equipment, leisure time and its utilization, institutional organization and utilization, recreational habits, health, hygiene and sanitation, crime and delinquency, depen-dency and modes and methods of social control and the prevention of personal and social maladjustment." In addition he includes various other social manifestations, trends, and comparisons of social phenomena.

Thus the regional survey is passing through some of the same phases as the local survey. It is only when the methods and techniques have reached a reliable degree of accuracy that we may begin to measure, evaluate, and compare the social processes, attitudes, and resultant phenomena.

Regional social planning, if it is to be effective and of any per-manent value, must include areas which go beyond or cut across political subdivisions. While this principle has been recognized for a long time, it has been difficult to overcome the restrictions of geographical or political subdivisions in order to carry out a regional plan successfully. For the regional plan to be effective there must be a maximum of free-dom to vary the program, when accumulated information and the results of further research indicate variation. The program for societal planning must represent the unrestricted choice of the participants, even though standardization is an important factor in research and in planning. Such standardization must be based upon the results of carefully checked, scientifically conducted research. It must not be standardization based merely on a desire to carry out some particular program or to obtain uniformity.

James H. S. Bossard called attention to sociological fashions in planning and warns us against losing the right of free choice. Whatever the extent to which a planned program and procedure will serve as the blueprint of the society of the morrow, let it be hoped that the disciplines enforcing it will be self-imposed, representing the free choice of an enlightened and participating citizenry. Recourse to any other method is but to substitute for the tryanny of planlessness the greater one of detailed coercion. Conformity delighteth the autocrat and the centralized administrator, but if its price is the enshrinement of mediocrity, the inevitable outcome is social bankruptcy. Bossard cautions us that while social planning may be the alternative to social chaos, yet to plan wisely through intelligent cooperation is the alternative to ultimate social ruin.

Social research developed through a long and varied background. The early attempts were abortive in many cases because they involved criticism or restatement of philosophical principles which were not accepted. This lack of acceptance was due in some cases because of the uneven progress in social understanding. Many phases of social research were proposed, but failed for reasons comparable to the failure of early automobiles and airplanes. The basic principles were recognized and understood, but certain techniques and additional developments were necessary before completion. The development first began to make progress within the realm of statistics, and then gradually gave in to include social phenomena of varying types: increase and decrease of population, community organization, the general social survey, regional studies, covering overall aspects. By the end of the nineteenth century the application of principles of social observation to the analysis of social phenomenon, sociology and statistics, inductive sociology gradually grew into community surveys. This naturally led to research of particular aspects of community life, such as women in industry, work accidents, housing, and migration. Each aspect required continuous and diversified effort by many individuals. Sometimes the value of the techniques and procedures was obscured by the bizarre and striking nature of the findings. This slowed up development in social research on the one hand and gave rise to spectacular studies on the other, which not only interferred with social progress, but frequently did harm to the development of sociology by giving emphasis to minor and unusual aspects of the field.

VI

Sociology Applied to New Areas

LIFE IN America began bursting the seams of tradition toward the end of the nineteenth century. A new trend of social thinking began to appear in America, much of which had not yet reached the dignity of being considered as sociology. It was seen everywhere in the general life of America and took in extensive expansion of new areas of interest, industries, the growth of new demands, organizations, and other activities which gave rise to political and economic machinery to protect or to control the results. Unplanned growth, the uncontrolled exploitation of natural resources, selfish opportunism gave rise to a reign of destructive aspects in our social life, which like tornadoes, drought, grasshopper or chinch bug plagues, raised a demand for information and for improvement. A large group of journalists and writers began to protest.

Jacob Riis (1849-1914) *How the Other Half Lives*, Lincoln Steffens, (1866-1936). *The Shame of the Cities*, Ida Tarbell (1847-1944) *Prison Reform*, Josiah Strong (1847-1916) *The New Era — League for Social Service, Safety First Movement*, Upton Sinclair (1878-   ) *The Jungle, Anthracite, Brass Check, Goose Step and Goslins*, are representative of the books by a group of men and women sometimes called "muckrakers." They dug beneath the surface and told us how the other half lived. They wrote of the shame of our cities, of crime and corruption in the treatment of our criminals. They called attention to atrocious working conditions. They demanded better housing and sanitary conditions of food preparation. The injustices of big industry, suppression of thought by newspapers, tradition riddled schools and colleges, undirected immigration and mob control became their areas of protest. Colleges and universities offering courses in sociology, influenced by the social trend, began to emphasize social pathology, urban problems, crime, poverty, housing, charities, and corrections. Courses were put into a prominent place in the curriculum that had been limited to formal presentation of general principles. The dominant figures in sociology continued to be Mayo-Smith, Giddings, Ward, Sumner, Small, Howard with a group of younger men like Blackmar, Ross, Ellwood, and Hayes beginning to loom up. However, C. R. Henderson, a relatively minor member of that group of sociologists was playing a bigger part than was recognized at that time.

Charles R. Henderson (1848-1915) was the actual founder of courses in applied sociology in American colleges and universities. He was a great teacher and an ineffective writer. He taught courses at the University of Chicago in the applied field before such courses were considered of academic value, and they were sometimes taken by students without credit. In 1894, his 'Catechism for Social Observation' was an attempt to do scientifically what the "muckrakers" were doing in magazines and newspapers. It was really the forerunner of the social survey movement. In 1897 he wrote the "Social Spirit of America" and in 1893 "Dependents, Defectives and Delinquents." These books began to give academic respectability to journalistic themes, and where a dozen people were taking the formal sociological courses there would be 40 to 100 students in Henderson's classes even though such courses carried only minor credit, and some of them were admittedly for general information, but not to apply towards a degree. These courses were designated as Social Technology, and were specifically, The Family, Crime and Social Insurance. Hundreds of courses sprang up all over the country, and were based on books such as those listed above by Henderson. Titles such as *The Trail of the Immigrant* by Edward Steiner, *Christianity and the Social Crisis* by Walter Rauschenbush; *Poverty* by Robert Hunter; *Penology* by Robinson; *Punishment and Reformation* by Frederick Wines; *Charities and Corrections* by Amos Warner; *Social Problems* by C. A. Ellwood; *Social Settlements* by Jane Addams; and, *Sin and Society* by E. A. Ross. The popular leadership in applied sociology became crystallized around such persons as Veblen, Ross, Ellwood, Thomas, and the symbolic Jane Addams.

Social trends as shown by social reforms had shifted a little beyond the muckraker and clean-up stage and began to go farther into the causes of negative situations. Public interest began to manifest itself in group movements, non-partisan leagues, welfare work, and community surveys.

In 1913, at Minneapolis, C. R. Henderson proposed: that the general movement for increasing research should be encouraged by the American Sociological Society. "The movement requires expert direction and wise plans. Investigation should be directed to promising fields. Schedules and methods should be carefully worked out by competent statisticians and should be uniform enough to secure comparable figures indicative of large and significant forces and tendencies, without dulling the ardor of persons of independent thought and power of invention."

He then proposed the appointment by the society of a committee to study the problem. The new president, E. A. Ross did so. The following year, December, 1914 before the meeting of the American Sociological

Society at Princeton, Henderson became seriously ill and did not attend. He sent in his partial report recommending a Standing Committee with a permanent secretary:

1. To formulate plans for joint action by the American Sociological Society, the Economic Association and the Statistical Association.
2. To stand ready to advise with organizations and private individuals intending to make investigations of any kind.

The coming of World War I paralyzed efforts along this line for several years, and when revived Henderson's work was largely forgotten.

In considering the trend toward applied sociology in the early quarter of the nineteenth century, an outstanding figure in England, who influenced sociological thought in America, must be given due credit. Patrick Geddes (1854-1932) might be compared with William Sumner from the point of view of the enormous mass of data, unfinished monographs and books which were left behind. Born in Scotland, Geddes in the earlier part of his life was interested in biology, and for many years was a lecturer in zoology at the school of medicine in Edinburgh. He was also professor of botany at Dundee, where he remained until about 1918. Thus his life was largely spent in fields comparable to that of Lester F. Ward. At the same time that Charles Booth was making the monumental Survey of London, Geddes was making a survey of Edinburgh (1886). Booth's study indicated the amount of work that could be done, but was filled with many inaccuracies and showed much lack of general understanding. The work of Geddes, while less spectacular, was more soundly based and resulted in a much more useful study. He was one of the pioneers who sold to social workers and social reformers the idea of the need for a careful survey of the situation before proceeding with a reform effort. Early in 1894, Charles Richmond Henderson and Charles Zueblin were directly influenced by Patrick Geddes's small book on how to study a community, and by the efforts and programs which they set in motion in Chicago. Geddes, like Ward in America, may be spoken of as England's first contemporary sociologist. A chair in sociology was established at the University of London, but after Geddes gave one lecture, the professorship was transferred to Leonard T. Hobhouse. For four years from 1920, Geddes was a professor of sociology and civics at the University of Bombay. Much of Geddes actual contribution aside from his continuous enthusiasm and encouragement to sociology in general is centered around his survey of Edinburgh with the resultant attention to slums and the use of open spaces for recreation, gardening, and other uses. Louis Mumford compares Geddes' knowledge of civics, climates, counsels and governments with Aristotle's and the scope of his understanding and outlook into the future with Leonardo da Vinci's.

In 1903 Geddes and Victor Branford with the approval of Spencer and others started the Sociological Society in London. Galton was the first president. After a number of years the society with its organ "The Sociological Review" seemed to point to an effective future. However, differences of opinion by those who wished to emphasize social philosophy, those who wished to bring about economic and political reform, the advocates of social amelioration of living conditions and the more rigid scientific research group gave rise to conflicts and recrimina- tions by Geddes and Branford, who accused some of the British sociologists of being verbalistic, fragmentary, and unscientific in the name of sociology. Sociology in England remained in large part social philosophy, while the efforts toward municipal reform, charity organi- zation societies, settlements and similar activities, grew into the fields of surveys and regional studies with some emphasis upon housing, garden cities, and improvement of living conditions. Regionalism and city planning were seen as definite future projects by Geddes, and his contributions need to be definitely recognized by the development of these fields in America.

One of the most generally known men of this period who even today is recognized was Thorstein Veblen (1857-1929). There was probably no social scientist during the latter part of the nineteenth and the early twentieth century who carried his social philosophy over into the details of his everyday life with greater personal satisfaction than did Thorstein Veblen. He was reared in a rural community of Wisconsin and graduated from Carlton College in 1880. Already at this age, he is reported to have expressed himself vigorously against the established procedures and points of view which arose in the discussion of science and religion in that community. He began doing graduate work at Johns Hopkins, but was dissatisfied and went to Yale, where he took his doctor's degree in 1884, writing his thesis on the philosophy of Immanuel Kant. He won a University award for a study of the Panic of 1837, which may have influenced his continuation of the study of economic problems. Reportedly because of ill health, but probably in part because of social unadjustment, he was not engaged in any active intellectual work for the next few years. But, in 1891 he went to Cornell, and despite his unkempt appearance, was granted a teaching fellowship. In 1892 he went to Chicago along with Professor J. Law- rence Laughlin, and remained there until 1906. The intellectual freedom existing at the University of Chicago, together with the stimulating group of young men brought together by President Harper, were a fer- tile soil for the brilliancy and originality of Veblen. He left Chicago in 1906 for Leland Stanford University, and later was connected with the University of Missouri and for a short time with the New School of

Social Research in New York. He eventually retired to a farm in Wisconsin where he died in 1929.

Veblen was a stormy and often irritating but stimulating influ-ence on the development of economic and social thought. Apparently holding himself aloof from established points of view, he sent stinging barbs, mingled with characteristic humor, at his contemporaries. Some-times with apparent childish histrionics, he launched his protests against accepted formalities and procedures, carrying these to carelessness in his own dress and personal appearance and in his attitude toward formal social and economic order, religious institutions, and the family. Whether his brilliant and unusual verbiage and his personal disregard for the amenities of life in general served as a better vehicle to put over his ideas regarding the social and economic order, it is impossible to say. He did call attention to himself and his point of view by many of these characteristics, but on the other hand, his active and professional life might have been longer and more effective if he had not so consciously been different. While most of Veblen's work was centered around the institution of property and the social system which it supported, he maintained a thread of thought which is of general interest to the sociologist. Cumulative change, rather than social reform, was recognized by him, and his work which probably had the greatest influence on sociological thinking was his *Theory of the Leisure Class* (1899). This study, while giving credit to diversification of ideas and the development of more and greater variety of production, was still colored by what he threw together under the terms, *conspicuous waste,* and *conspicuous consumption.* While Veblen claimed to avoid moral judgment, his caustic remarks were continually directed towards what he considered contaminating institutions and habits of thought which interfered with effective development of life. His vigorous writing, satire, sometimes rude humor, may have done more to call attention to many of the foibles of our social structure than any other procedure would have done. Whatever his faults and his strength, as a social thinker he was one of the great influences in the direction of social thought from 1890 to 1915.

A man who represents an important area which merits considerable attention is John Lewis Gillin (1871-   ). He steadily increased in recognized capacity from the time he was thirty years of age until long after his retirement. He wrote extensively in the field of social problems and criminology. The first outstanding work was as co-author with Blackmar, in an introductory text. This set the standard for texts in introductory sociology for twenty-five years. Gillin's early writing tended to be a little heavy, but later showed real effective literary style. He was a Divisional Director of the American Red Cross during the First World War, and in charge of courses in social work at Wisconsin until his retirement. Gillin continually increased in the respect of his colleagues and other sociologists. He was never a spectacular writer like his colleague Ross, but was always effective as a writer and as a teacher.

In these fields Professor Gillin made significant contributions:

1. *Religion*   Religion represents a system of social values, realized in an organized complex of practices and beliefs, characterized by processes, some of which are common to all social interrelationships, but some of which are peculiar to religion, since they are concerned with relationships to a supernatural being. These religious values, beliefs, and practices are connected closely with the other elements of the culture. Religious sects grow out of conflict of values between those held by small groups and those cherished by the rest of the population.

2. *Recreation*   Recreation, as an expression of leisure-time activities, functions as a release from the purposive activities of society. But they are limited by the system of values held by the dominant group.

3. *Poverty*   Poverty is a function partly of the economic organization, but partly of the social values relating to social status inhering in the social order. To be poor or dependent in our society, except for the pioneer, or the religious or artistic devotee, is to occupy a lower social status.

4. *Crime*   Crime likewise is a function of our economic and social systems of value. In part it is a reaction against entrenched power and prestige, and in part a struggle to act a role and obtain a status denied by the dominant group.

5. *The Pathology of Social Institutions*   The pathology of the various social institutions eventuates from the lack of adjustment between the values and practices of one or more institutions and those of other institutions in the culture.

In defining sociology he states that it "studies man in his social relations as affecting and being effected by association together with all the products and processes consequent upon such an association; it is closely related to all fields of science, especially to social sciences, economics, political sciences, history, philosophy, psychology, eugenics, euthenics, and education. As a general social science it is concerned with the broad field of human association while others are concerned with only special phases of human relations."

John L. and John P. Gillin state in their joint publication *Cultural Sociology,* "the aftermath of the Second World War has made monstrously clear the necessity for a more widespread knowledge of a theoretically sound and practically applicable science of human relations. If science can organize the forces of the atom so as to flatten whole cities with a single blast, but is not able to organize forces inherent in human beings and in human society so as to render holocausts impossible, science has become a Frankenstein's monster which may destroy us all. Thus the mastery of social sciences has become a task which is not only something we ought to do, but an obligation we must fulfill in material self-defense."

Of criminology and penology Gillin states, "As one looks back over the history of penal treatment, he cannot fail to be impressed by the somewhat meagre results of society's immemorial struggle with crime and the criminal; experiments of Society in dealing with the criminal have been based on false theories. Unconscious of the role of custom, tradition, superstition, and prejudice, society has largely based its treatment of the criminal on fear, hate, lust for power, and selfishness. Treatment has been begotten on emotional reaction to a situation rather than rational consideration of the conditioning factors of crime and of the purposes of punishment." He further states, "We cannot be content with gathering up and trying to mend those who fall over the precipice; we must build a fence along the top."

A request for what Dr. John L. Gillin considered his more significant contribution brought the following statements: "Of course, I feel flattered to be asked by you or anyone else to state what I think I have contributed to sociology. It is a terrible thing when a man has to face his past and look at his work as objectively as he can and try to evaluate it. However, here goes.

"As I see it, sociology beginning as a social philosophy did an important service to the social sciences in calling attention to phases of social life, ignored by history, by political science and economics. Its analysis of forms of social organization, of the social processes and of the social pathology created by change broke ground for a better understanding of the nature of social relationships in all the fields of social activity. But, too often its methods if one judged them by the papers read at the meetings of the American Sociological Society and the discussions heard there are methods in logic, and too often we have been a bunch of logic-choppers, dealing with what might by a stretch of imagination be called the prolegomena of sociology. 'The definition of definition, operational definition' and such abstruse subjects have diverted and confused a good many promising young scholars from the real job of sociology. Above almost everything else, we need research to justify or refute the many hypotheses that some have mistaken for 'gospel Truth.' No wonder some scoffers have said that 'sociology is more and more about less and less.' Theory is all right, and by that I mean hypotheses about how individuals and groups in a society interact, the patterns of behavior they form, etc. But, those hypotheses must be tested by actual study of social interaction and the products thereof by scholars who know what science means. That we are beginning to get. A small but increasing number of our younger men are attacking various aspects of social life in the scientific spirit. Much more needs to be done along that line to bring our theories in line with the facts. I have seen that growing, and therefore I'm not pessimistic about the future of sociology. Some of our theories have been substantiated, others refuted.

"I hesitate to point out what seems to me to have been my own rather limited contributions. I'm not sure that I have selected for mention any that are strictly my own. I owe so much to suggestions from others. But, I think that some of the matters I have emphasized are in part some that resulted from my observations that other sociologists either neglected or treated in an inadequate way. Let me try to name a few.

    a. "Growing out of my interest in religious organizations, especially my own church, I attempted to discover how it originated, and the social complex out of which it grew. That led me to write my Ph.D. thesis on *The Dunkers: A Sociological Interpretation*. Giddings thought this was the best piece of work I had done up to the time he died. He often urged me to work it over and publish it as a book.

    b. "Out of that grew my wonder whether the sociologists had given adequate attention to religion as an element in the whole cultural complex. I was not satisfied with Spencer's 'Ecclesiastical Institutions' in his great work on sociology. In the first book I wrote (on the basis of Blackmar's *Elements*) I developed a theory of the part religion played in the development of social organization and life, noting both its constructive and divisive functions.

    c. "As I gradually worked over into the field of social pathology, I became conscious that the 'social reformers' had done most work there, but had not attempted to apply strict scientific methods to a study of the various aspects of social disorganization. In only one part of that large field have I done what I consider careful scientific work. That is in the field of criminology. I studied the reports of others—the Italian School, the German School, the French School— but, I did not feel that they had meticulously gone to the source of information as to why criminals had become criminals. Hence, I undertook to interview 486 of the inmates of the Wisconsin State Prison, to check what they told me with information from people in the communities from which they had come and who knew them and their backgrounds. I then compared events in their history with that of their non-criminal brothers. That appeared, so far as I got reliable results, in my latest book, *The Wisconsin Prisoner,* published about a year ago by the University of Wisconsin Press. In that I made my most strictly scientific contribution. Closely connected with that study was a study still unpublished, on what conditions in a prisoner's background affect his failure or success on parole, or if he was a probationer, what his social background had to do with his success or failure. I found that neither Burgess' nor Gluck's criteria worked on the Wisconsin criminals. I also studied by the same methods the after-careers of those who had been granted executive clemency over thirty years. That was the least satisfactory of these studies.

d. "In all these studies, I considered that criminology was a part of sociology, not something distinct from it. Their behavior was *social* behavior. It was a deviate behavior, but it was a part of the whole social complex. It was the result of social conditions. I tried to find out how it fitted into the social whole, and why it departed from the norms of the group in which these individuals were reared, or in what respect their behavior was a part of the pattern of behavior that was normal to their subgroup. It is in this field that I think I have made my greatest contribution to sociology.

"The greatest opportunity before sociologists today is careful research on every phase of social relationships. That research need not be limited to statistical methods. The anthropologists have something to teach us there. They study the cultures of various primitive peoples. The sociologists in this atomic age should be studying the cultures of our so-called civilized societies. Are the sociological processes that we have assumed to be universal really so? We have already a good deal of knowledge about the primary institutions in civilized societies, such as the family, business organizations, and political institutions. But what do we know about the underlying psycho-sociological motivations of the various civilized societies? We talk about a Latin culture, an Anglo-Saxon, a German, a French, a Chinese, a Japanese culture. But what we need, it seems to me, is a much more meticulous study of the underlying psycho-social factors that account for the patterns of national behavior."

The approach suggested by Gillin was rather well done, in 1918 by Maurice Parmalee who effectively presented the scope and field of criminology. His world wide contact and experience particularly fitted him to introduce subjects of crime, poverty, social progress and world problems to an eager upsurge of young sociologists. He helped differentiate social problems in the period following World War II. Some of his excellent work was not given its due because at times he

tended to irritate people by his persistence in attempting to enlist their
enthusiastic support for problems concerning which they either had no
interest or at best did not wish to divert energy or effort to support
the program.

When the scope and the function of sociology began to be more
extensively recognized by the general public, the application of sociological principles was applied to many new areas. Social maladjustment,
poverty, health, and gross forms of social injustice began to attract the
attention of many individuals. Many of the persons concerned were
social reformers who exploited the bad situations for purpose of personal
publicity or to sell a story without much concern about the truth of the
presentation. This was met by a new group of sociologists who began to
apply the principles which were beginning to take form to the study
and analysis of particular situations. New interests began to develop,
both among teachers of sociology and groups of persons who were concerned about a particular phase of social life such as the urban or rural
community, education, social organization and control, with more
emphasis upon the constructive activities and less upon the destructive
forces.

Rural Sociology

In 1908 President Theodore Roosevelt appointed the Country Life
Commission. This resulted from various individual efforts ranging from
conservation of natural resources, the establishment of rural free
delivery a few years earlier, health organizations, and perhaps even at
earlier periods the granger movement and the sporadic efforts toward
consolidation and improvement of rural schools. Following the report of
the commission, courses in rural sociology were introduced into colleges
and special studies of rural life began to appear. C. J. Galpin, The
Social Anatomy of an American Community; Carol Aronovich, Community Studies; Warren Wilson, Quaker Hill, 1907; Newell Sims,
Hoosier Village; Paul Vogt; J. M. Williams and American Town 1906;
Nat Frame of West Virginia and many others began to make a
significant impact.

John M. Gillette (1866-1949) is considered by many as the first
major rural sociologist. He wrote one of the first textbooks on the
subject of rural sociology, although he had previously written a book
on the family and a study of South Chicago. In the year 1915 when the
American Sociological Society met in Washington, John M. Gillette
rounded up a small group of men who gathered in a sample room of the
hotel to discuss the teaching of rural sociology and the problems of
rural sociology, and Gillette made the suggestion that this group should
attempt to have the American Sociological Society at some future time
have a program dealing with that subject. The group which met with

John M. Gillette was composed of Warren Wilson, Paul Vogt, C. J. Galpin, George H. von Tungeln, E. L. Morgan, A. Z. Mann, and M. C. Elmer. The following year the annual meeting took note of the Sociology of Rural Life.

Gillette spent practically all of his teaching life at the University of North Dakota. There were years when his salary was reduced to a virtual minimum. But he stayed at North Dakota, exerting a tremendous influence on those with whom he came in contact. Many of his early students continued their work and became well known in the field of sociology: O. Myking Mehus, George Davies, and George Lundberg are examples. Gillette was never a social reformer, but was always ahead of the crowd in this thinking. My early contact with Gillette was typical. Scores of people in all parts of the United States were inspired to study rural social life by John M. Gillette.

In 1914, I was teaching sociology in Fargo, North Dakota. One day a sturdy looking man walked into my office and told me that he was John M. Gillette; that he did not have any classes that day, and had heard there was a young man teaching sociology down in Fargo. So he drove down—a distance of one hundred and twenty-six miles to welcome another sociologist to the state of North Dakota. He said that he knew our library would be meager and if there was any way he could help by sending books they had at the University, or any other way, I should let him know. That act was typical of John M. Gillette. It causes some of us to feel rather embarrassed when we remember the times we have not taken a trip of one hundred and twenty-six miles one way to help a young man to get started in his first teaching course.

At the annual meeting of the American Sociological Society in Philadelphia in 1917, a few persons interested in rural sociology held another informal conference and appointed a committee on standardization. This committee formed a report. Charles J. Galpin, Walter J. Campbell, and Paul L. Vogt were the committee. Their purpose was to establish a cooperative plan of national rural research. The significant point for our purpose was the formulation of definitions which were recommended to form the basis for planned cooperative research. These were published in the American Journal of Sociology, November, 1918.

Definitions

"1. Rural sociology.—It is recommended that the co-operative research in rural sociology be directed primarily to the social problems of farm populations. This limitation, however, is not to be construed as shutting out treatment of the relations of farm populations either to village populations or to city populations.

"2. Rural.—Usage has established many meanings in connection

with the term rural—often vague, sometimes contradictory. It is recommended, therefore, that the term rural be discontinued in statistical
calculations and that there be substituted the more specific terms country, farm, village, small city—as the case may be. The term rural should
be reserved for very general reference to country and village conditions
and relations, or used in the sense defined by the United States Census,
or else should be carefully defined.

"3. Country.—It is recommended that the term country, when
used in a rural sense, apply to the areas outside the limits of villages and
cities incorporated or unincorporated.

"4. Farm—It is recommended that the term farm be used according
to the definition of the United States Census.

"5. Village.—It is recommended that the term village be used to
designate the small type of commercial and residential cluster, whether
it be incorporated as a 'village' or unincorporated. It seems premature
to set a numerical population standard, however, for the village.

"6. Small City.—It is recommended that the term small city be
used to apply to commercial clusters larger than the village, but still
small enough to have decided immediate relations to farm populations.

"7. Country neighborhood.—It is recommended that the term
neighborhood be employed to refer to a geographical group of farm
families having some distinct social cohesion.

"8. Community.—It is recommended that the term community,
when construed in a technical sense with reference to farm populations,
be employed to designate the population group which is formed by a
village or small city, together with all the farm families making this
village or city their regular business center.

"9. Urban.—It is recommended that the term city or village be
employed. The term urban should be reserved for very general reference
to the relations of life in the clustered type of residence, or used in the
sense defined by the United States Census, or else should be carefully
defined.

"10. Farm population.—It is recommended that the term farm population be construed as relating to population living on farms. It is evident, therefore, that farm population will be found in the country, in
unincorporated villages, in incorporated villages, and also in cities; that
is, wherever there are farms as defined by the United States Census.
Owners of farms will not constitute a part of farm population unless
residing on a farm.

"11. Country population.—It is evident that besides farm population living in the country there is also a certain amount of suburban
non-farm population.

"12. Rural or agricultural economics and rural sociology.—In order to relate rural sociology as closely as possible to rural or agricultural economics, especially on the statistical side, it has been deemed wise, in defining rural sociology, to make its general field coincide with that of rural or agricultural economics.

"13. Rural education and rural sociology.—It is recommended that the field of rural sociology, as discriminated from the field of rural education, include the specifically social aspects of educational agencies relating to farm population, but not the technique of educational agencies, problems, or administration."

Hence, by the end of World War I, rural sociology had reached the point of being recognized as a distinctive phase of sociology, and had arrived at an agreement of terms which did much to define the areas of interest and work. A good beginning had been made, which during the next generation, made more progress than a number of other divisions of sociology. Much of the research during the next twenty years was largely descriptive, which gave rise to some criticism by persons who had never done any pioneer work to the effect that "rural sociologists are not doing any *real* research." Actually, the tremendous amount of diversified stock taking and descriptive studies has built a backdrop against which specific sociological processes may be effectively analyzed and studied.

VII

Extending Particular Interests

THERE used to be a saying that a man was only interested in what occurred one day's ride on a mule from where he lived. When transportation and communication was limited and slow, interest only extended to what was on the other side of the mountain. With the means of communication and transportation accelerated, the interest in "What" soon extended to "How" and "Why". This new interest was no longer the special mark of a few selected individuals. A desire for an explanation for the different attitudes of friends and relatives who differed only in occupation or neighborhood began to be of general interest.

The application of the principles of sociology began to occur in life in general with increasing momentum. This was because sociological concepts were beginning to be accepted and understood by people work-ing in widely varied areas, and because in the general public there was a growing understanding of the interaction of social activities and the effect of the entire configuration of social life upon its particular situa-tion. The new growth of industries, of cities, the resultant immigration, population change, and the resultant changes in every phase of social life gave rise to new situations, new demands and pressures, with the need for meeting the social changes. It meant the readjustment of every type of social agency, and reorganization of all forms of established pro-cedure which had met our earlier requirements and the needs of the nineteenth century. Even the attitude of the early "muck-rakers" had become passe, although many of their criticisms had become a part of the accepted language. An example is a phrase, "The Smoky City," applied to Pittsburgh, Pennsylvania in 1907 and continued by comedians and even by an occasional writer for many years after the city was less smoky than any other industrial city in existence.

In the fall of 1911 Emory S. Bogardus (1882-   ) went to the University of Southern California to teach sociology. There was not much interest in the subject in that city nor in the University. Within a few years, however, interest began to grow. Young Bogardus was not satisfied with the type of text books available so he began to write books for students rather than to impress other college professors. He was soon surrounded with a staff which caught his enthusiasm although few persons had his energy and vigor. He was a part of the University, but

also an active participant in every important group of persons concerned with the life and social relations of Los Angeles. His activities
were so numerous, that it was difficult for a person who did not know
him to understand how one person could do so much. His energies were
not dissipated. Each job was recreation and rest from the preceding
one. When a situation arose, he quickly classified its major aspects, and
went to work at what needed to be done. Experience made him increasingly proficient. About 1916 he headed up a group of people interested in sociology. He encouraged each to concentrate on a particular
topic. A few reports were fairly good. These were published in pamphlet
form. The number increased and a regular publication *Applied Sociology*
appeared, later becoming *Sociology and Social Research* which was soon
accepted as one of the major sociological publications. Bogardus represents the type of American who see that something needs to be done,
then starts to do it—always busy, but never too busy to give attention
to a problem of his fellowmen. The following partial list of concepts
emphasized by Bogardus are typical of the way in which sociology was
being made a part of social thinking everywhere.

1. *Social distance*
   a. By *social distance* is meant the degree of sympathetic under-
      standing that exists between people.
   b. *The social distance differential* is the greater distance that
      one person feels toward a second person than the second
      feels toward the first; or vice versa.
   c. A *social distance scale* is an objective measurement device
      for recording quantitatively the different degrees of racial,
      religious, political-economic, and occupational distances that
      exist among people.
2. *A Public opinion scale.* A method for measuring public opinion
   which gives the person a chance to state his attitude on a question with greater freedom than "yes" or "no". With such a
   scale it is possible to measure relative intensities of opinion, as
   well as to note variations in attitude.
3. *Occupational attitudes.* Dr. Bogardus says in *Sociology,* that
   "an occupational attitude is an acquired and established way to
   act with reference to some value offered by a regular means of
   earning a living." A person who has carried on one type of work
   for a considerable time finds that his whole life is influenced
   by the way he does his work and by what he does. He reacts
   toward or against a value outside of his occupation in much the
   same way as he would on the job.
4. *Group priority.* All people are born into groups. The group
   comes first and the individual second; as the individual is helpless

when he comes into his world of established and well-organized society.

5. *The fifth wish.* To W. I. Thomas' four wishes, (the urge for new experience, the urge for security, the urge for response, and the urge for recognition) Dr. Bogardus had added a fifth, the urge to aid others. Evidences of assistance given with no expectation of regard even under dangerous circumstances, or with great hardship, has prompted Dr. Bogardus to point out a natural tendency of the individual to give aid to another person.

6. *Race concepts*
   a. *Race relations spirals*
      1. An unfavorable human relations spiral is described as follows: one member of a race may call a person of another race an uncomplimentary name; there is an unfavorable reaction from the second person who responds in an un-friendly manner. This response is a stimulus which leads the first person to be more sure than ever that the second person and his race are bad.
      2. The favorable human relations spiral develops in the same manner with an expression of friendship and appreciation resulting in a friendly response which in turn produces still more friendly reactions on the part of the first person, and so on, with the first person concluding that the second person and his race are good.
   b. *Racial enclavement* is the opposite of enslavement. The con-cept is used to describe a group which has withdrawn into itself in order not to be enslaved. The group in this way maintains its culture for its people and does not become assimilated.

7. *Groupistic error.* The groupistic error is the popular tendency to judge a person by the stereotype that one has of the group to which the particular person belongs. If that stereotype is un-favorable, then one reacts unfavorably to the person who is identified with that stereotype.

Interest began to be shown in population from the approach of its biological aspects early in the Nineteenth Century. Many of the early critical evaluations were presented at Clark University during the period of mass immigration to the United States before 1910. This early ap-proach, as presented by Frank H. Hankins (1877-   ) was not pre-sented in the manner of another writer of the same period, Edward A. Steiner and his *Trait of the Immigrant,* 1906; *The Immigrant Tide,* 1909; or *From Alien to Citizen,* 1914. Hankins was interested in basic hereditary factors, and racial basis for civilization, and the response of the hereditary organism to stimuli. This approach did not grip the popular attention at a time when the press was kept busy with human interest stories relating to current immigration problems.

Hankins states, "In the first place, I have always thought of myself as a teacher rather than a researcher. However, I have felt that in order to keep alive the teacher must have some field of intellectual inquiry in which he was endeavoring to extend the boundaries of knowledge, or clarify basic concepts. I have been gratified by the very considerable number of my students who have gone into academic sociology and are now teaching in institutions all over the country—California at Berke-ley, Minnesota, Pennsylvania, Florida, North Carolina. As a recruiting agent for sociology, I have done full service, though this is largely due to the fact that most of my teaching has been undergraduate.

"The biological aspects of social life have consistently held a central place in my interests since my study of Galton and Pearson over forty years ago. Associated therewith have been my interest in the heredity-environment problem, the inheritance of human traits, race and popula-tion questions, and problems of sex and family life. I make no claim to special originality in my contributions to any of these fields. My *Racial Basis of Civilization* was the first direct attack on the Nordic doctrine and all its ramifications after World War I, but it was about ten years too early to receive attention outside a limited group. It was translated into French in 1936. On the Heredity-Environment problem, I consider my most important contribution to be the concept of Organic Response as over against the concept of Organic Plasticity, so widely accepted by sociologists. This was set forth in my presidential address as first president of the Eastern Sociological Society and afterwards published in *Social Forces* in modified form.

"The principle of organic response is based on the following propositions:

1. 'An organism and this includes man can make no response to a stimulus except in terms of its own organic constitu-tion.'
2. 'Whether a response is made depends on the hereditary constitution.'
3. 'The nature of the response depends on this same constitu-tion, and'
4. 'The only mediation or source of correlation between the stimulus and the nature of the response is to be found in the nature of the hereditary constitution of the responding organism.'

"These propositions would be accepted at once by a biologist; but the sociologists—at least many of them—continue to believe that the environment can do most anything with the hereditary human constitution and that the only source of human differences is to be found in the social environment. We live in an age or are passing through a period when the ideal of human equality elicits almost universal approval; we prefer equality and security to liberty and personal distinction. It is a period in which we no longer say 'Blood Tells', but 'the social environment explains all'. This is a part of the culture drift toward a socialistic-communistic ideology. Another evidence of this drift of which I have been made keenly aware is the gradual decline of interest in eugenics. This interest is much less evident among intellectuals than it was a generation ago. Why be interested in the quality of the human breed when a good kindergarten can make a near genius out of a moron? One could cite many illustrations of the present emphasis on the environmental factors—in education, in criminology, juvenile delinquency, divorce, poverty, and indeed all other social problems. No doubt some of this was needed as a corrective to the aristocratic flavor often given to the older Galtonian ideas. Whether there will be some reversal of the trend depends fundamentally on the basic drift of our culture. If we move strongly toward a socialistic-communistic society, the environmental emphasis will intensify.

"For several recent years I have been trying to make a study of the basic trends of western culture from its backgrounds in the middle ages to the present. The purpose was to work out a few tenable ideas regarding the basic factors in social dynamics. There is literally nothing in this field that one could call systematic. Yes, there is Sorokin's mysticism, Parson's obscurities, and on back to Hegelian antitheses. Over the long view the economic changes seem to be primary; political theories arise as rationalizations of new class or sectional interests; new religious doctrines grow up as sanctions of economic modes. Basically, culture change must be seen as the slow changes in the every day activities of increasing proportions of the population, these change in daily routines carrying with them changes in folkways, mores, technique-ways, and stateways, and eventuating in new values and new ideologies.

"Moreover, this process of social change, when viewed from the secular angle, although it is the result of the operation of human wills, does not seem to be amenable to special human manipulation. It does not seem probable, for instance, that any act of any government or class or church could have stopped the gradual emergence of the bourgeoisie in Western Europe and the gradual transformation of all aspects of social life, including the rise of democratic ideas in all spheres, political, economic, and religious, in consequence of the changes in the customary routines and life expectancies of increasing proportions of the population. This gives to cultural change a deterministic and an evolutionary

character that ties it firmly into the body of scientifically studied phenomena. We may well end our sociological search with a social physics
—the first adumbrations are now beginning to appear in the work of
the demographers, of Zypf, Stewart, and others. This would also get us
back not only to Comte and Quetelet, but to some of the best insights
of Spencer and Giddings."

Jerimiah W. Jenks, in 1913, also emphasized some of the social
results of immigration, not agreeing with the group on the one hand
who looked upon all immigration as a social catastrophe nor on the
other hand with those who felt that opening our gates to unlimited
immigration was the way to pave a road to eternal glory. However, the
work of Hankins, by effective teaching and careful writing, has become
representative of the best thought developed during the first quarter
of the nineteenth century in the realm of the biological aspects of social
life. Without becoming a "professional social reformer," he was one of
the influential men in developing a balanced and scientific viewpoint.

Population

Since the work of Johann Peter Sussmilch in 1745, population has
been a subject of major interest to students of human relations. Many
of the leading sociologists during the period covered by our study have
devoted their efforts toward an analysis of the control of population,
population growth and decline, migration and the various phenomena
arising in connection with population changes. These studies have varied
from the early writings of Mayo-Smith and Carrol D. Wright, which
were largely factual presentation of census data to such studies as
Standing Room Only by E. A. Ross (1927) and *Danger Spots in World
Population* by Warren Thompson (1929). Early leaders in this field
were Frank Hankins, previously mentioned, and Henry Pratt Fairchild.

"There appears to be no practicable solution for the problems of
over-population, and therefore of world peace, as long as the over-
crowded countries, which include the largest aggregates of humanity
continue to multiply beyond the possibility of comfortable support
through their own domestic economics." This belief was voiced by Dr.
Henry Pratt Fairchild, of New York University's Department of Sociology, at the 1942 annual meeting of the Birth Control Federation of
America.

Henry Pratt Fairchild was born in Dundee, Illinois on August 18,
1880 the son of Arthur Rabbitt and Isabel (Pratt) Fairchild. Later his
parents moved to Nebraska. His interest in population began, as stated
by him, while he was a boy in this rural region of Nebraska, "which
had a predominantly foreign citizenry, a large proportion of which
could not speak English." After getting the B.A. at Doane College,
Crete, Nebraska, in 1900, his interests in immigration problems took

him to Yale University to specialize in that field. Shortly afterward he left for Smyrna, Turkey to become an instructor at the International College, where he remained from 1900 to 1903.

Dr. Fairchild prepared two studies on immigration, published in 1911 and 1913: *Greek Immigration to the United States* and *Immigration. Outline of Applied Sociology* (1916) and *Elements of Social Science* (1924) were useful as textbooks as well as for the general reader. *The Melting Pot Mistake* (1926) was a further analysis of the immigration question; and in 1927 came *The Foundations of Social Life.* The depression years saw the publication of two studies on the national economic situation; the problem of the paradox of poverty and plenty was presented in *Profits or Prosperity* (1932), and in *This Way Out* (1936) an explanation was given of why the profit motive is breaking down, and of how our resources and technical plans could become the means of producing enough goods to create a far higher standard of living for everyone. Fairchild advocates collectivism as the "way out" of our economic impasse, and shows how it may be accomplished by peaceful means. *People: The Quantity and Quality of Population* published in 1939 was a popular exposition of present trends in population, their probable causes, and possible means of changing them.

A more recently published book is *Economics for the Millions* which appeared in 1940. This book offered an explanation for the layman of the elements of economics and the workings of the present economic system.

Dr. Fairchild exerted much influence as a lecturer and as a writer. His topics were drawn from the subject matter of his books or his extensive travels in this country, in Europe, and in Russia.

The interest in population from the point of view of sociology will continue to be extensive. Most of the work in this field may be represented by the work of Warren Thompson at the Scripps Foundation. There are, however, an increasing number of studies such as those by H. A. Phelps and David Henderson which are tending to emphasize the analytical and minimize the factual data.

Shortly after completing his academic training, Warren S. Thompson (1887-   ) was selected to head up the Scripps Foundation for the study of population at Oxford, Ohio. Thompson has never written anything for the sole purpose of getting it into print, and many studies were made by Thompson which were never printed, merely because he did not feel they added sufficiently to what was already generally known. He has consistently refused to publish material that was not a definite contribution or step ahead. As a result, Warren Thompson has become one of the most respected authorities on population and population problems. His work has influenced population studies throughout the world and he has contributed much to the development of research, both by private individuals and by national government.

"If I have made any contribution to social thinking, it is probably in helping people to see population movements as *natural* phenomena which can be studied scientifically with a view to their control just as all other *natural* events. This was inevitable as a development and all any of us can claim is to have added our mite to increase momentum. As a simple and useful tool for measuring growth, although not as accurate as desirable, the *replacement index* is of some interest. As far as I know, my use was original although the reproduction rates have been much more widely used and probably were developed earlier. Whelpton and I also feel that our empirical method of calculating future populations has been of some value."

* * *

Just as the last quarter of the nineteenth century marked a period of disorganized growth in urban communities due to the rapid increase of unassimilated populations, so the middle of the twentieth century is significant for its attempts, not merely to clear out the decaying remnants of growth in that earlier period, but to develop a new urban pattern. The first quarter of the twentieth century was the period in which the earlier experiments in garden cities were introduced on an increasing scale. Perhaps a natural growth of this idea evolved into the efforts toward metropolitan decentralization. Some industrialists like Henry Ford shortly after World War I advocated the decentralization of industry with more or less practical demonstration. It was, however, not until after World War II that extensive efforts were put forth along this line. A problem which the early decentralization of industry met was the lack of adequate provision for American planes of living. This included not merely adequate housing, but the additional comfort and necessity services. After World War II housing projects were developed commercially and the increased wages, salaries, and available credit enabled middle class people who formerly felt constrained to live within walking distance of their work to move out of the urban center by ten and fifteen miles. They purchased homes selling for eight, ten, twelve, and fifteen thousand dollars. Trade centers, schools, church centers followed and our early efforts to move industries out of concentrated areas was nearing the completion of a cycle. Population of all levels of interest, service agencies, stores, theaters as well as industry, began decentralization. At first recreation centers such as theaters merely took the form of an occasional drive-in theater. The results exceeded the expectations. Trade centers were arbitrarily built up out in the country supported at first by the increasing population in out of center areas and in turn stimulating study of population and migration, such as, Metropolitan Decentralization by Donald J. Bogue, and Research and Planning in New Economic Areas.

Mr. Caradog Jones stated, in *Journal of the Royal Statistical Society,* 1931, "It would be an immense boon if the country could be mapped out into a number of suitable regions, each with a statistical officer attached, whose function would be to present periodical reports upon the social conditions and industrial development of his own area, supplementing existing data by inquiries conducted on uniform lines so that the different regions might be effectively compared. There should, of course, be close collaboration with the central and local authorities, and especially with the General Register Office, to prevent overlapping. We should then begin to see our problems, not in isolation, but as parts of an ordered whole, and we should approach them with less bewilderment."

Sociology Applied to Education

Just as theoretical sociology and principles of sociology were manifested in a wide variety of approaches to the general subject, so the application of sociological principles or applied sociology took a variety of forms. Generally applied sociology was considered as dealing with some particular situation or area which showed irritation spots if not socially pathological situations. However, the application of sociological principles and procedures to education was recognized by early sociologists and followed an interesting development. At first this interest like that of sociology in general, stressed the *social phases* of education. Socrates, Quintilian, Abelard, Pestalozzi, Froebel, and Thomas Arnold were all concerned with the social phases of education. Attention to the sociological aspects of education began to take form with the emerging of sociology toward the end of the nineteenth century. In 1883 Lester F. Ward considered education as the proximate means of progress, and in 1896, William T. Harris, the United States Commissioner, of Education, stated that education to be fundamental must be based on sociology. He specifically stated, "Education is founded on sociology." In 1897 Albion W. Small, in discussing some demands of sociology upon pedagogy said, "While sociology proper is not a desirable subject for young pupils, our educational methods will be miserably inadequate to their social function until every teacher, from kindergarten on, is sufficiently instructed in sociology to put all his teaching in the setting which the sociological viewpoint affords." The same year John Dewey in "My Pedagogic Creed" said, "I believe that the school is primarily a social institution, education being a social process." This was reiterated by S. P. Dutton, Superintendent of Schools in Brookline, Massachusetts, saying, "The school is a social institution, its aims are social, and its management, discipline of methods and instructions should be dominated by this idea." Two years before this, in 1895, the Board of Regents of Normal Schools of Minnesota made social science a required subject, and in 1896 the normal schools of Winona, Minnesota and Milwaukee, Wisconsin introduced a course in sociology. By 1902 sociology was offered in all teacher training schools in Wisconsin. That same year John M. Gillette introduced a course in the normal school in Valley City, North Dakota in which he attempted to apply the principles and procedures of sociology to education. He called this course Educational Sociology. Frederick R. Clow offered a similar course in the Oskosh Normal School in 1904 and in 1908 Henry Suzzalo began giving his very popular course on Educational Sociology at Teachers College, Columbia University.

During the next few years interest in Educational Sociology developed rapidly and by 1910 forty normal schools in the United States were offering courses in sociology. By 1914 seventeen institutions of higher learning made sociology a required subject for teachers in training. This indicates the extent of the trend to apply sociology to education. Much of what was written still harked back to the earlier philosophers and teachers, resulting in books on the general social phases of education typical among which were Colon A. Scott's book on *Social Education,* 1908, and M. V. O'Shea, *Social Development in Education.* In 1919 William Estabrook Chancellor wrote a book on *Educational Sociology* definitely based upon sociological approach. This was divided into three parts: 1. Social Movements; 2. Social Institutions; 3. Social Measurement.

This latter topic was becoming a very pertinent topic for sociological research in isolated cases.

From 1915 to 1930 marked a second era in the development of Educational Sociology. This was given emphasis in 1916 when Edwin A. Kirkpatrick wrote his *Fundamentals of Sociology with Special Emphasis on Community and Educational Problems.* In 1917 Walter R. Smith followed with his *Introduction to Educational Sociology.* That same year David Snedden prepared an elaborate digest and syllabus for Educational Sociology, which he followed during the next eight years with *Sociological Determination of the Objectives in Education, Educational Sociology, Civic Education, Sociology for Teachers,* and finally *Educational Applications of Sociology.* Because of his extensive contacts with teachers who attended Columbia University for graduate work, Snedden's influence in this field was probably more extensive than any other writer of his period. Snedden, Clow, and others in 1923 organized the National Society for the Study of Educational Sociology. During this same decade Frederick Redman Clow played an important part in emphasizing sociological principles within the area of teacher's training both as author of *Principles of Sociology with Educational Application* and as the first editor of a yearbook for the study of educational sociology. He was also instrumental in establishing a section on educational sociology in 1928 in the American Sociological Society which functioned until 1948. In line with the emphasis of the leaders in educational sociology, Charles C. Peters in 1924 wrote a significant book on *Foundations of Educational Sociology.* This was generally recognized as setting a new pace within that area. Joseph K. Hart backed up this developing field with *Social Life and Social Institutions.* In 1925 Ernest Groves wrote the first of what proved to be an epoch making series of books dealing with social and educational problems. In this study he wrote a very thought provoking section on Problems of the Family as Related to Education and this in turn started the demand for his many books dealing with various problems of the family, including the Education for the Family Life. Work in this field continued to grow. Alvin Good placed special emphasis on development of sociology and their place in education. And in 1928 E. George Payne, in addition to writing a book on *Principles of Educational Sociology,* was instrumental in beginning the publication of the *Journal of Educational Sociology.* George Payne presented his point of view as follows: "By educational sociology we mean the science which describes and explains the institutions, social groups, and social processes, that is, the social relationships in which or through which the individual gains and organizes his experiences."

"These social interdependencies include not merely those in which the individual gains and organizes his experiences as a child, but also those social groups and processes in which he must function in adult life. These social relationships are furthermore regarded particularly in relation to the educational system in its evolution and changing function."

In 1928 Ross L. Finney wrote *The Sociological Philosophy of Education.* This book, while drawing on the achievements in the philosophy of education since the Rennaissance of the twelfth century, made an outstanding contribution by recognizing and applying twentieth century developments in social psychology, sociological research, and sociological analysis to that foundation of educational philosophy as presented and developed by the great minds of the past.

The volumes of material that appeared from 1930 to the present time tended to emphasize three particular areas. Willard Waller in the *Sociology of Teaching,* 1933, emphasized the social processes. He analyzed the school and the community showing the school's place in the social process and the relation of the school and the community. His interpretation of life in the school dealt with culture manifesta tions in the school and factors of social control varying from crowd and mob psychology to the primary group among children. In connection with teacher and pupil relations, Waller speaks of teaching as *institu-tionalized leadership*. The social relationship is manifested in a variety of forms, of prestige and of disrepute, of social distance, attitudes and roles in class room situations and in the focal points of student-teacher responses and antagonisms.

A second focalization of educational sociology was presented by Francis J. Brown. Brown gave a place in individual approach, societal approach and the interaction approach. The first dealt with individual group interaction. Consideration was given to the cultural heritage of the group, the distinction between the individual and the person and the social processes found in social interaction. Under the second divi-sion, he dealt with person-group interaction, discussing the part of the school in relation to activities groups, to the family, and to the person-group interaction within the school as manifested by its development of the in-groups, the curriculum, its relation to the community as well as active and passive agencies of social interaction. Brown's third ap-proach deals with the carry-over of the resultant activities into such matters as community health, vocational proficiency, purposeful living, social attitudes, social planning, and social control.

The third area in which educational sociology tended to receive consideration is found in Lloyd Allan Cook's *Community Backgrounds of Education*. This was revised and published as a *Sociological Approach to Education*, which is a more effective title and, in view of the develop-ments that had taken place since the earlier book and Cook's participa-tion in these developments, it really constituted a new book. The main divisions of this book deal with the community frame of life, the com-munity, child, and school, in which the theory of child socialization, the development of social class in the school are significant contributions. This material and the way of working on school problems in which established sociological and social-psychological findings are applied make up the significant contributions.

The conclusions of this third group of educational sociologists are in line with the statement of Charles A. Ellwood in his article "What is Educational Sociology" where he said: "Educational sociology is the science which aims to reveal the connections at all points between the educative process and the social process. It is the science of the educa-tional phase of the social life, or more exactly, of the educative aspect of the social process. Its business is to show the origin, development, and function of the educative process in human society."

Willard Waller stated that educational sociology was a systematic application of the concepts of sociology and social psychology to the social phenomena of school life. And so, as summarized by Francis J. Brown, "Educational sociology is the study of the interaction of the individual and his cultural environment which includes other individuals, social groups, and patterns of behavior." Cook and Cook state, "Educational sociology is particularly interested in finding out how to manipulate the educational process (social control) to achieve better personality development. Application of sociological knowledge and techniques to educative problems in the field of human relations and material well being." There has often been some confusion as to the place of educational sociology and of its particular significance. Many sociologists have ignored its development and function. However, it has been one of the most effective and significant phases of applied sociology during the fifty years since it was first introduced by John M. Gillette, Frederick R. Clow, and Henry Suzzalo.

Secondary Schools

Another trend in the development of sociology and social thought is the attempt to introduce it into secondary schools. By 1920 there was a wide acceptance of sociology in the courses of study offered in high schools. This was a natural result of its extensive adoption by teachers' colleges. The status it had reached by 1940 may be noted from the excerpts given below, based on a paper by George W. Strong, "A Suggested Plan for High School Sociology," presented at the Annual Meeting of the Southern Sociological Society in Knoxville, Tennessee, April 5, 1940. This marked a great step since Small's statement forty-three years earlier.

There is a growing need for the study of sociological materials in the secondary schools. It has become an integral part of our public education system and a recognized part of everyday life. What physical scientists have accomplished in making the school boy and the routine worker science conscious, is being done to make them socially conscious. The whole network of education has been wrestling with this problem. It is just as much the task of the secondary school as of the college, but the more specialized college had to determine the basic principles involved. Education is as concerned with the development of desirable social attitudes and philosophy for the individuals who never go to college as for those who do.

We need a course giving students an insight into how social experiences are consistently related, and which will give a sane social philosophy. What about their problems? What about their community? Here it is proposed that an experience course of this sort should be developed for the senior high schools.

It is difficult to prescribe the field of content for sociology on the secondary level. First, because there is such a great bulk of current material which appears to the layman to be what he conceives as sociology. To him sociology is confused with the accumulation of startling data which call attention to needed social reforms. It is usually composed of spectacular situations which are subject matter for propaganda or for shocking people to take some action. Secondly, there is a popular trend even among teachers toward associating sociology with that which is fascinating, curious, unique, and pathological. We do need a better insight into what is *wrong* with our social lives. However, overemphasis of this view can be carried to the point where we fail to point out standards and values on what is *right* with society.

Basing our conclusions upon the texts that are available, we find five or more approaches. First, there is the Current Problems approach which emphasizes disorganizing factors in society. The attempt is made to shock students into a consciousness of deplorable social conditions about which they become more hopelessly helpless since plausible solutions are vague. Problems of social welfare, crime, unemployment, international relations, slum conditions, and democracy are a few examples of the questions students and teachers set about to answer. The classroom atmosphere often becomes rarified with prejudicial and opinionated discussion. This presupposes that reforms will thereby be attained. The conglomerate mess is too big for them to untangle.

A second approach is what we may call the General or Topical approach. Very little thought has been given to order and organization of material. The pedagogical value of such an approach is questionable since it follows any number of non-related topics.

A third approach deals with Personality Development and Social Etiquette. A number of books have recently appeared ranging in material from business to recreation and their effect on personality. The material may be good and well organized but woven around one or two cores of thought. There is danger of developing only a tangent of the sphere.

A fourth approach, the Institutional, has been rather widely followed. If the material is well planned, such material can contribute successfully to an understanding of social living. Treatment of material should not be topheavy with structure and superstructure. The tendency has been to overstress government and the economic order and neglect a comprehensive discussion of other institutions closer to the conception of the individual student. When institutions are used as the basis of organization, they should be viewed as parts of a changing social process.

The Process approach has been fairly well employed in recent developments of the social sciences. Most of this work has been carried into the social sciences from history. Whatever we call the material presented in social science courses, there are some basic principles which are characteristic of any pattern of societal phenomena, to be followed in the treatment and presentation. Any social activity, regardless of time or place, can be analyzed and studied on the basis of certain re-current phenomena. These are found in similar sequential patterns of relationship. The recurrent purposes, activities, and sequential relation-ships we are defining here as *societal continuities.* Continuity is con-gruous with one of the chief objectives of education, that of growth. Learning experiences must be continuous from one situation to the next if they are to be any more than unrelated boxcars in the educational train distributed on various sidings or coupled only by association. Based upon suggestions by Dr. C. A. Buckner, eight societal continuities and the blocks or areas of content to which they apply are formulated in Chart I. Each of the recurring activities or fundamental continuities is considered in its application to each of the major blocks of content. It is the study of these recurrent activities which make up the content of our subject matter.

Most high schools do not teach sociology as a distinct discipline. What is taught is a general social science. Of this a small part is com-posed of history, economics, political science, and sociology, or consists of a general medley of problems. These problems presumably are dealt with from the viewpoint of these special social sciences. However, whether sociology is taught as a distinct subject, as a part of a group of subjects, or as incidental in explaining a medley of social problems, it is necessary that the sociological principles shall be exact and correct.

The plan proposed here should be flexible enough to meet the needs and material of any community. Its success will depend very much on the personality, ingenuity, and background of the individual teachers. We must translate these continuities into understandable terms and learning situations for the student. He should be encouraged to help guide his own learning as well as to follow our guidance. A major aim in this approach is to organize teaching material to show relationships rather than to stress innumerable unrelated facts. Less emphasis should be placed on speed in digesting and regurgitating bulks of subject matter and going through motions of educational activity. More emphasis should be placed on developing individual and group methods of study-ing and sampling characteristic areas of society. Instead of teaching subject matter, let us help students in their learning.

G. W. Strong's proposal for sociology on the Secondary School level as published in *Social Forces,* October 1940 gives a good view of the development that had taken place in fifty years.

CHART I

OVERVIEW FOR HIGH SCHOOL SOCIOLOGY

RECURRING ACTIVITIES OR FUNDAMENTAL CONTINUITIES	BLOCKS	SOCIAL INSTITUTIONS							
		I. Community and Its Groups	II. The Family Group	III. The Leisure Time Group	IV. Religious and Moral Group	V. Educational Groups	VI. Occupational Groups Economic Structure	VII. Cultural and Racial Group	VIII. Civic Groups and Political Organization
A. Individual's Adjustment to Society									
1. Social World Encountered 2. Individual's Place in It									
B. Social Origins and Elements									
C. Factors in Social Change									
1. Biological 2. Geographical 3. Psychological 4. Cultural									
D. Social Processes									
1. Contact and Interaction 2. Conflict 3. Competition 4. Cooperation									
E. Social Function and Purposes									
F. Social Organization, Structure, Type									
G. Problems of Social Change									
H. Social Control									
1. Use of Scientific Method									

When the general basic principles had become generally accepted, there began to be a wide-spread application of these principles to increasingly extended fields. Sociology began to consider problems of social adjustment as effected by population, race, public opinion, rural life, urban development, the community, and the general problems of education. The educational aspects, while less spectacular than a startling novel, made a more positive impact. The sociological approach was extended into the secondary schools and into the teaching of geography and history in the lower grades of the public schools. In fact, the seeds planted in the lower grades and high school prepared a receptive soil for response to suggested social changes and to social organization and legislation which took place during the years from 1910 to 1955. When future historians evaluate the first half of the twentieth century, their first observation may be the great technical and industrial changes, with a tendency to speak of it as the electronic age. A further evalua- tion will, however, undoubtedly give rise to the question of whether the great material changes would have been possible without having been preceded by a recognition of great underlying sociological principles.

VIII

Some Selected Areas of Research

AFTER World War I social research, building upon the past, was able to concentrate on more particular aspects of human behavior: human ecology, race relations, collective behavior. Emphasis found in such studies as *Hoosier Village* (Sims), *South Chicago* (Gillette), *Sociology of a New York City Block* (Jones), *Manhattanville* (Woolston), *Quaker Hill* (Wilson) began to be broken down along lines of more specific emphasis. Albion W. Small expressed the general trend by stating that special techniques were required for history, economics, political science, and "There are areas of knowledge which can be explored only by use of the techniques which are in process of development among structural sociologists on the one hand, and psychological or behavioristic sociologists on the other for analyzing and interpreting human group phenomena in general.[1]

In short, a different technique must be mobilized for each type of situation about which something has been learned. Small sent out a warning, however. "I seem to see evidence that some sociologists are thinking of 'research' as a sort of ritual, a performance of mystical or ceremonial merit, detached from any objective utility."

Shortly after World War I social research had received additional impetus. Many of the research techniques had reached an effective level of development, and by combining the different procedures some real progress was possible. As stated by Thomas, "progress in method is made from point to point, setting up objectives, employing certain techniques, then resetting the problems with the introduction of still other objectives, employing certain techniques."

The historical surveys of the early Columbia University group had developed into the more intensive research of a particular community project, within the setting of a comprehensive community survey. Human ecology and regionalism, mentioned earlier, after 300 years of development, took the form of the studies by McKenzie, Burgess, and others from the spatial relations approach, with J. Quinn emphasizing more specifically social interaction.

[1] "The Future of Sociology," *Publications of the American Sociological Society,* Vol. 15, pp. 185-86.

During the 1920's research methods of sociologists began to take the form of application to a particular problem of interest: race rela-tions and social distance (Bogardus), social aspects of the business cycle (Dorothy Thomas), indexes of social trends (Ogburn), parole predic-tion studies, predicting success and failure in marriage. Then sampling methods became increasingly refined and corrected for errors (Stephan, Sletto). The tedious work of early community studies and surveys was eliminated by increased and broken-down census data.

Life history studies and personal documents became an approach used by special research projects, particularly dealing with problems of crime, delinquency, the family, and personal adjustment. Thomas and Znaniecki, Clifford Shaw, E. H. Sutherland, E. Franklin Frazier, and Robert C. Angell have made effective use of these more refined methods. Likewise, the selection of documents and cases based upon a particular attribute or type has received considerable attention. The increasing emphasis on the importance of integrating different research methods known as sociometry emphasized the need for integrating the concepts and methods of two or more fields in the study of a situation.

The universe of research to which different sociologists have devoted themselves has varied. Some of the early men felt that the best source for observing phenomena and collecting data was among unique, peculiar situations. It was rather an innovation when Charles H. Cooley observed the conduct of his daughters in order to test the definitions he gave of human nature, primary contact, and similar statements.

While it is discouraging to work against popular recognition and at the loss of remunerative acceptance, one sometimes tends to wonder whether some of the best research done was not that which was accom-plished independently along with other regular employment, rather than what was done as a part of a widely acclaimed program. It is my belief that real progress is made by taking cognizance of the results of centuries of development of the techniques of mathematics, statistics, and the general rules covering empirical procedures which have been developed in hundreds of instances.

The development of the foundation for social research has been slow. There was first the need for the tools of statistics and other research techniques. Second there was the need to recognize the exist-ence of specific social activities; third, to understand the nature and process of causal relationships; and, fourth, to recognize the dynamics of the specific act. We are now ready to continue work already begun toward effective social research. Criticisms of the past sometimes tend to overlook the many steps necessary before we were ready to measure a situation, an attitude, or a process removed from values and opinions. To reach relative accuracy, establish adequate units of measure, differ-

entiate consistent patterns of response, and predict trends, there is a
background of immeasurable effort.

A few of the representative types of development of sociology and
social research during the years following World War I are given here.
This may be expressed by associating trends with representative persons.

It is quite in order to consider the contribution to sociology made
by Ernest W. Burgess at the same time we are discussing Robert E.
Parks, although Burgess made many contributions to sociology after
Parks. He did work in community social surveys, with F. W. Blackmar
and others in Kansas, before Parks became active in the field. During
Parks' most active period, Burgess worked with him and with other
persons in the Chicago group. In fact, many of the excellent studies
which originated in the Department of Sociology at Chicago bear the
imprint of both Burgess and Parks. Several representative studies will be
cited in the following pages which bear signs of the brilliant "pointing
up" of Parks and the careful analytical insight of Burgess. Ernest
Burgess suggested that his efforts have been to develop six main concepts in the realm of sociology. These are:

1. The concept of transition of the family from institution to
   companionship.
2. The differentiation between society and the ecological community.
3. The zonal pattern of urban growth.
4. The family as a unit of interacting personalities.
5. Four types of mobility.
6. Prediction techniques.

In recent years, the study of the family has been much more
definitely recognized as a sociological speciality. Beginning about 1917,
a course in the family was given at the University of Chicago by
Burgess, and was taken by nearly all candidates for higher degrees is
sociology. The influence of this course was extensive. He was instrumental in establishing and developing the National Council on Family
Relations and the publication of "Marriage and Family Living."

In 1921 Parks and Burgess wrote an *Introduction to the Science of
Sociology,* which set a new standard for introductory texts in the field.
It lay the basis for a new emphasis in the points of departure of social
research, and in many respects marked the end of the second and beginning of the third phase in the development of sociology since 1890. A
few of the studies which typify the Chicago group and which were
reflections of the point of view of Parks and Burgess may be cited.
Of course many additional persons played a part in their development.
In fact these studies represent one phase of the third period in the
development of sociological thought in the years covered by this account.

In this third period, the individual had become merged into a stream which represented aspects of the work of many individuals and few individuals contributions were limited to any particular contributory stream.

The University of Chicago *Sociological Series* include many of which the following are typical. *Suicide* by Ruth Shonle Cavan; *The Natural History of Revolution* by Lyford P. Edwards; *Family Disorganization* by Ernest R. Mowrer; *The Gang* by Frederic M. Thrasher; *Sex Freedom and Social Control* by Charles W. Margold; *The City* by Robert E. Park, E. W. Burgess and others (1925); *The Urban Community* edited by E. W. Burgess (1926); *Personality and The Social Group* edited by Ernest W. Burgess; *Press and Politics in Japan* by Kisaburo Kawabe. *Social Currents in Japan* by Harry Emerson Wildes; *An Introduction to the Science of Sociology* (revised edition) by Robert E. Park and E. W. Burgess; *Chicago's Gangland* by Frederic M. Thrasher; *The Hobo* by Nels Anderson; *The Social Base Map of Chicago; Domestic Discord* by Ernest R. Mowrer; *The Family: Its Organization and Disorganization* by Ernest R. Mowrer; *The Gold Coast and the Slum* by Harvey Zorbaugh; *The Ghetto* by Louis Wirth; *The Strike* by E. T. Hiller; *The Saleslady* by Frances R. Donovan; *The Negro Family in Chicago* by E. Franklin Frazier; *Small-Town Stuff* by Albert Blumenthal; *The Pilgrims of Russian-Town* by Pauline V. Young; *The Taxi-Dance Hall* by Paul G. Cressey.

Robert Ezra Park (1864-1944) after studying at the University of Michigan he became a newspaper reporter. Interested in ways of dealing with human activities, he returned to college—first to Harvard and then to Heidelberg, Germany. Having adequate means to do the work which interested him without financial worries, he was associated from 1905-1914 with the work of Booker T. Washington. He came to the University of Chicago in the summer of 1914, and remained there until 1935. In 1936 he went to Fisk University and in the meantime studied race relations in various parts of the world. His work at the University of Chicago is significant, since he was fifty years old when he began his career as a sociologist. But in the ensuing thirty years he did more than all but a very few sociologists to develop the field of his final choice. Many significant contributions were made by Park. His students of the community, the city, human ecology, social institutions, with special emphasis on the newspaper and collective behavior, left a deep imprint on sociological thinking. Park's interest in depressed human beings was given an outlet when he worked as a press agent for the "Congo Reform Association," which was concerned with the regime of Leopold II. This was followed by his interest in Tuskeegee Institute. By 1920 Park had become recognized leader on the University of Chi-

cago campus. Ellsworth Faris, has given us a most succinct summary
and evaluation of Park's contribution to the development of sociology
in Park's obituary (Volume IX, American Sociological Review).

"His success was not immediate. In 1914 Small was an outstanding
figure on the campus, Henderson was still remembered for his brilliant
work, and Thomas was at the height of his fame, attracting students
into his courses by the hundreds. By 1920, however, when the students
swarmed back after the war, Park had become the outstanding member
of the department. He was no speech-maker and his reputation did not
depend on his lectures, profound and stimulating though they were. His
practice became to make appointments with each of his students and to
have protracted interviews with each one of them, learning their background and interests and planning definite problems for investigation.
This procedure was enormously time-consuming and Park was usually
late to meals—but he loved it.

"If his literary output is not impressive in quantity, the reason is
obvious. He did plan many books which he did not write. Several
volumes were projected in collaboration with his colleagues. These were
never produced, but the books he caused to be written and the ones he
laboriously edited and corrected are numbered by the scores and the
men he trained will yet write many more because of him. He held it was
better to induce ten men to write ten books than to take time off to
write one himself.

"His criterion of acceptability did not always commend itself to the
rest of us for he insisted that, if a man had done his best and that more
work would not improve the thesis, it should be approved. This is not
quite so bad as it sounds for many were eliminated before they came to
the point of writing, but he was very charitable if a mediocre man had
worked hard and done his best. He often said that the best results in the
long run could be expected, not from the most brilliant men, but from
the competent ones who could be depended upon to take a continuing
interest in a problem and stay with it. It must be confessed that the
results often justified his contention.

"His conception of sociology as an objective science, 'a basic science
of human nature,' made him oppose any effort to turn sociology into a
propaganda instrument. He steadfastly opposed what passed for 'reform.'
Because of this he sometimes encountered opposition from his Social
Worker colleagues on the campus who wrongfully interpreted his position as implying indifference to human welfare. But, he steadfastly
insisted that sociologists must not become agitators for he held that this
would only mean partisanship, the loss of the scientific temper, and
above all the loss of that influence and authority which objective science
should command."

The interest in community organization began to grow about the time of World War I. Jesse Steiner (1880-   ) was a teacher in Japan for several years. He returned to this country about the time of the first World War, becoming active in Red Cross administration, and along with E. W. Burgess, Fred Croxton, M. C. Elmer, Shelby Harrison, Phillip Kline, Louise Mark, and several others, worked on the reorganization plan for the American Red Cross. He did extensive work in community organization at North Carolina University, Tulane; and the University of Washington, Seattle. His work on community organization dealing with principles has long been recognized as a classic.

Steiner's statements below are what he considers as his contribution to sociology:

1. "Clarifying the relationship between sociology and social work and pointing out the necessity of making the social sciences the basis for a social work training curriculum. While with the Red Cross, I helped establish the first schools of social work in university departments of sociology.

2. "I developed the concept community organization from a vague phrase used by social workers into a well established sociological term. I gave the first university course in community organization at the University of North Carolina and wrote the first text dealing with this subject.

3. "In the field of community studies, I published case stories of small communities in which the emphasis was not upon a cross-section of the community at any one time as in a social survey, but upon the dynamic side of community life. The emphasis was upon the factors and forces responsible for community action rather than upon social problems or social institutions.

4. "I made the first nation-wide study of recreation in which the emphasis was upon the collection of quantitative data showing the changes that had taken place over a period of years. My statement and analysis of receational trends was perhaps my greatest contribution in this field.

5. "In my later years most of my time and energy have been given to a study of Japanese social institutions and Japanese traits and characteristics. If time does not run out, I hope to make this my magnum opus. Thus far I have only made a beginning in the publication of data I have collected. During my retirement I hope to complete this work."

One of the earliest writers and students of community organization was Bessie A. McClennahan (1885-   ). She pioneered in this work at Iowa, Missouri and Southern California. Her contribution expressed the emerging point of view of the early 1920's:

"The general decline of interest in local affairs does not necessarily mean that people lack social contacts and activities. Within contiguous communities people inevitably gravitate together into congenial groups. If they have common interests, they will get together, the only limitation being time and means of transportation. The place need have no special relation to their place of residence, but is determined only by its convenience as a meeting place. It is this type of association which may be called 'a communality.'

"The communality is an interest-circle characterized by the social nearness of members whose places of residence may be widely separated. It may be a formal or an informal group, as close-knit as a fraternity, as fluid as a public dance hall crowd. Its members belong, not because they share a place of common residence or are identified with the same community, but simply because they share like interests, ranging from the ephemeral to the relatively permanent. They meet together whenever they find it convenient . . .

"Communalities are as varied as the interests of people. They form a kind of shifting, shimmering overlay above the more stable, earthbound community. They are territorially detached social groupings, and their activities run the gamut of social, economic, political, and religious concerns. They provide for the socially popular, as well as for the so-called social misfit. Their varied type and makeup permit the crossing of many social boundary lines. As a consequence, they provide opportunities for the expansion of personality in the easy give-and-take of social interaction."

* * *

There was perhaps no individual in the period from 1925 to 1945 who was more representative of social thinking in America than *William Fielding Ogburn,* (1885-   ). He was born in Georgia; educated at Mercer College and at Columbia University; taught at Reed College, Columbia, and Chicago. He was president of American Statistical Association and president of American Sociological Society. *Social Change,* one of his early contributions greatly affected social thinking. He was an editor and director of the monumental "Studies on Social Trends." *Social Trends,* published in the latter part of 1932 under Ogburn's editorship, formed in large part a summary and re-evaluation of the threads of development of sociology of the preceding two decades. He has written and edited several volumes in this field bringing trends up to date. While one does not include the average introductory textbook as a significant factor in the development of social thought, the general text by Ogburn and Nimkoff, like the one by Park and Burgess, was so extensively used as a basic approach, that one may mention them. Their effect was not quite the same as the earlier pioneer works by

Stuckenberg, Blackmar and Gillin, or Small and Vincent, but neverthe-less are indicative of trends in emphasis. Ogburn was recognized as an outstanding authority in social change and technology during the genera-tion from 1920 to 1950. In a brief statement of what he considered his main contributions he states:

"The most widely known of my contributions is the measurement of unequal rates of change between the correlated parts of a culture, giving rise to maladjustments between the parts of culture which can be measured.

"I also think that the problem of social evolution has been solved by the discovery of four factors, as brief and general as those used by Darwin to explain biological evolution—mutation, inheritance, and natural selection. The factors are:

1. Invention—material and non-material.
2. The measurement, by exponential equations, of the accumulation of inventions.
3. The diffusion of inventions, and
4. The adaptation of culture to an invention.

"Number (2) above is largely mine. I have added greatly to (1) and (4), but have done nothing with (3).

"The application of these four factors to social change has revealed in the Western World in modern times the tremendous impetus to change in civilization due to technology and the lagging adjustment of non-material culture.

"I have applied these four factors to prediction, as in my book on the social effects of aviation, and developed methodologies of prediction. In the measurement of trends and my discovery that trends seldom change their course radically and my explanation thereof I should con-sider as a major contribution."

Ogburn believed that statistics are often misinterpreted because their presentation is such that, in the reader's mind, they are divorced from the nature of the data which they represent. One purpose of sta-tistics is to present information. This they fail to do adequately unless the nature of the data is presented in connection with the figures. Therefore, the meaning of an average is limited and indefinite unless there is a knowledge of the data from which it has been derived.

Statisticians sometimes make exaggerated claims for their subject with little understanding of the limitations of statistics. In 1934 Ogburn discussed several limitations.

"First: Statistics have a limited value for the discovery of the new in social science.

"Second: They are not applicable to unique phenomena or to the non-quantitative phases of personal and social life.

"Third: The method is inadequate for prediction because it does not include all variables involved in a situation.

"Fourth: The figures of language symbols of statistics are limited as conveyors of meanings.

"Fifth: Statistics must be aided by interpretations which of themselves are subject to much error.

"Sixth: Statistics add to knowledge, but do not enhance our understanding of the meaning of phenomena.

"Seventh: Statistics deal with segments and do not give an adequate composite picture of reality."

The interests of Hornell Hart (1888-   ) were probably more diversified than those of most sociologists of this period. His diversity of interests was more like that of the scholars of earlier periods. With an exceptionally keen insight, he has penetrated deeply into the fields of social psychology, religion, child welfare, the family, social theory, and statistical research. Hornell Hart has a saving grace sometimes lacking. He is never averse, after thoroughly studying a question, to recognize an error in the point of view he has been advocating, and start over again. This is a definite variation from some writers who having placed emphasis incorrectly, spend the rest of their lives trying to justify the error or obscure it by excessive defense.

He states: "Among the topics to which I may have made some original contribution, the following would seem to be relatively more important:

1. 'The fitting of logistic and log-log (continually accelerating) mathematic trends to various social trends, and the analysis of such trends as fitted by other sociologists.

2. 'The development of the Verifiability Rating Scale for measuring the scientific quality of sociological writings.

3. 'Various contributions to the objective analysis of social values.

4. 'Development of the operational approach to social problems, exemplified, for example, in the textbook *Personality and the Family*.

5. 'Various pieces of statistical pioneering, as in the first comprehensive measurement of urban unemployment, the first demonstration of the predictability of parole success, and the like."

In 1920-1921, a young musician visiting in Prague came in contact with a Russian sociologist, Pitirim A. Sorokin. Sorokin had been a teacher in the University of Petrograd, editor of a newspaper, private secretary to Kerensky, and had carried on some experimental research regarding the effectiveness of persons working in a soviet and in individual enterprise. He was imprisoned by the Bolsheviki, but on the intervention of former students, he was allowed to leave the country.

This young musician wrote to his father, Professor E. A. Ross at the University of Wisconsin, and Ross encouraged and aided the young sociologist to come to this country. Dr. Sorokin gave lectures at the University of Wisconsin, Illinois, and Minnesota. He remained at Minnesota for several years as a professor of sociology, later going to Harvard to head up the newly organized Department of Sociology.

Dr. Sorokin has been a prolific and suggestive writer. *Leaves from a Russian Diary, The Sociology of Revolution, Contemporary Sociological Theories, Social Mobility,* and a very extensive work on rural sociology which traces the history of social thought since the Middle Ages, which was written in collaboration with Dr. Carl Zimmerman. These constituted his earlier writings. Dr. Sorokin's method is forceful, with a resultant positive reaction by those who hear or study him—either vigorously agreeing or definitely disagreeing with him.

Dr. James Steele Gow, Jr. has made the following evaluation: "Pitirim Sorokin is worth studying because of his attempt to order, arrange and evaluate social data collected by other sociologists, historians, political scientists and the like. He has elements in common with Spengler and Toynbee in the grand sweep of his historical analysis, with Mosca and Pareto in his generalizing of the data of social stratification, mobility and political dynamics, and with Comte and Spencer in his synthesizing of the great mass of social data to provide a perspective the better to guide future work in the field. His most spectacular contribution that of the ideational, idealistic and sensate super systems of culture, appears to me to be less worthwhile than a subordinate concept of his, that of the logico-meaningful. Sorokin insists that a social science, while it is causal like physical or natural sciences, also is logico-meaningful, in that the significant relationships often are those of volution, aesthetic conformity, ethical judgments or rational thought structures. A culture, he insists, is more than artifacts—it is the men who make the artifacts and their reasons for doing so. Only by recognizing and scientifically studying logico-meaningful relationships can we learn the full significance of social data, he says. This, it appears to me, is valuable as an antidote to some of the over-emphasis on reasonable physical data to the exclusion of all else."

After World War I there evolved a type of sociologist, particularly during the '30's, of whom George Lundberg is a good representative. After he had completed his undergraduate work at the University of North Dakota he was introduced to sociology by John M. Gillette. He joined the armed forces in the first World War. A personnel officer noting his broad shoulders and the fact that he was from North Dakota, decided that unloading ships at Bordeaux was what he was equipped to do. Lundberg has never been heard to complain about what he was asked to do. About his war experience he would say—"I got tired then, but I have been tired before and since." After the war he did graduate work at the University of London, at the University of Wisconsin and at the University of Minnesota. His "stick-to-it-tiveness" was shown as a graduate student, when I assigned him a project which several others had given up as impossible. A typical Lundberg stunt occurred one night on our way home from a trip in Wisconsin. The car stopped because of carburetor trouble. I rolled in a blanket for the night. Sometime before morning I was awakened—the car was running. Lundberg had gone on eight miles into the next town. It was Sunday and everything was closed. He found out who had a shop, found him in church, and after the services persuaded him to sell repair parts and then walked back to put the car in shape. His procedure was always "when anything needs to be done—do it." He probably did more than most sociologists in alerting them to the use of statistics and objective research.

Regarding his contribution he writes: "In my own opinion my most important contribution to methodology has been in helping to explode the notion that the case method and the statistical method are in some way opposed to each other. My most important research, I think, has been my inquiry into the basic structure of the human community as represented by my study of "Social Attraction Patterns in a Village" (*Sociometry*, 1938) and also discussed in "The Sociography of Some Community Relation (*American Sociological Review*, June 1937). That type of research has since become very common. Over and above these specific contributions, my central interest has, of course, been to break down the barrier which still exists between the physical and the social sciences. Most of my serious writing has been directed at that end. I am convinced that the so-called problems of values is a pseudo-problem and that the field of ethics and values does not represent the separate world that it is frequently assumed to be, and that it, therefore, does not require a different technology and approach from that of other social problems.

"I do not see that the so-called value problem is a unique problem at all. Whenever man acts at all, his action may be regarded as evaluative in the sense that he does, in fact, act one way although he could conceivably have acted in any number of other ways. In this sense, all of the data with which sociologists have ever worked, including the bulk of the data in the census volumes, are data on human values (valuings). Nor does it matter whether these values lie in the past, in the present, or in the future. We react to past events that we have valued in the form of cherished memories (symbols); we react to present situations in terms of what we presently value; and we react to future values by reacting to the symbolic forms in which we have cast our aspirations for the future. I think the whole confusion over this subject is due to the still persisting philosophical preoccupations with which most sociologists have approached the problem. I predict that the next generation will wonder what all the noise was about."

In "The Growth of Scientific Method," (*The American Journal of Sociology,* May, 1945), he expressed the opinion that sociology was at present in process of transition from the natural history stage of scientific development (in which men were interested in gathering huge masses empirical data from all over the world from every traveler to distant countries and attempting to reduce the whole to some kind of order), to the atomic stage where scientists turn their attention increasingly to more and more intensive studies of increasingly small areas on the theory that, as happened in atomic theory in physics, the relationships observed in small microcosms will also throw a flood of light upon the microscopic universe in its farthest reaches.

Lundberg said, "I sometimes wonder whether the most important research done in the world is not what people steal time from their regular employment to do, rather than what they are paid and honored for doing. I retract nothing of what I have said in the past about the importance of large-scale studies and quantitative methods. In short, I intend to devote myself, as far as possible, to intensive work on what will appear to be relatively small problems and I would rather work on those with an assistant or two than be the head of a very large research institution with dozens or hundreds of subordinates.

"The most discouraging thing that occurs to me as I look over the field is the fact that sociological training seems to be still a pretty thin veneer for many of the fraternity. For example, when a war comes along they become hopeful and starry-eyed as little children in their capacity to entertain hopes of results for which there is absolutely no ground whatever. In the same way, there is an incredible amount of naivete about what can be done about certain social ills, many of which are inherent in the nature of society itself. Much of the more idealistic agitation regarding minority problems is of this character. It is still possible to secure the support of sociologists for programs which violate all known principles of sociology and which have not the slightest prospect of success. At the same time, I know of no way of correcting this defect except to continue along the lines we are working."

Efforts Toward Sampling of Mass Data

Giddings called attention to the fact that when in the world of external things we find objects so much alike that we may classify them, such objects are "seldom scattered in a wholly random distribution." With the wide acceptance of social survey procedures, including regional studies as well as particularized studies of specific areas of group activities, the problem of extensive data was simplified by use of scientifically determined samples.

The term *random sample* is quite generally used in a discussion of the collection of statistical material. It is understood to mean a rela-tively small number of units selected from a great mass of supposedly similar units in such a promiscuous manner that the different character-istics found among them will be presented in proportion to their existence in the entire group. Even when all possible variations are not present, it is presumed that enough variations are duly represented to enable a representative curve to be constructed from the data thus made available.

There is no objection to the use of a random sample in making an analysis of social phenomena, providing it is truly representative. There are, however, serious difficulties in choosing a representative random sample.

When we are making a study of units composed of single items, obtaining a random sample is easy. For example, it is easy to secure a random sample of individuals for the purpose of estimating the curve of height or weight, or for determining the relative variation in the intelligence quotient of a given group of individuals. The study of society, however, involves more than a variation in individuals. It is a study of social process, of group activities, and the interrelationship of activities and processes. The unit of investigation consists of an indi-vidual human being if we are trying to show an increase or decrease of population, or movement of population. It may consist of a study of individual members in a church or benevolent organization if we are attempting to show the relationship to the total expenditure. When the investigation involves a study of social processes, however, it is not the individual who is the unit of investigation, but rather the activities of the group of individuals, the social processes. *A Sample of Social Pro-cesses Must Have a Unit Large Enough to Include the Functioning of the Social Process.*

In dealing with social phenomena, the problem of choosing a ran-dom sample is more difficult than when individual items are the units of investigation. The sample should be a complete unit. If a study is being made of social activities, each unit must be studied completely. In making a study of health agencies in county seat towns, for example, it would be inaccurate to consider scattered inquiries within scattered towns as reliable samples. Each town should be considered as a unit and studied as a unit in its entirety. That is, a complete, comprehensive study must be made of each sample unit. If a study of community reaction is being made, the sample would involve a complex and com-prehensive study of random selected communities.

A random sample of the recreational activities of selected communities would not be a satisfactory basis for drawing conclusions since the unit of study consists of all phases of recreational activity and the conditioning phenomena within each sample community. A sample study of families would involve making a complete study of all of the activities and the conditioning factors involved in the life of each selected family. Selected individual members within the sample families would not be adequate. A sample study of group activities involves consideration of conditioning phenomena affecting each sample group, and not sample individuals within the sample group, such as pseudo-scientists are sometimes tempted to use in order to avoid tedious work and to get to results quickly.

One of the first essentials of social research is willingness to do routine tasks, to take careful notes; to make precise use of figures, dates, and references; and to stick to a line of procedure until it has been carried out. Persons who have been interested in general philosophies and comparative evaluations find the routine work of observation, recording, checking, and testing for accuracy tedious and boresome.

In a recent investigation of trade centers, the investigator started out collecting samples by taking selected or random stores in community trade centers. After a short time it was seen that the results would be entirely inadequate and would have no value in making a statistical study. The method of sampling was changed. Instead of picking random samples of stores in representative trade centers, the representative trade centers as a whole were taken, and all stores, in each of the trade centers, were carefully studied. This gave all of the variations of the unit of measure found in each of the different representative trade centers.

Likewise, in a study of the ownership of homes in a large midwestern city, the first thought was to take one home at random in each block in the city, the idea being that this would give a sample of homes owned, with additional data concerning nationality, occupation, length of residence in community, group interests, and activities, from which conclusions might be drawn. However, instead of following that method, another and more desirable method of sampling was followed. In several sections of the city an area was selected varying from 3,000 to 12,000 population, which was representative of the particular section of which it was a part. Within the area selected every unit of measure for which data was desired was taken, so that the *entire range of information within each sample area was secured*. In short, any data should be comprehensive enough to insure its covering all probable cases.

A very practical discussion of problems of sampling procedure was made by Frederick F. Stephan in the American Sociological Review (Aug. 1936) where he discussed the problems of sampling from schedules or files and sampling in field inquiries. Under general rules of sampling, he particularly calls attention to the need to draw the sample from items "as numerous and nearly similar in size and characteristics as possible," and to include samples from subgroups, appropriately weighted or adjusted when making up the aggregate. It should be in conformity with theoretical assumptions. Further, "Each item in the universe must be assured an equal chance of being selected for the sample if the sample is to be truly random." The same errors of bias occur both in sample and in complete enumeration.

Because of the excessive cost and effort of taking every item into consideration, the sampling method is extensively used in all types of social research. The causes of error may be controlled in this method as effectively as though every item in the universe were being considered. The great weakness of students of sociological problems is the desire to make a sweeping generalization of all similar phenomena, instead of limiting the conclusions to the data obtained.

Even in dealing with samples, it is well to consider all types of related data and information. The apparent effectiveness of statistics sometimes causes the investigation to suffer through the failure to appreciate the like values of qualitative estimates of the data assembled. There should be complete knowledge of all compilations of the same or similar material, and sufficient familiarity with all related phenomena to enable one to make sociological analyses.

Sampling Public Opinion

In discussing the sampling of public opinion, Giddings said in the Scientific Study of Human Society 1925, that, "A practice has grown up of interviewing individuals in various walks of life to ascertain their reactions to innumerable matters of belief, morals, domestic legislation, and world politics. Another is that of straw votes. Most of the samples obtained by either of these methods are invalid; they have little value even as indications of an actual state of public prejudice or conviction. Now and then they are taken at random, and would meet scientific requirements if taken from a homogenous field; but attention to this point is rarely discovered."

"When there is a vast amount of data, or when the field of investigation covers an extensive area, and time and funds are limited, sampling or the study of a selection number of cases is resorted to. Sampling is sometimes used when it is desired to check on data secured at some previous time in order to see whether any marked changes are evident. At best sampling is only what the term indicates. It can never be anything more than an approximation. This is to a certain extent true of any statistics, but the probability of error may be decreased by the method used in the gathering of the data. Above all, the samples should

not be too small, or representative of only part of the elements represented in the factors under consideration." In short, while the principles
of sampling have been well established, great amounts of pseudo-
research have been piled up by persons whose objectives were to secure
acclaim rather than secure reliable data.

A specific illustration of the error which may occur in sampling
is given by Clyde V. Kiser in a study of population found in the Journal of the American Statistical Association for September 1934. The
test revealed that the number of persons in the households included in
the sample were larger than those of the areas in which they were
located. This difference was due not to faulty selection so far as nati-
vity, race stock, and economic status are concerned. It seemed probable
that the selection of large families might be due to the failure of enum-
erators to revisit missed families, since married women who work away
from home are more likely to be childless. The primary objective of the
study was a morbidity survey and, hence, the chief concern was to
secure a sample representation of the area with regard to sickness rather
than size of household. Other errors likewise resulted due to a change
in the final use of the data from its original purpose. Regarding this
point, Kiser concludes: "So far as samples of population are concerned,
a definite bias is introduced unless the sample is selected with care, and,
once selected, is thoroughly canvassed. It is a persistent bias which cannot be corrected by mere extension of the sample."

The work of Frederick F. Stephan (1903-   ) of Princeton University presents a very definite tie-up of statistics with sociological
studies and research. This involves special procedures in sampling methods
other than the standardized work. Most of what he has done, especially
in recent years, has been connected with the organization and development of research and is representative of what other sociologists and
social scientists were doing. He particularly made some contribution in
the development of sampling methods for surveys, which are becoming
more and more significant. He states, "Recently I worked up a history
of the use of sampling, and was impressed by the slowness with which
efficient sampling methods were adopted in surveys. For example,
Bowley's work in 1912 was not imitated until his assistant, Margaret
Hogg, applied his sampling method in New Haven in 1931. The same
slow adoption of efficient sampling methods appears to have been
characteristic of other countries. I suppose that it was due, first of all,
to the preoccupation of people who were making surveys with other,
more pressing, practical problems, and secondly, to their meager knowledge and interest in statistical methodology."

Another example of the trend in the work of Kurt Lewin, who by
the middle of the century, gave emphasis to more refined analysis of

group dynamics than was possible in the earlier years of the century. While the problems of learning development and regression and the differentiated aspects of group dynamics have long been recognized, many other specific developments in study and research had to take place before certain types of problems could be dealt with. This need has been amply demonstrated in the mechanical and physical sciences and is of even more subtle significance in the social sciences.

The development and testing of new research procedures, however, has not been a smooth procedure agreed upon by all persons interested. The reactions to different attempts have usually been very positive and vigorous. A typical representative of the group who demanded the best and was most intolerant of slip-shod research, or any attempt to build up a personal following was Read Bain. In a most vigorous article in *Social Forces,* October, 1951 on "Action Research and Group Dynamics," he called to task some of the presentations in the newer fields of social research.

⸱ ⸱ ⸱ "The ideas conveyed by the terms action research, or group dynamics, are neither new nor original. It is pointless to argue whether Lewin or Moreno "discovered" this approach since neither man did. Perhaps it is also pointless to note that the followers of both men seldom mentioned the other man. Lippitt writes a book in which socio-dramatic techniques play an important part, but does not mention Moreno.[3] Jennings is more generous to Lewin and mentions Lippitt's important studies of leadership with approval.[4]

"Sociologists should not be surprised that social psychologists, social anthropologists, and others almost ignore the contributions of sociology to what is called action research and group dynamics. It is not unusual for the contributions of sociology to be overlooked by men in other fields. More than fifty years after the death of Adam Ferguson and nearly twenty-five after the death of Comte, social psychology and social anthropology began to develop. Eventually there appeared social geography, social biology, sociological jurisprudence and political science, institutional economics, the sociological interpretation of religion and all the fine arts. Even atomic physicists, long contemptuous of all social science, are now somewhat vainly and belatedly trying to become "social" physicists. Unfortunately, most people in all of these fields still remain highly critical and woefully ignorant of sociology.

"Action research deals with what sociologists have been calling social problems and social conflicts for over fifty years. Group dynamics and social processes appear to mean about the same thing. After 1850,

[3] Lippitt, Ronald, *Training in Community Relations* (New York: Harpers, 1949)
[4] Jennings, Helen H., *Leadership and Isolation: A Study of Personality in Interpersonal Relations* (New York: Longmans, 1943.)

the sociological point of view became widely disseminated. Many people think they have made novel discoveries when they invent new names for what sociologists have known for years. When one reads Laski's *Grammar of Politics,* one wishes Laski had read some elementary sociology. One feels the same about studies of "quaint" communities by social anthropoligists who have been driven out the South Seas and are running short of Amerinds. If they knew some elementary sociology, they would not make so many (to them) new and revolutionary discoveries.

"It is easy to find some sources of action research in the history of sociology. One notes the shift from the static, descriptive concepts of Comte and Spencer to the *Dynamic Sociology* of Ward (1883), the *Gemeinschaft und Gesellschaft* of Tonnies (1887), *Die Soziologische Erkenntnis* of Ratzenhofer (1898), Small's processes in *General Sociology* (1905), and the social work "action" writing of C. R. Henderson and Graham Taylor. E. A. Ross, influenced by Tarde and Ward, furthered the trend by *Social Control* (1901), *Sin and Society* (1907), and *Social Psychology* (1908), William James, James Mark Baldwin, and later, John Dewey and G. H. Mead were powerful influences on sociologists like Cooley and Ellwood. Settlement houses, the community organization movement, and social surveys around 1900 were doing much the same sort of thing now called action research and group dynamics. Books like A. F. Bentley's *The Process of Government* (1908), Mary Follett's *The New State* (1918), and Cooley's three volumes (1902, 1908, 1918) set forth the theory of group dynamics. Later, but still antecedent to action research, was the emphasis by Cooley and L. J. Henderson on the importance of small social systems and actual research of that sort by Carr, Newstetter, and D. S. Thomas.[5] The work of Elton Mayo and associates in industrial sociology and the earlier work of educational researchers like Piaget should also be mentioned. In short, there is nothing very new or original about so-called action research and group dynamics.

"The idea that scientists are doing research for the purpose of

[5] C. H. Cooley, "Case Study of Small Institutions as a Method of Research" (1927) in *Sociological Theory and Social Research* (New York: Holt, 1930), pp. 313-327; L. J. Henderson, Pareto's *General Sociology* (Cambridge, Mass.: Harvard Press, 1935); Lowell J. Carr, "Experimental Sociology," *Social Forces* (Sept., 1929), pp. 63-74. See also Carr's *Situational Analysis: An Observational Approach to Introductory Sociology* (New York: Harpers, 1948); Wilbur I. Newstetter and M. J. Feldstein *Wawokiye Camp: A Research Project in Group Work* (Cleveland: Western Reserve University Press, 1930); Dorothy Swaine Thomas, Alice M. Loomis, and Ruth E. Arrington, *Observational Studies of Social Behavior,* Vol. I, *Social Behavior Patterns* (New Haven: Yale University Press, Institute of Human Relations, 1933).

solving moral and ethical problems shocks the minds of many scientists. They insist that science and scientists are essentially amoral, non-ethical, and non-utilitarian. This leads to some curious confusions. Logically, it would seem that a scientist who took such a position could sell his services to the highest bidder with no moral qualms or scruples. He is merely a technician; he takes no moral responsibility either for the knowledge he seeks or the use to which it may be put. He admits that science may be used for logically and morally contradictory purposes, and he may even make the moral judgment that this fact is unfortunate; it is in the same category as the fact that a knife may be used to kill the king or cut a carrot. Science and its results are as amoral and non-utilitarian as rain and uranium in a non-teleological world. If this causes anyone pain, our amoral scientist is quick to assert that in his capacity as *citizen,* he is as moral as the next man; it is only in his role as *scientist* that he is non-moral."

"This position may be tenable for purposes of abstract analysis, but it is untenable for purposes of action in a real world. When a man acts as a scientist, he is bound by a most austere morality. He will not falsify data; he will process all data by the rigorous rationale of science; he will publish his results; he will gladly change his views when new evidence warrants it; he will not violate law or ethics to advance research; he will aid colleagues in every possible way; he will act like a lobbyist and publicity agent for the advancement of science. By his calling, he is inescapably moral and ethical; he promotes values that promote science and opposes values that harm science. The scientist is non-moral only in the sense that he will not violate the ethic of science to retard or ad-advance non-science or anti-science values. Science is his supreme value. If he has any other values which will induce him to violate the ethic of science, he is not a 'true scientist.' He might practice 'expediency' morality to save his life by *saying* he thinks the earth is flat and motion-less when he knows better, but this does not invalidate the central argument in cases where we say the man has "freedom of action.""

Reform "researchers" often deceive themselves by being uncritical of their methods and findings. They often want the results they expect so strongly that they unconsciously violate the ethic and logic of science. They often are quite impatient with the cautious and critical scientist. If a scientist is full of reformation zeal, he may make errors he could have avoided easily if he had been critical of the goals the action group was seeking.

With the basic principles, techniques, and procedures for general social research fairly well established, research in specific areas began to make their appearance. By combining different procedures, real progress was possible. As long as 1901 Franklin H. Giddings stated,

"Sociology legitimately uses all known methods of scientific research, inductive and deductive. Its chief reliance, however, is necessarily upon inductive method." By the end of the first quarter of the twentieth century, research methods began to be applied to particular problems of interest. Social distance, the business cycle, indeces of social trends, prediction studies, and refined methods of sampling began to appear. There were short periods and sometimes particular areas of the country, or even individual universities where emphasis was placed upon special fields of inquiry. These varied studies with their widely divergent emphasis sometimes caused controversy when persons incorrectly assumed that the type of research under consideration was to become the major trend. However, as the controversal points had their sharp, conflicting edges worn down to size, the overall picture of social research is becoming increasingly understood. The evolving social scientist is beginning to understand the use of various techniques and his use of them will be as particularized as the tools in a mechanic's chest.

IX

Social Work and Social Reform

WHEN A SITUATION appears which is not in harmony with what is generally recognized as desirable, a usual reaction is to prevent its continuance. When any considerable number of persons get the same impression, a concerted effort may be made to remedy the situation. The situation may be one which is destructive of established values. It may be a replacement of a deteriorated social order. It may, even more frequently, be the result of certain areas of the social order moving ahead and others remaining static, causing a stress due to a cultural lag. Whatever the situation may be, the effect tends to give rise to a feeling that negative forces or deteriorating factors are at work, and the result is a condition of social pathology.

During the first half of the nineteenth century, the attitude towards social pathology has changed. In the beginning any variation from the normal, particularly downward or unapproved, was given an absolute designation. Gradually, however, it was recognized that any factor, whether we speak of poverty, crime, inadequate housing, child labor, infant mortality, or of disease is a relative factor and without any absolute significance. Emphasis began to be placed upon conflict of values instead of specific personal behavior.

In the late '90's much of the material in this field was designated as practical sociology as indicated by Carroll D. Wright. Interest in the development of social insurance in many of the European countries was brought forth by Charles R. Henderson, along with his university teaching and his work in developing charity organization societies in America. With Jane Addams and Graham Taylor establishing settlement houses and with Edward T. Devine and others trying to establish schools of social work, we began to use the term *social technology*. By 1914 this interest in social pathology had changed to applied sociology and social problems. Particularly after World War I and again in the early '30's social disorganization became the keynote term within this field. Following President Hoover's conference on child welfare in 1929, the term was extended to include personal and social disorganization. Many of the studies, whether spoken of as social pathology, social disorganization, applied sociology, social technology, or social problems, contained substantially the same material and covered the same general field.

At the University of Chicago Charles Richmond Henderson em-phasized social technology, which culminated in his "Dependence De-fectives and Delinquents" (1901). Amos Warner whose ideas were crystalized in his book on American Charities, and many others began to express their ideas to such an extent that from 1895 to 1900, 21 percent of the articles in the American Journal of Sociology were on the subject of social pathology and social reform. By 1940-1944 only 5.5 percent dealt with those topics. The approach in the beginning of the twentieth century was very largely to present first a point of view based upon inadequate factual data, but substantiated by the logic of accepted ethical and moral principles, and second a presentation for organizing and promoting remedial measures. This development was summarized by E. H. Sutherland in The American Journal of Sociology Vol. 11 No. 6 as follows:

"*First,* the social scientist makes the appraisal of any social unit. Since this involves or need involve no ethical judgment, it is not correct to say, as has been said, that social disorganization is social organization of which the social scientist disapproves.

"*Second,* the criteria used by the social scientist in appraising a social unit are the internal inconsistencies in that unit, as a result of which common objectives are relatively lacking. *Third,* these internal inconsistencies may be of two kinds, namely, anomie, or lack of internal organization, and conflicting social organizations within the unit. The emphasis has been on the latter, and in that sense disorganization is differential group organization. When a community is disorganized with reference to crime, for instance, one or more groups within that community are organized for crime and one or more groups within the community are organized against crime. *Fourth,* the relativity of social pathology has been recognized throughout this period, but has become an essential part of the definition in the later part of the period. *Ward* stated that 'the criminals are the geniuses of the slums.' *Small* and *Vincent* recognized that pathology is defined in relation to the mores and that the mores are variable. *Thomas and Znaniecki* defined social disorganization as 'the weakening of the social rules of behavior upon individual members of the group' and demonstrated that this generally means the development of conflicting rules of behavior. *R. C. Fuller* defined social problems as 'conflicts of values.' The common element in these definitions is the relativity of the pathological: what is one man's disease in another man's cure. The conflicts of values range from one person deviating from the other members of the group, at one extreme, to 50 percent of the members deviating from the other 50 percent, at the other extreme. Because of the absolutistic connotations of the term 'pathology,' it is not an appropriate designation for these relativistic phenomena, and on that account it is being supplanted by other terms, such as 'social disorganization.' A few authors have stated absolutistic criteria of social pathology, but have not in any case developed these in a systematic manner. *Cooley,* for instance, defined social disorganization as the lack of harmony between human nature and the institutions in the larger society. Since he conceived of human nature as approximately universal, being the product of primary groups which are approximately universal, this definition appears to be absolutistic. But since it was not developed and is inconsistent with Cooley's general point of view of society, the meaning is not clear. *Ogburn,* in his theory of cultural lag, implies a definition social disorganization which apparently eliminates the ethical evaluations by the participants, namely, social disorganiza- tion is the inconsistency in a culture which occurs when the material or technological elements change more quickly than the adaptive elements. This definition, however, does not succeed in eliminating the evaluative features, since the condition prior to the change in the technological elements is assumed to be organization and the criteria for appraising it as organization are not stated. *Fifth,* the social pathologists are not interested in every inconsistency or conflict of values in society, but they have not made a concerted effort to define the limits of the con- flicts of values in which they are interested. Blumer suggests as a limita- tion that social disorganization is the condition in which 'a society in the face of disturbance loses the ability to re-establish concerted be- havior.' The general practice among social pathologists is to use criteria such as the number of persons involved or the intensity of the conflict."

Early Beginnings in Social Work

The National Association for the Promotion of Social Science of Great Britain was organized in 1857. The American Social Science Association, modeled after the British, was organized in 1865. Both associations were concerned with the application of science to the prob- lems of human relations, and with the possibility of new discoveries and improvements in social relationships. The area of their interests was designated as "whatever concerns mankind in their social, rather than their individual relationships and shades off easily and imperceptible into metaphysics on the one side, philanthropy on another and political economy on a third." The purpose of the association was stated "to develop the study of social science—to increase public wealth and to insure its proper distribution—(and) the diffusion of those principles which make the strength and dignity of nations," as stated in the Ameri- can Social Science Association *Transactions,* July, 1866.

In 1863 Massachusetts created the first board in the country to supervise and administer charitable, medical, and penal institutions of the state. Within twelve years, eight additional states had such organizations. As early as 1872 Frederick H. Wines, secretary of the Illinois board, and Andrew E. Elmore, president of the Wisconsin board, after visiting institutions in Wisconsin called together representatives from the upper Mississippi valley for a two-day session. This was repeated at Milwaukee in 1873 and attracted so much attention that the American Social Science Association took up the idea and included all boards of charity and health in the United States. The leaders of these activities represent as significant a group in this phase of the development of social thought as the individuals mentioned in the chapter on emerging sociology were to social theory. We find among the intellectual group leaders Samuel Eliot and George William Curtis, who is sometimes spoken of as the Father of Civil Service in the United States. Enoch C. Wines, secretary of the New York Prison Association; Bebulon R. Brockway, who was putting reform and penal philosophy into practice. Before 1880 the charity organization movement inspired and molded after comparable efforts in England had taken definite form. The old Social Science Association began developing areas which represented particular fields of interest. These took the form, after separation from the parent body, of the American Sociological Society and the National Conference of Charities and Correction. This later subdivision retained that name until 1917 when it was changed to the National Conference of Social Work. On separation from the Social Science Association, it became a body interested, not chiefly, in scientific inquiry, but to an increased degree emphasized administration and methods of practice, with some secondary consideration to prevention. Frank Bruno states, "Its leaders were challenged by the assistance of their day by day problems; the numbers of insane were increasing at an alarming rate; children were being brought up in alms houses; the mentally deficient were an increasing menace to the well-being of society; dependency was placing an ever-increasing burden on tax payers. - - - They were pressing exigiencies which could not wait long for an answer."

By the end of the nineteenth century, the idea that indigent able bodied persons should be placed in institutions had been practically discontinued.

The Insane and Feeble-Minded

Until well into the second half of the nineteenth century, insane persons in this country were usually relegated to alms houses. The few exceptions were the state hospital of Virginia erected in Williamsburg in 1773 and one in Philadelphia in 1775. A hospital exclusively for mentally ill persons was built in New York in 1843 and within the next thirty years there were seven such institutions in New York. The first problem, which indicated the point of view of the times, was how to manage and treat mental patients without physical disturbance. Phy-sicians were put in charge of institutions at a very early period and while it was admitted that these institutions functioned better under a physician frequently the physician, in charge was a person with inferior qualifications. Beginning in the later part of the nineteenth century, individuals were expressing the need of a change in treatment of the insane and significant examples such as the program followed at Ghepl, Belgium have gradually become a part of the thinking and of the prac-tice throughout the country.

In 1888 many persons were shocked when the Reverend S. J. Barrows, editor of *The Christian Register,* took issue with the accepted view that a feeble-minded person was incapable of receiving any in-struction.

Richard L. Dugdale made a study in 1876 of certain groups of criminals. In this study he attempted to demonstrate the continuity of delinquency and mental deficiency within a family. He recognized the variety of influences affecting the personality of the individual,—dis-ease, standard of living, education, and particularly family status in the community. In his study of the Jukes family he showed that mem-bers who have become a part of a satisfactory social environment had secured effective social status when they were removed from their frus-trating environment of economic want, and the social stigma of asso-ciation with criminal groups. This point of view did not have an in-terested or understanding audience, and Dugdale's contention was diverted so far into the limits of biological heredity that in 1901 Frank-lin H. Giddings brought out a new edition of the study in order to show how the original contention had been lost.

The idea that feeble-minded persons could be educated found ex-pression in the work of many individuals such as Samuel Gridley Howe, who, while disappointed with his own efforts, attempted to work out a program at the Perkins Institute. Similarly, William Pryor Letchworth (1823-1910) and Hasting H. Hart who in 1892 contended that feeble-minded could be restored to normalcy. On the other hand, Dr. Issac N. Kerlin and Alexander Johnson were more pessimestic. The general idea that there were effective classifications of feeble-minded became an accepted point of view and they were generally grouped as idiots, im-beciles, and feeble-minded until Henry H. Goddard at the beginning of the twentieth century popularized the term moron for the group form-erly spoken of as feeble-minded.

The Delinquent

The idea of probation was actively illustrated by John Augustus (1785-1859), a Boston bootmaker who persuaded the courts of Boston to release certain convicted defendants into his custody. Between 1848 and 1858 Augustus produced bail and received on probation 1052 men and 794 women. Z. R. Brockway and John Augustus stand out in crystallizing thought in regard to the care of delinquents. Just as we mentioned in the case of community studies, the work of novelists and writers called attention to certain situations. In the field of treatment of delinquents we find during the last quarter of the nineteenth century the novelist George W. Cable writing about the leasing of prisoners to private contractors. Much of what he wrote was well known to penologists and a few selected individuals, but they needed the popular interest created by a novelist to back them up. In fact a most interesting and valuable study of trends of social thought should be made by the study of literary and fictional writing of any period. This would not represent the origin of these principles, but there is no question that it would give a true picture of public and popular recognition and backing of those principles. As stated elsewhere, Upton Sinclair's *The Jungle* crystallized public opinion and focalized political administrators' attention to pure food requirements.

Protection of Children

Shortly before the Civil War, Charles Loren Brace began rescuing abondoned children from the streets of New York and sending them to western states to be distributed among farmers. This practice continued up until the early years of the twentieth century. Thousands of children were taken care of in this way. It was considered a real step forward from the practice of placing children in alms houses and orphanages. This point of view was not agreed to by many, and there was a period when orphanages grew with tremendous rapidity. The advocates of orphanages and children's institutions objected to foster homes. Their objection had some foundation which in turn was due to the inadequacy of proper investigation and follow-up methods. It is, perhaps, a human tendency to be afraid of admitting a flaw in a program and as a result, spend more time trying to justify some procedure rather than eliminate the mistake which gives rise to the criticism. In the intensity of the struggle between the point of view advocating institutions and advocating foster homes, the point suggested by J. Prentice Murphy in 1922 was that it might have been wiser for society to have directed its efforts toward preserving the home rather than to have spent its energies to save the child after he had been damaged. In short, preventive work as a function of child protection did not receive as much attention as rescue work. It is so much more thrilling and spectacular to do disaster relief than to spend one's time in the non-spectacular work of prevention. A. E. Elmore of Wisconsin, Hastings H. Hart of Minnesota, John P. Erly of Indiana, A. G. Byers of Ohio, F. M. Gregg of Chicago and many others became actively interested in improving methods of caring for children. However, as early as 1890 John H. Finley of New York and Homer Folks of Pennsylvania called attention to the need for careful investigations of both the foster home and the child to be placed. Homer Folks was particularly emphatic in his opposition to reformatories to which children might be sent for delinquencies.

In 1896 a committee on children for the National Conference of Charities and Corrections definitely recommended that a special court should be created to try children's cases in which there would be no semblence of formal criminal procedure. Under the influence of Hastings H. Hart, Alexander J. McKelway, Owen R. Lovejoy, John H. Findlay and Florence Kelly, a special conference on child saving was held in 1893 in connection with the Columbian Exposition in Chicago. These persons represented a vanguard of individuals who were probing into social situations, frequently making more mistakes in their evaluations than instructive conclusions, but by means of trial and error experience the residue of their findings became the gold dust which was eventually molded into the bricks of established thinking.

Children's Bureau

It is reported that in 1906 Lillian Wald, reading a statement in the paper that the President had called a cabinet meeting to consider the menace of the boll weevil, commented on the relative importance of the boll weevil, fish or pigs as compared with governmental interest in children. She and her companion Florence Kelly secured the cooperation of Edward T. Devine and the matter was taken up with President Theodore Roosevelt who wired back, "It's a bully idea, come to Washington and let's see." This resulted in the first president's White House conference on child welfare in 1909, and by 1912 the bill first introduced by Murray Crane of Massachusetts was passed as finally revised by Senator Borah of Idaho and signed by President William Howard Taft six years after its first suggestion. Homer Folks was an important factor in setting up the U. S. Children's Bureau and under the effective leadership of Julius C. Lathrop and Grace Abbott, the federal government entered the field of social services in areas other than publication, education, and health. We mentioned these aspects since it signified the trend in social thinking.

The Settlement Movement

1. Early Beginnings

The beginning of the community organization movement is usually spoken of as originating in England in 1869. There was, however, a well established idea in the general cultural pattern of a large proportion of the American people long before that time, which was in effect similar to the community organization movement as such. The district school-house was long and generally recognized as the center of the community and neighborhood activities. The type of activities ranging from spelling-bees to services of particular religious sects represented by an occasional itinerant preacher, or to an entertainment consisting of anything from a one-man band or a sleight of hand performer to a lyceum lecture. They consisted of pie socials, basket suppers, and local singing and debating societies. Long before the Civil War, circulating singing masters organized classes in rural schools. These meetings were in reality forerunners of the type of thing the modern group worker is attempting to achieve. The method and techniques may vary, but the objective has always been socialization of community attitudes, development and adjustment of personalities, and building up individual interests and skills. It is sometimes difficult for the person evaluating a situation or a movement to realize that an earlier or a cruder effort may have been a necessary forerunner of a point of view. The more efficient functioning of the present day was built upon the successes and failures of the past.

Dr. Jesse Steiner speaks of the early settlement movement as having been essentially a missionary enterprise, beginning with the work of Barnett, Vicar of St. Jude's in Whitechapel, who tried to persuade Oxford University students to take an interest in some of the poorest parishes of London. An organization was formed in 1884 and university students made use of temporary quarters until Toynbee Hall was completed. This led to similar social settlements in other sections of London. In 1887 Dr. Stanton Coit established the Neighborhood Guild in New York. Jane Addams and Ellen Gates Starr organized the work at Hull House in Chicago in 1889. This was soon followed by Andover House in Boston, now known as South End House.

While we are emphasizing trends in social thought from the last decade of the nineteenth century up to the middle of the twentieth century, the immediate routes of social thought and activity sometimes reach back a little further. In the years before the Civil War, there was a man living in Cedarville, Illinois by the name of John Addams. He was of Quaker background and because he ministered to the physical needs, as well as other human requirements, he was known as Dr. Addams. During one winter in the late '50's he came to a Swiss settlement about fifteen miles north of his home in the state of Wisconsin. Here he conducted a day school for the immigrant children. The parents paid fifty cents a month tuition and met in the various homes. During the morning hours they would sing the multiplication tables, rules of syntax, weights and measures, and geography to the tune of some familiar song. In the afternoon he would talk to the children about various things concerning which they asked questions. He told them about plants, explaining fibro-vascular bundles and differences between monocotyledonous and dicotyledonous plants. He told them how fossils which they found in abundance in limestone came to be there. He helped them to become adjusted to life in America. In 1860 his daughter, Jane Addams was born. There is no question that her interest in immigrant groups was encouraged by her father's activities. After graduating from the Rockford, Illinois Female Seminary in 1881, Miss Addams spent some time in Europe and in England where she was greatly impressed with the establishment of settlement houses by a group of university students in London. This began the crystallization of many attempts to adjust the millions of people who came to this country to the American way of life. It gave impetus to often widely diverse branches of applied sociology and social work which have developed in this country. Not only did the Hull House become a successful settlement house, but throughout the United States great settlement houses became established, each emphasizing the needs and characteristics of its neighborhood.

2. The Philosophy Movement

The religious motive played a strong part in much of the early settlement movements and since the churches were not socializing their programs to any great extent, it drew leaders with this type of interest to the settlements. Jesse Steiner states:

"One of the outstanding features of the settlement movement as contrasted with the charity organization movement, is its direct concern with the people themselves rather than with the various agencies that are working in their behalf. By drawing the people together in a neighbor' hood center and giving them opportunity for wholesome social inter' course, the social settlement strives to build up community solidarity. When the purpose of the settlement is stated in this manner it appears very similar to the modern community center movement. The social settlement movement, however, possesses distinctive features of its own that have been colored by its early beginning in the congested slums of the large cities. Its early founders conceived their mission to be the alleviation of the sufferings of the poor. Their method of accomplishing this purpose was to take up residence in the poorer quarters of the city where they could share with the disadvantaged their heritage of culture and education. The very nature of the movement made it a contribution of the rich to the poor. The initiative for the organization of the settle' ment as well as its financial support comes from outside the neighbor' hood in which it was located . . . The social settlements never accepted the traditional idea that leadership was a divine right of the upper classes. At a time when such an idea was widely prevalent, the social settlements set themselves firmly against attitudes of condescension in their relation with the poor, and sought to break down the undemocratic cleavage between the social classes."

3. The Growth of Settlements in the United States

Neighborhood work in the United States showed signs of greater flexibility and extended itself beyond its academic parent. It became known as the "Social Settlement."

Settlement workers have in the past few decades embarked on a course of social action. They have emphasized social justice in industrial relations, housing, health and sanitation, and recreation. They have opposed and agitated against negative social situations of all kinds, whether unsanitary living conditions, adverse labor relations or other civic, industrial, and social ills. Some of this agitation resulted in social amelioration through legislation. Further interests in recent years have led settlement leaders into the struggle for large scale public housing, social insurance, internationalism and world peace. Some workers today appear to avoid these problems while they engage themselves in leisure time programs. Many are "courageous" enough to say what they "stand for" and sponsor any movement to alleviate or improve social well-being. The work of the settlement has been criticized as superficial, that it stands aside and backs down in the economic struggle when its endeavors run counter to the controlling groups which permit its existence. However, this may be due to devious methods being employed to bring pressure to bear against business and government for the adoption of some new scheme of social betterment. There tends to be fewer revolutionary movements and in their stead a slower process of reform is hoped for through education.

Settlements have been termed obsolete by some writers and it is held their activities are being absorbed by the public school and public supported community center. This has not happened yet to any great degree in many cities, but it is rapidly under way. The progressive settlement worker strives to keep the settlement from becoming a "part of the established order of things." The problems of interest to settlement workers probably will reach some semblance of solution in time. After experimentation by the settlement has proven projects workable, it has given them over to public institutions, which leads a number of settlement executives to comment that they are "working themselves out of a job," "putting themselves out of business." What is their business? Settlements are often regarded as recreation centers. Their real purpose, however, said Jane Addams, is "to provide a center for higher civic and social life, to institute and maintain educational and philanthropic enterprises, and to investigate and improve the conditions in industrial districts." It is to investigate the new, make discoveries, tap new sources of potential and growing resources. They must change with their neighborhoods. Their functions may change, but settlements are still needed as centers of contact and understanding. At present the group-work technique is spreading among settlements as another device to fulfill the settlement purposes.

The most obvious difficulty the settlements are facing is that of the encroachment of industry and the disappearance of the neighbor-hood. Population is constantly shifting and the configuration of the community is rapidly changing. Older institutions having adapted them-selves to a former population have had to move with the people or modify their programs to meet the changed communities. Some have not done this. The true settlement does if it is to carry out its purposes. Reorganization becomes necessary when functions and clientele have been altered. Industrial communities have been dissected by heavy traffic arteries, spreading factories, railroads, and super-highways.

Thus there are two apparent approaches which become evident, namely that having a community objective and that having a neighbor-hood objective. A centralized program while it emphasizes neighborhood needs continually, is organized likewise for a general community objec-tive. In the decentralized program of each unit it places greater em-phasis on the neighborhood specifically, but the combined neighborhood programs of the different units become the functioning community program. The determination of the program followed depends then, as was stated, on the factors relating to the founding of the settlement, the size of the area to be covered, natural and artificial structure of the community, topography, economic condition of different areas, num-ber of agencies, availability of space and equipment for leisure time programs; and on the amount of available funds for administration, supervision and leadership; in fact, the entire social configuration.

Education for Social Work

The source of inspiration for the development of new ideas is often overlooked because any record of its designation does not come within the accepted term of such work. Just as Herbert Adams, historian of Johns Hopkins, played an important part in the lives of a group of young men, who became sociologists, so Dr. Francis G. Peabody at Harvard University apparently influenced a group of young men towards social work during the last quarter of the nineteenth century. Peabody's course was listed as Philosophy 11 and described as "The Ethics of Social Reform." "The questions of Charity, Divorce, the Indians, Labor, Prisons, Temperance, and problems of practical ethics—lectures, essays, and practical observations." The inclusion of this course was seriously questioned by officials of the University. Among the men who had contact with Peabody and Philosophy 11 were: Dr. Richard C. Cabot, Homer Folks, Sherman Kingsley, Robert A. Woods, William H. Pear, Charles Birkwell, and Judge Harvey Baker. Such an array of leaders seems more than accidental. In 1871 Professor White of Cornell recommended a course "to fit young men to deal intellectually with such important social questions as the best method of dealing with pauperism, intemperance, crime of various degrees and among persons of different ages, insanity, idiocy and the like." In 1884 Franklin B. Sanborn gave such a course. Another person with wide influence in inspiring young men to go into social work areas was Simon N. Patton of the University of Pennsylvania, among whose students Edward T. Devine and Francis Tyson are most generally known. An outstanding person represented the culmination of social thought up to 1900 was Amos G. Warner, (1861-1900). He held a professorship at the University of Nebraska in 1889 and in 1893 he went to Leland Stanford University as professor of economics and sociology. While there he brought out his classical book *American Charities*. This book was the only text within that field for many years and together with C. R. Henderson's *Dependents, Defectives and Delinquents* determined the trend of thinking within the fields for a quarter of a century. Amos Warner died at the age of 39 after three years of suffering from tuberculosis. In this connection Zilpha D. Smith should be mentioned. Much social work was done by volunteers and other well meaning people. Someone about this period made the pungent remark that "one half the time of the wise was spent in correcting the work done by the good. Miss Smith was a firm believer in the possibility for training paid workers and of developing comparable and reliable procedures for social inquiry. She insisted on the use of exact records of activities such as case records and minutes of meetings. Her point of view was brought out in a paper on "Methods Common to Social Investigations." This paper printed in Charities and the Commons, became the basis and inspiration for Social Diagnosis by Mary Richmond. For many years it was the most useful book for persons in various areas of social work.

Social Insurance

While individual efforts dealing largely with the feasibility of insurance had been discussed by individuals for over 200 years, it was not until 1884 that under the administration of Bismarck was German social insurance introduced. This covered loss of accidents, sickness, old age including mother's pension. John Graham Brooks presented a complete report of this at the St. Louis World's Fair, which gave it wide publicity although Charles R. Henderson of the University of Chicago in 1902 had suggested that a commission be appointed to study "the best practical method of insuring the working people against extreme need in case of accident, sickness during the period of invalidism and helpless old age." A committee was appointed by the National Conference of Charities and Correction with Henderson as chairman and the committee consisting of Frederick L. Hoffman, Dr. Samuel G. Smith,

John Graham Brooks, Amos W. Butler, Frank A. Fetter, and Edward T. Devine. Two years later Hoffman criticized government insurance on financial acturial and economic grounds and Brooks, differing from Hoffman on the crippling effect of social insurance, felt that the scale of German pensions would be quite adequate for American workmen. Not until 1917 was there effective consideration of social insurance when the outstanding spokesman as Royal Meeker, John B. Andrews and Governor Hiram Johnson of California, Professor Ernst Freund pointed out that while there was no legal precedence for such a law, the law might be sustained on the basis of "its essential equity." Not until twenty years later, 1937, was that question decided by the Supreme Court, making the decision on the basis of "its essential equity." In 1911 Louis D. Brandeis indicated that social insurance should cover all contingencies which endangered his economic independence. Thus we see that the ideas expressed by C. R. Henderson and others were beginning to take root. This has not yet been achieved, although in the middle '40's New Zealand made an attempt in that direction.

Social Change and Social Reforms

Every succeeding generation brings with it changes which give it a distinctive mark in history. Often these changes are of such minor significance that there is little to distinguish the generations from each other. To those who are a part of one era, or who are affected directly by the change, even a minor event looms up out of all proportion to its actual significance. Every social situation, whether it is caused by a new turn of events or whether it is something that has suggested some modi-fication, may become the rallying cry for a social change.

The new social reforms proposed are as numerous as the days of the calendar. They are as varied as the people who sponsor or accept them. They are proposed by every group of persons whose attention has been called to any situation which might be used as a handle for pulling a new program out of "Pandora's Box." Certainly the proposals add no more to the peace and prosperity of the world than that fabled receptacle.

Reform movements are spasmodic rather than continuous. Attempts to bring about a reform may be as diversified as the individuals or groups who attempt them. Sometimes different groups who have the same ultimate objective become as bitter towards each other as they are toward their mutual long-time objective. This is well illustrated in the controversies which arise between opposing elements interested in labor reform, in political reform, or in some project such as prohibition or public health. A split in a church group or a voters' league may have no basis other than friction of personalities, the mutual objective being overshadowed by the conflict of participating workers, officials, and fund raising groups.

A reform movement may continue, however, even when the specific effort has been burned out by the local bickering and controversy of a particular effort. To the extent that the effort was based upon sound social principles it will tend to rise to the surface and continue in the general stream of development. Each effort leaves a residue which gradually builds the movement to a new plane—just as the Plains of Lebanon and the rolling wheat lands of the Palouse Hills of South-eastern Washington have been built up by the soil carried by the divergent winds. In the case of many consciously planned efforts, this residue builds up toward a better social condition. In other cases the idea or objective may become lost in a useless accumulation of selfish aims, just as once fertile land may become waste lands and desert, or an area in a community may become blighted and eventually a slum by an accumulation of unsocial residue as persons with other objectives give up the struggle and moved on. A social reform movement, consequently, is a series of concrete attempts to define and redefine the rights of man. The result may be called a social reform, but the series of efforts con-stitutes the social reform movement.

Whenever a new movement is started, one usually finds a number of similar names sponsoring the activity. Some of these consist of "always available cash" and are persuaded to be included among the sponsors of a "Liberal Movement." There are a few who contribute nothing but are eagerly sought because of the organization with which they are associated—a professor in a university, a pastor of a church, a city official. A third group are the enthusiasts who are "all out" for any reform. They are the professional reformers. They have no sense of humor. If a man has only one idea, that idea is as serious as can be; when he has another idea, he may laugh, and is less serious. Usually he knows little about both sides of the question and often no more than a minor phase of one side. In fact, the less he knows the more enthuiasti-cally he will participate in the reform. The fourth group consists of a small number who are selfishly trying to manipulate their fellow men for the benefit of a special group.

How then may we avoid being a contributor to a "fake reform" or be sure of giving worth-while projects the support they deserve?

In a democracy, one finds a continuous stream of efforts to bring about change. Many of these resemble the little dust spirals which occur on a hot day on the plains. When a number of these little whirlwinds unite, or when a combination of circumstances occurs, an effort may present itself which reaches the proportions of a tornado, and we have riots, violent strikes, civil wars, or revolutions. While many of the particular efforts are wasteful and give rise to more negative results than improvements, this continuous restlessness is, nonetheless, of value and is a definite part of a working democratic system. It is necessary for some momentum to arise which will bring about the means for making social adjustments and prevent the social order from settling into stratified lethargy. Many proposals to bring about a change have not been carefully thought out. Some of them are unnecessary. Better results could be obtained by less effort and upheaval. Some of them are instigated for a selfish purpose which would benefit only a few people or some special group. Many of them fail because there is not a general understanding of the purpose nor of the methods used. One might trace the growth and development of a Progressive Party movement, of the Labor movement, of the Child Welfare movement, or educational changes in our history. There are sometimes violent as well as spasmodic efforts which rise to a considerable height, and then recede, giving the impression of having failed. Individuals throw the entire weight of their lives into an effort and become discouraged that the Nirvana they hoped for was not achieved.

It is essential that citizens of a democracy distinguish between desirable, non-desirable, fantastic, or impractical efforts, and where a desirable objective is under consideration, that the efforts become constructive rather than self destructive. A standard of measures is needed which may be applied to any new program presented and which may serve as a guide in our evaluation of social reforms and reformers. Such a proposed standard may be used to evaluate a reform movement and furnish a basis for an attitude other than the list of names of persons who are listed as sponsors.

1. *Is a change essential to secure improvement?* Frequently a social, economic, or political situation appears to need a change when all that is needed is a minor correction in some aspect of administration. A particularly spectacular event occurs and at once the cry arises, "all is wrong, we must do away with what we have and start a movement for a new procedure." Reform efforts are most frequently aimed at some short range objective. Long range reform movements usually show an increase in techniques and organizational machinery. This cumulative effort was noted in the Prohibition movement and is also found in the Labor movement. Many movements die because of the short range objective, where a minor adjustment may correct everything.

2. *Is the purpose for the general good, and not for class benefits only?* This is the greatest weakness found in attempts to establish social reforms, and it usually provides us with the most intensive proponents. There is always a half truth to be found in their arguments, and it is necessary to calmly study the entire situation to see all possible results of the proposed innovation. Unfavorable conditions or distress may not be the incentive for a reform effort. A program for the benefit of a

special class may arise during periods of prosperity or when a group has a special advantage which they wish to perpetuate.

3. *Is there a general consciousness of the need for the proposal and a recognized measure of its values?* Every major reform effort has had set-backs because different groups interested in the same general objec- tive varied in regard to their common point of view. Without such general recognition and a measure or standard of the proposed values, the resulting confusion and ineffective results may cause a permanent obstruction to the present as well as later worthwhile effects. Sometimes the effort is short-lived because it is dependent upon popular interest which can usually be maintained at a high pitch only when the objective is immediate. If the objective is too distant, interest will be lost.

4. *Is there equalization of knowledge on the subject?* Unless there has been a general effort to acquaint everyone concerned with the true purpose and meaning of the proposal, knowledge will be limited to the prejudicial propaganda of the proponents, without the means for sound judgment and evaluation.

5. *Recognition of personal responsibility.* Probably the greatest social problem which confronts America today is the lack of a sense of personal responsibility. No social reform, whatever its value, will succeed without a well established sense of individual responsibility. If this does not exist, among the persons concerned, the effort will be largely wasted.

6. *Time, place, circumstances and beliefs must be taken into con- sideration.* Worth-while plans and reforms are frequently swept into discard because there was not due consideration given to other events, trends of social thought and beliefs within the area. The attempt to rush reform through is a temptation which often results in new situations more harmful than the one the reform seeks to remedy.

7. *Counting the cost, means for carrying forth the program, and the necessary patience to permit development are important considera- tions.* If every proposal for a change were tested by the above standard, rather than by the claim of its sponsors that it was "Liberal" or a "great forward looking plan," much more would be accomplished and less waste and obstruction to real progress would occur. Within our political, economic, and social organized life, many movements have been success- ful in having reforms adopted which actually have been harmful in the ultimate results obtained.

The further application of principles of sociology in specific areas and an interpretation of the social processes concerned has given rise to extensive studies, all of which add to our general understanding of sociological theory and principles determine social action. Sometimes these areas of study appear to be an entirely new dicipline. Frequently the increase of understanding demands a re-evaluation of a concept which was fairly well established. A good example is the change in the concept of social work.

Speaking at the 1948 Conference of Social Work, Arthur J. Altmeyer elaborated this point, which is well worth bearing in mind throughout the following pages. ". . . . Our evolving concept of social work is dependent upon our evolving ideas of the responsibility of community and State in promoting the well-being of its members. As our sense of social responsibility develops, our concept of social work inevitably grows. At one time, not so long ago, our concept of social work included, almost exclusively, relief and service to the underprivileged and disadvantaged. Our concept was based rather largely upon the spirit of *noblesse oblige*. Our attention was focussed upon the needs of the specific individual rather than upon the social institutions, the presence or absence of which affected the needs of individuals. Social work was thought of largely in terms of adjusting the individual to his environment rather than in terms of bringing environmental forces into play to assist the individual . . ."

The newer concept of social work is that it consists not only of counselling and assisting the individual and family in making the necessary adjustments to environment, but more importantly, it consists of combining all community resources for the general well-being. We do not think in terms of a few under-privileged and disadvantaged persons, but we think in terms of *all* individuals and families. The trends in social work which have been undertaken may be summarized:

"1. Philanthropy and social work were not differentiated until the twentieth century. Philanthropy now includes the wide range of activities voluntarily supported by a private individual or organization without expectation of pecuniary return and for purposes of public interest. Social work, as one division of philanthropy, is the channel for direct efforts to mitigate the consequences of social living which are unfortunate in their effect upon certain groups and certain individuals. Its varied activities center upon social adjustment.

"2. Voluntarily supported social work is primarily for the benefit of those individuals who are economically unable to pay for the services required for their social well being. It is, in this chapter, differentiated from welfare activities supported out of tax funds.

"3. During the past 25 years there has been a marked increase in private social welfare activities. This increase is manifested in the number of social work organizations, in the size of their personnel, in the volume of their expenditures, in the number of their clients.

"4. The development of individualized treatment of maladjustment —social case work—has been of primary importance in shaping the methods and objectives of private social agencies. The adaptation of

social work methods to other fields, and in a variety of situations involving social maladjustment, has been an important correlative
development.

"5. Emphasis upon prevention of poverty and degeneracy has
characterized social work during the last quarter century. Changing
concepts as to the causes of destitution have resulted in the concentration of attention at different times upon heredity, general physical
health, environment, mental health, and economic conditions. The
general depression of 1930-1932 has brought out clearly the economic
origin of much maladjustment.

"6. Social legislation, surveys and investigations, and the development of activities of preventive and constructive nature have been
promoted by social work for at least twenty years.

"7. Since 1915 there has been a definite trend toward a higher
standard of relief for dependent families and individuals. This is
evidenced in the items allowed in budgets and in the increased per capita
relief expenditures. Before the depression, the maintenance of satisfactory standards for all families assisted was a cardinal principle of
private welfare agencies and the intake of new cases was determined by
resources available. With the greatly increased demands upon the agencies in 1929-1932, the principle has been somewhat violated.

"8. From 1915 to 1930 there was marked emphasis upon the
psychiatric approach to all social maladjustment. The expansion of
facilities, such as child guidance clinics and mental hygiene clinics, for
special attention to the mental condition of clients was considerable.
The influence was wide-spread and has led to permanent modifications
in social treatment. There is less belief than formerly, however, in the
possibility of solving the major part of the problem of dependency
through understanding of mental processes.

"9. The coordination and systematizing of social work activities
since 1915 constitutes a major trend. It is evidenced in the growth of
associations and national agencies for standardizing work and centraliz-
ing authority, of chests for the financing of all community social work,
of councils for planning a unified community program, in the number
and size of conferences, and of social service exchanges.

"10. The effort of social workers to obtain professional status has
been constant during the past twenty years. Several definite accomplish-
ments in this direction have marked the last five or six years.

"11. The growth of professional schools, of research by social work
organizations, and publications has been especially notable within the
period since 1920.

"12. The development of social work has proceeded very unevenly
in the United States as a whole. There is a lag, due to sluggishness in

adopting new ideas and to lack of economic resources, and a difference in point of view between the country and the city, the west and the east, the south and the north. The lag and the difference in outlook may be less great in 1932 than in 1920, but it is still impossible to generalize as to standards and methods in social work for the country as a whole.

"13. The trend which is most important in marking the probable future developments in social welfare is the absorption of activities as a part of public administration in increasing number and at accelerated rate. The government's obligation to provide for certain types of dependency and delinquency has long been recognized; the addition of new categories of need requiring the government support or supervision is an outstanding development of the last fifteen years. The private agency has experimented with methods of meeting various situations, demonstrated the effectiveness of certain methods, and stimulated social legislation to make possible the transfer of social services to public funds.

"14. During the past five years the administration of relief giving has become decidedly more a function of public than of private agencies.

"15. The privately supported social agency should continue to have an important place in American life, since it can supplement public welfare work successfully. In experimenting, in promoting and main- taining standards, in using imagination and a flexible approach to social problems, the private organization has great advantage.

"16. The growth of organizations for the financing of philanthropy has been marked since 1900. The community chest and the community trust are chiefly concerned with social work; the foundation covers the whole area of philanthropy and give some support to social welfare activities.

"17. Though there is no dependable body of complete information upon the extent and the financing of social work, within the last ten years a beginning has been made toward such records. The registration of social statistics, now carried on by the Children's Bureau, the data of the Research Bureau of the New York Welfare Council, the work of the Department of Statistics of the Russell Sage Foundation, the studies of the Association of Community Chests and Councils, and the income and estate tax returns of the United States Bureau of Internal Revenue are important sources of information both upon the extent and the financing of general social welfare activities. During the past 25 years, increasing amounts have been contributed, but the data are not sufficiently complete to permit population and national income."[1]

---

[1] *Recent Social Trends in the United States,* Volume II; McGraw-Hill Book Company, Inc.; 1933; Chapter XXIII, pp. 1220, 1221, 1222, 1223.

X

Formation of Concepts

The Formation of Accepted Vocabulary

A STATEMENT to be understood by everyone who hears it or sees it in print must present to all a generalized meaning which suggests only one type, and which is never confused by a particular object or unique situation within the type. Especially, in any scientific discussion it is necessary to have clear cut concepts if there is to be mutual clear cut understanding.

A *pencil* is never a pen, a stylus, or a nail, yet it does not specify any particular kind of pencil, any particular colored graphite, nor any specific size or structure. Because of the numerous concepts which occur as any field is being studied, the new combinations, and in fact the new ideas appearing grow into new concepts. Many of these are peculiar to each field of inquiry, and are not duplicated in any other area, but because of the lack of accepted terms, use is made of concepts already formulated. Attempts are made to carry over these concepts from other fields, or terminology is constructed which is not distinctive enough to give it a permanent and a singular meaning. The result is confusion.

The conceptual vocabulary in which the early writers in sociology attempted to express themselves was for the most part carried from some other subject to sociology. As a result much was written which was misconstrued as being an aspect of a related field; it was as recent as October, 1949 that a well known professor of economics expressed his difficulty of knowing what sociologists were attempting to do. He stated, "At best, it seems to me that sociology is economics poorly taught." The ideas of Comte, Spencer, and Ward in a very marked degree were expressed in the terminology, and by the use of concepts of their non-sociological training and background.

Sociological Concepts

When any new field is in the process of developing there is a tendency for one of two situations to arise. Undue authority will be attributed to a writer, and any concept he uses or approach that he follows in building his structure will be accepted as patterned by him, and others will follow that pattern without exploring into possible by-paths, thus failing to discover newer and better procedures or more effective concepts and terminology. The other situation which arises is that each person writing will attempt to use a classification, terminology, and concepts which may have been logically determined, but which are not generally accepted. This may be done with the hope of creating a new approach for which the author will be accredited, sometimes, because of unfamiliarity or knowledge of comparable terms already used by others. Irrespective of the motive, the result tends to give rise to confusion. It is because of this that an attempt is being made to follow threads of thought which are related to each other and indicate growth in conceptual understanding that make up the warp and woof of the pattern of sociological thinking since the latter part of the nineteenth century.

Social phenomena are so varied, and the point of view from a particular situation toward a principle so unique that the angles of vision may be as numerous as the persons making the observation. This is merely restating the old tale of the "blind men and the elephant." Each approach permits a rich fund of illustrations and examples, which are so interesting in themselves that the principle sometimes is lost in the verdure of delightful new facts and unexpected results. Only by most extensive reading on each aspect of a subject in sociology is one able to trace the threads of thought which actually permeate the discussions.

In order to give permanence to the findings in any field of sociology, it is necessary to have certain concepts whose meaning are used in the same sense whenever applied to any situation of combinations of facts—a clear cut and accepted meaning which is not complicated by a variety of interpretations. Where that is not possible, a working definition of the way a term is used needs to be explained. The first reaction to this point of view is that the results will be "stuffy."

If well written, nothing is dull reading. Even humor depends upon a clear cut meaning which brings out the humor. The general effort to establish an accepted body of concepts in explaining group relations, have brought forth much useful data and material, but often left the concepts themselves in an increasingly confused state. A recent excellently written book covered the general topic of group organizations. It was informative and attempted to be objectively analytical. Certain generally accepted concepts dealing with group activity in modern society were discussed. Extensive excerpts and quotations were given in explanation. The quotations, however, were all pointed toward a given subjective interpretation, with no attempt to evaluate or check on their accuracy. The result was a delightfully written book, which was an excellent example of the kind of one-sided propaganda the book set out to describe.

The social value of such works must not be minimized. Upton Sinclair's novel, *The Jungle,* developed a germ of enthusiasm which did much to help establish pure food and drug laws in the first decade of the nineteenth century. However, it is often the desire to do something which will have observable results, or the attempt to get public approval of a reform movement as quickly as possible, which has done much to retard exact sociological thinking. In spite of the many factors which retarded sociological progress, much has been accomplished.

A particularly obvious handicap in the discussion of group thinking is a lack of clearly understood terminology. This has been a recognized situation since Bodin in the sixteenth century called attention to the need for exact data as a basis for controlling social disorder, and since William Petty (1682) called attention to the need for more correct nomenclature. The very basic terms, "social" and "society" have caused endless confusion. However, it is usually left to the general context to give the desired meaning. This is a rather general attitude and was so expressed by Charles A. Ellwood, who felt that common usage has given "social" the meaning "pertaining to society—or to the social group." Eubank suggests that "social" should be understood to mean "those orders of phenomena in which individual consciousness becomes by reason of reciprocity with other minds, inter-individual consciousness." A. G. Keller gave us the term "societal" while A. W. Small presented the basis for use of the term "societary." It must be definitely understood that the term used has reference to associated human beings and refers to collective life and thinking, rather than individual thought or action. Even the individual who is part of society and acquires from them and contributes to them is a societary self rather than strictly an individual.

After a term is accepted, it is difficult for us to appreciate the impact made by new interpretations and by sociological concepts when they were first proposed or introduced. Many of the principles, terms, and concepts which are now an accepted part of everyday conversation and thinking were startling when first presented. Just as in the fourteenth century when Chinese gun powder was being introduced as a military weapon, the very individuals who beheaded and disemboweled their victims by the thousands spoke of the use of gun powder as highly immoral and ethically shocking. So, we find people disturbed by any new idea. In May, 1909, the *Cosmopolitan Magazine* contained an article by Harold Bolce on the subject "Blasting the Rock of Ages." This article was preceded by an editorial comment on the shocking disclosures of the kind of teaching that was going on in our American universities. Among the examples which astounded Bolce was the statement of Charles Horton Cooley that, "Every man's mind is the theater of a conflict of standards." Frank W. Blackmar shocked the writer and editor by the statement that "standards of right perpetually changed in social life, these varying standards being found not only in different races, but in the same race from age to age." Lester F. Ward, J. Z. Dealey, William Graham Sumner, Simon Patton, Shaler Mathews, Franklin H. Giddings, E. A. Ross, along with Blackmar and Cooley are held up as "blasting the rock of ages."

After the first vigorous efforts by Ward, Giddings, Sumner, Small, Ross, Cooley, Thomas, and others to formulate basic concepts in sociology, there were many individual efforts covering a wide scope of sociology and related fields. Much of the controversy occurring was the result of a lack of uniform understanding and agreement. From time to time efforts were made to bring together the basic concepts as we will see at the end of this chapter. In the intervening pages are listed individual sociologists who represent more or less specialized areas and who have given me statements which seem to them to focalize the efforts with which they were associated. In a few cases, in addition to their personal statements, we have taken a quotation from something they have written which seemed to express the point of view they had in mind.

One of the most effective attempts to make clear the concepts in use by sociologists was made by Earle Edward Eubank (1887-1946). In 1913 he returned to the United States from teaching in the Philippines and began graduate work at the University of Chicago. Most of the group of young graduate students were interested in some specific project which they were anxious to discuss with their colleagues. Eubank soon became popular. He was always willing to take a long walk and discuss anyone's project. He was interested in knowing their point of view. He was particularly ready to discuss the different interpretation of a concept. Often after one of Albion W. Small's lectures, Clarence Blachley, Neil McIntyre, R. D. McKenzie, M. C. Elmer, G. S. Dow, and E. E. Eubank would stay on for an hour or more to discuss the concepts presented. Eubank usually seemed able to pull the different views together in an understanding summary. It seemed a natural result a few years later to have Eubank summarize sociological concepts in a most effective manner.

Like many other men, some of Eubank's most valuable contributions were his efforts toward the understanding of life which he passed on to his family, his students, and his associates. A teacher for five years in the Philippines, George Williams College in Chicago, 1915-1921; a student of disorganized families and desertion in Chicago; and his years of active work at the University of Cincinnati, are all apart from the phase of his work considered here. Recognizing the need for some standardization of concepts, Eubank summarized his interpretation as follows:

"I *Societary Composition:* the tangible 'substance' of which society is composed, viz. people, singly and collectively.
  1. *The Single Human Being:* the individual, especially considered as a person, or situation-self.
  2. *The Human Plural:* the combination of individuals; especially the group, which is an entity of interacting persons.
"II *Societary Causation:* the elements responsible for the fact of change, and for the forms which changes take.
  3. *Societary Energy:* motivations, conations, psychic impulses to action.
  4. *Societary Control:* whatever way any individual or group influences or constrains the behavior of another individual or group.
"III *Societary Change:* the alterations and modifications that occur within, or in relation to, societary composition.
  5. *Societary Action:* the movements and processes that are participated in by the group and its members.
  6. *Societary Relationship:* the connection between the members of a group, especially as manifested in their mutual and reciprocal states of being.
"IV *Societary Products:* whatever comes into being as a result of human association, especially:
  7. *Culture:* the customary ways of action and inner feelings of the group, plus all its objective creations, both artifacts and mentifacts.

"Sociology is concerned with *human beings associated in activity.* By re-stating our major points of attention in terms of action a basis of synthesis of the entire body of material becomes at once apparent.

  I. The Actors (Composition)
  II. The Causes of Their Actions (Causation)
  III. The Action Itself and Its Accompanying Relationships, existing as Association (Change)
  IV. The Outcome, or Results of Their Actions (Products)[1]

"Reduced to a paragraph, the synthesis which we have been endeavoring to develop is the following:

"Human society is composed of a vast totality of single human beings, each a psycho-physical organism biologically self-sufficient, but endowed with capacity for many desires whose satisfactions are impossible without group-life. Association with his fellows once established, life for each person within the group is a continuous sequence of activi-

---

[1] Eubanks, E. E., *The Concepts of Sociology,* D. C. Heath & Co., 1932, p. 384-386. Permission to quote from the above publication by the courtesy of D. D. Heath and co.

ties, in company with others for the fulfillment of these desires. During this time relationships are established among them, the group itself becoming a major factor in shaping his volitions, controlling his actions, and providing the culture in which his life is set and by which it is conditioned."

Another important contributor to the social thought of the period was Luther Lee Bernard (1881-1951). In his social contacts he was very retiring and one might even say bashful. He was very sensitive to the reactions of others and was always kind and sympathetic. However, his intellectual honesty which in some respects was as severe as a Puritan's standards of "right living" at times gave rise to misunderstanding. The head of a large university who was considering Bernard for a position asked me if Bernard was difficult to get along with. When I told him the opposite was true, he seemed surprised saying various persons had said that Bernard was unfriendly. During the seven years I worked on the same faculty with him, there was never once when he was the cause of controversies between members. He did, on several occasions, call attention to some weakness in something that I had written. This he did in such a blunt, undecorated manner that if one had not known the purpose for his criticism it might have caused offense. When Bernard got an idea he worked at it with a degree of minute attention to details and a disregard for the amount of effort required beyond the range of stick-to-itiveness which most people possess.

At the time when many sociologists were unsure of their ground and were attempting to compromise with meta-physical or pseudo-psychological pronouncements, we find Bernard a young man in 1911 presenting a doctoral dissertation which plunged into the controversy of the "transition to an objective standard of social control." This led to his contention that social control was the objective of any scientific work. For several years Bernard led the discussion with some psychologists regarding instincts. This culminated in 1924 in a book, *Instincts*. This actually set a new approach to the subject and today many have forgotten or never knew who made that contribution to social psychological thinking.

Read Bain[2] summarizes Bernard's contributions to social thought:
1. By viewpoint, method, and purpose, sociology is essentially a natural science.
2. All instinctivist explanations of social behavior are unsound.
3. Culture is the product of interactions of fourfold environment.
4. Invention and technology are of major importance in cultural change.

[2] Bain, Read, "L. L. Bernard, Social Theorist," *American Sociological Review*, June, 1951.

5. All social interaction is mediated by the symbolic process.
6. Social control is the basic problem and logical end of sociology and all the social sciences.
7. Supernatural religions, superstitions, magicmindedness, and their meta-physical surrogates will gradually disappear as sanctions for social behavior and will be replaced by a religion of science and humanity.
8. He had an intense personal hatred of war, poverty, disease, waste, intellectual dishonesty, and undemocratic behavior.

Adding to the development of sociological concepts the results of thorough Scottish training and experience in social science, Robert MacIver (1882-   ) helped establish an approach to the community as an aspect of our social life while still a professor of political science at McGill University. After coming to Columbia University, his clear-cut and effective writing soon caused him to be recognized as one of the ablest social theorists of the second quarter of the twentieth century. His outstanding contributions to social thought of the period may be stated as follows:

1. The concept of community, as a democratic totality of social life, especially in its relation to and contrast with the *state,* with which it has often been fused and confused.
2. The analysis of social structure, based on the distinction between associations, institutions, and formal patterns of social behavior.
3. The distinction of the areas of technology, basic and secondary ("civilization") and of culture, as entering differently and behaving differently in the processes of social change.
4. The analysis of social causation, seeking to find a procedure that gets beyond unrelated "factors" and thus to give a more coherent account of the processes of social change.
5. More recently the application of research methods to the discovery of effective modes of social strategy—in other words, an experimental approach to the data of research in order to derive from them some leads for social policy: the field in question being that of intergroup discrimination in the United States.

Like many other writers in the field of sociology, Thomas D. Eliot (1889-   ) is best known for certain phases of his work and not as well known for other phases which he considered of even more importance. For example, everyone is familiar with Eliot's study on the standards and planes of living, and with his study on conspicuous waste. However, Eliot was in the vanguard of many ideas which were later emphasized by others in addition to a consistent scheme of thought in the social economics of standards and planes of living, and the relation of these to family integrity and normal life. Some of his efforts and contributions related to particular aspects of social thinking such as, the situational approach on interpretation of social causation and prediction beginning with his contributions to The Survey in June, 1922 to his article in the *American Sociological Review,* August 1937 on "Human Controls as Situation Processes." Eliot protested against "Observable trends toward dehumanized, sterile, fragmented 'research' and toward disparagment or ignoring of humanistic, useful, or evaluative aspects of our field." He further stated, "More dangerous is the noticeable process of selection for new courses from texts and teaching personnel in which ignorance of the history of ideas myopic time-span and culture span, and absence of philosophic background or of purposes other than professional prestige or 'advancement' becomes apparent."

Likewise Read Bain, with keen insight into social realities, did much to deflate effervescent bubbles of enthusiasm which tended to divert sound thinking from a pertinent objective.[3] For example he shows how confusion, fear and hysteria are perpetrated by emphasis on acceptance of one approach to a situation instead of another, or the assumption of an unavoidable tragedy following the failure to accept one of two values. Similarly, Walter B. Bodenhafer[4] presented a criterion by which to distinguish between amateurish and scientific procedure in sociology. Not only on the basis of logic, but as a development through experience and practice. The recognition of group structure, group processes and group behavior are bases for integrating and controlling group situations.

Basing his conclusions upon specific research projects, James H. S. Bossard in his conclusions helped build up conceptual thinking rather than merely suggesting treatment for a particularized case.

Important phases of his contributions include:

1. *The specificity of social problems* indicative of the fact that all problems are specific as to time, to place and particular combination of circumstances.
2. *The concept of the territorial lag.*
3. *The situational approach in sociology* as developed in "Family Situations."
4. The idea of the family, as well as all other social institutions, as having three dimensions:
   a. Form or structure
   b. Process or interaction
   c. Content or culture

[3] Read Bain, "What is this Crisis," *Philosophy and Science,* Vol. 20, No. 1, January, 1953.
[4] *American Journal of Sociology,* Vol. 26, pp. 273, 425, 588, and 716.

Contributions to the development of concepts by Stuart Queen (1890-   ) have been largely centered around social problems and the urban community. He has been an alert and interesting teacher, and a capable organizer. Stuart Queen, a major in Greek at Pomona College and at the University of Nebraska,—"until, by a happy accident, I took a course in sociology with George Eliot Howard, whose ponderous three volumes on Matrimonial Institutions give no slightest bent of the fascinating personality and challenging teacher that he was in the classroom. This man's personal influence is directly responsible for my change to sociology and for the decision to do graduate work in this field at the University of Chicago." This is an interesting item showing the continuing influence of Professor George E. Howard on contemporary social thought.

In recent years Queen has been giving a great deal of attention to the development of a program of general education which is distinguished on the one hand from the old-fashioned liberal arts college and on the other from the pre-professional curricula which dominate the contemporary college of liberal arts. In line with the above Queen has been a leader in working out a program for the integration of sociology and anthropology.

His earlier work, which went under the label of Social Pathology was developed into something better represented by the term, Social Participation. Queen's chief concern has been the relationships between sociology and social work. He insists upon their differentiation as two distinct fields of interest and activity, and points out that they have, actually, and potentially, numerous points of contact and possible collaboration and looks upon sociology as one of the foundation stones for the profession of social work.

Queen gives us the following pertinent observation: "I think, through the American Sociological Society and our regional societies, as well as in other ways, we are laying, quite properly, great emphasis on research and the development of new knowledge in our field. I am sometimes fearful that we may forget our obligations to pass this knowledge on in a variety of ways, but particularly through effective teaching. It seems to me sometimes that our young sociologists are almost apologetic about devoting time and effort to the teaching job.

"In this teaching, it seems to me we must develop both general principles and specific applications. We must challenge students to relate their academic course work to the real world about them, but I would not have us confuse our function with that of the clergyman or the politician. I do not believe that it is the privilege or the responsibility of the sociology teacher to issue statements to the effect that 'so and so must be done' or 'such and such ought to be abolished'.

"Rather we should help students to assemble reliable information about them; analyze situations to see what they are, how they come to be, what are their implications; are there any alternative possibilities; if so, what are they, and at what cost might they be realized."

Typical of Floyd N. House (1893-   ) is the modest claim to any contribution to social thought. He has, however, put into a succinct statement what some social theorists have required many volumes to express. There is a need of a clear-cut statement of the categories, and of whatever it is we are measuring or counting before devoting too much time and expense to lengthy statistical inquiries. This most apt point of view was almost lost in the mass of private, organizational and official flood of publications, reports, studies, propaganda and "filler material" turned out during the later third of this period. House is considered a social theorist because of his work on the range of social theory and the development of sociology. Much research has been inadequate because of a lack of understanding social theory such as House has contributed.

"I do not believe I have contributed in any significant and original way to the present corpus of American sociology, either conceptually or in any other methodological way.

"I feel that I may have managed to convey to a few of the brighter of my students, both graduate and undergraduate, through lectures and discussions, a few items of concept and point of view which were not entirely identical with what can readily be gotten from the existing literature—notably as regards the importance of study, descriptions, and conceptualization of the actual stuff of experience with which, as I see it, sociology is concerned. As I briefly indicated in my paper, "Measurement in Sociology" (*American Journal Sociology*, XL, July, 1934, pp. 1-8, see esp. p. 3), I am not opposed to statistical work in sociology, or to the effort to be as quantitative as we can in the state- ment of our findings and generalizations; however, I believe profoundly that the effort which seems to be *implicit* in much of the recent litera- ture, even though explicitly denied—to reduce our statements as nearly as may be to purely quantitative form, is misguided and even absurd. After all, to have reference to the actual world of experience, quantities have to be quantities *of something;* and what I have emphasized in my teaching, where-ever suitable, of getting as clear and adequate ideas as possible of our categories—of whatever it is that we are counting or measuring, before we devote too much time and expense to elaborate and lengthy statistical inquiries."

* * *

While more generally known through his writings on social prob- lems, Harold A. Phelps' (1898-   ) major contributions might be considered under laws and principles. He presents certain concepts with statements of methods, analysis and results which show the extent to which various aspects of sociology have been developed by the integration of sociological methods and processes.

"Concept: Criminal behavior.

Method: Analysis, via statistical trends, of the legal records of crime.

Results: Most criminal records on file fail to indicate the nature or trends in crime because they do not connect:

    (a) actual criminal conduct with
    (b) apprehended offenders with
    (c) court dispositions

Concept: Social Work Administration and its problems.

Method: Case Analysis

Results: Case records are selective. They do not in consequence reveal either the actual problems of social inadequacy or clarify success or failure in social work administration. Constructive treatment in social work has had no great success because its policies are a combination of current ethical and legal norms without adequate factual bases. Ex: Red Cross rehabilitation; Children's agencies and security in the placement of children.

Concept: Sociological Laws

Method: Consensus or agreement

Results: Most writers since the publication of Giddings' *Principles of Sociology* confuse the content and nature of principles with laws on the one hand and approaches on the other. There is little or no support in sociology for the interpretation of laws as established relationships or of principles as the explanation of these laws.

Concept: Subjective Sociology

Method: Collection, classification and comparison of opinions

Objective: To obtain a wider interpretation of social insights through the experiences of scientists and artists in other fields than the social sciences.

Ex: The sociology of law, medicine, art, literature."

*   *   *

Among contemporary sociologists Talcott Parsons, (1902-   ) presents a line of thinking influenced by German social theorists, particularly by Max Weber. In some respects his thinking is a continuation of the work of Edward Cary Hayes, particularly with reference to the Social Realities. This may be expressed by the point of view that the processes of collective behavior are measurable. Intangible entities may be as real as physical elements. However, the factors which determine or limit social behavior must be considered in the study of any situation and the entire configuration recognized. The limit of variation in culture is set by different social units related to a particularized area of interest, such as beliefs, family relationships, financial status or dependency, age, sex, and their resulting complexes. This approach is illustrated by Parsons in a discussion on "The Kinship Systems of the Contemporary United States," in which he directs our attention to the effect which the functioning of our lives in innumerable aspects is modified by our form of family organization, and the resultant status of its members.

Talcott Parsons[5] shows the place of the concept of culture among the components of systematic sociological theory. Parsons indicates that Max Weber's concept of social relationship assumes at least a minimum of mutual orientation of each participant with the others. A social relationship can be of a temporary character or of varying degrees of permanence. Likewise, the meaning of a social relationship may change but any meaningful content which remains relatively constant is capable of formation in terms which may be accepted to a relative extent by the persons concerned.

In discussing the theory of social stratification,[6] Parsons emphasizes the symbolic role of income in social stratification rather than its intrinsic role. This treatment of stratification is based on differential valuation which tends to arrange social classes in hierarchial form and when translated into moral attitudes, may be expressed in terms of respect, disapproval, or indignation.

As stated previously, the first stage in the development of sociology has been that of outlining the field to be included, and then analyzing the scope and functions of the various areas. Not until there is a relative clear-cut understanding of what is involved can much specific research be done. Alfred McClung Lee illustrates a next step in effective sociological analysis.[7] He states: "A society's culture defines the values typically held by its members. It furnishes the ethical norms which individuals more or less accurately internalize and make part of their thought processes. Culture in turn cannot adequately be regarded as it is by many social scientists to be solely an over-all phenomenon available to all members of a society. But even those who recognize the fact of subcultural differentiation sometimes try to preserve the over-all conception of culture by contending that culture consists in part of free-floating elements, is it were, called by Linton "cultural alternatives,"

[5] *American Sociological Review,* April, 1948, pp. 56-64.
[6] *American Journal of Sociology,* May, 1940, pp. 841-862.
[7] Alfred McClung Lee, "A Sociological Discussion of Consistency and Inconsistency in Intergroup Relations," *Journal of Social Issues,* Vol. V, No. 3, pp. 12-18.

from among which members of a society as a whole can make their own selections.[8] A more tenable theory is to recognize that the alleged "alternatives" in a culture are functions of groups (including classes and castes). The various groups within a society, due to different traditions and apparent interests and problems, develop subcultural patterns which may differ from those of other groups and which may contradict over-all societal patterns. Individuals take such patterns, not through rational choice, but through membership in familial, play, educational, religious, gang, vocational, club, and other groups. And a person's life history and other statuses furnish more likely explanations for a given group membership than a discussion of freedom of choice.

In outlining this theory, it is useful to relate culture and cultural adaptations to the (1) *societal*, (2) *group*, (3) *personal*, and (4) *self* levels of social and personal organization. The central and integrating culture traits on these levels may be called respectively (1) morals, (2) mores, (3) apparent sentiments, and (4) sentiments. These are the constituents in the jerry-built aggregations of value determinants which a person exhibits in those of his behaviors which are covered by societal and group sanctions.

Morals are seen by members of a society as the broad major premises of discussion and action on a societal level. In terms of them, spokesmen attempt to utter statements which will strike as large a share of the people as possible as being "just what I was thinking" or "just what we really ought to do." The noble aspirations concerning civil liberties in the laws of the United States and, in a more derived form, of the United Nations are related to our morals. The civil liberties cases that get to the United States Supreme Court emphasize by their character the tremendous pressures against the literal maintenance of our moral codes. Increasing mass literacy, alertness, and representation through pressure groups have, of course, brought new pressures to give effect to the promises in the Federal Bill of Rights and subsequent civil rights Amendments.

As a person matures in our society, he learns that a moral pattern is a part of the societal ritual and that it has a special relation to his behavior. Otherwise, he has learned a whole series of rationalizations for avoiding or mitigating their stringency. Thus what a societal surrogate tells you is typically part of this societal ritualism and hence is to be discounted as being moral, religious, academic, or legalistic when compared or contrasted with the more compelling group or personal considerations. Dr. Jahoda illustrates this in mentioning the experiences of the teacher with the Brotherhood Week message, of the organizer of an

[8] Ralph Linton, *The Study of Man*, New York: Appleton-Century, 1936, pp. 273-274, 278-280.

interracial camp, and of the Detroit trade union officials during the 1943 riots.

Behind the cultural facade of an institution, defined by the morals, the folkways-mores patterns define formulas upon which an institution and its associated roles "really work." These patterns are the practical and expedient understandings and techniques, the customary ways of exercising power, of cutting corners on the morals, of handling aggressiveness, of exploiting submissiveness, and of making the best of public relations opportunities and other social action situations.

If mores are largely unrecorded, sentiments are even less open to general knowledge and inspection. Sentiments are among the more enduring, integrating, and consistent aspects of personality. They are more emotionally charged and less consciously organized than corresponding societal morals and group mores. People do not like to reveal their sentiments when they are at all deviant or delicate, and, to a marked extent, they do not actually put them into words or even understand the nature of these basic guides of their thought, feelings, and action. Sentiments are often apparently contradictory and even multivalent, but their owners ordinarily do not so regard them. Their contradictoriness and multivalence derive from their having societal and group as well as personal and self facets.

The personal and self levels of this social-structure-and-personality theory are significant chiefly, in this brief summary, to suggest the character of uncoordination and of the related potential and actual tensions. The growth and change in sociological concepts is exemplified in the writing of Mabel A. Elliott in another area. One of her major contributions to sociology is the nature of social disorganization and personal disorganization. A concept this material develops is the thesis that all social organization entails the acceptance of certain social values, either implicit or explicit, and that when conflicting values threaten the status quo disorganization is more or less inevitable.

In the field of criminology and delinquency, she has contributed some studies in penology showing how conflicting theories in penology make difficult any rational basis for punishment. Her study on "A Correlation Between Juvenile Delinquency and Racial Heterogeneity" was one of the first studies to show the importance of cultural conflict in producing delinquency. In her test in *Criminology* one aspect is the study of the Woman Offender and analyses of the differences in the private culture in which the average woman lives from the public culture in which the average man commits his offenses.

Sociological thinking which took form in the decade from 1940-1950, is well expressed by John F. Cuber, (1911-   ). Founded upon the contributions of the past, it is likewise modified by contemporary research, and a certain amount of prediction. In an attempt to formulate a list of principles underlying sociology to which most sociologists agree, Cuber presented the following set of eighteen which he suggested as basic in establishing a beginning in the study of sociology:[9]

1. When groups of people live in prolonged association, they develop and enforce standardized overt behavior patterns and ideological systems. ("Culture," "the superorganic," "the social heritage.")
2. Cultural phenomena can be studied by the scientific method. What the detached observer may call "myths and superstition" is real to the person who regards it as "true" and as such, it has objective reality.
3. Some cultural practices are physiologically injurious to the people practicing them, but are approved nevertheless.
4. Single biophysiological "needs" have widely divergent culturally approved modes of overt expression in different cultures.
5. The concepts of "right" and "wrong" are intra-cultural definitions and do not have intercultural applicability.
6. Logically inconsistant cultural patterns may and do coexist.
7. Every known people is ethnocentric.
8. The geographic (biophysical, "natural") environment does not determine what cultural practices will prevail; it does preclude certain practices, but always permits numerous alternative adjustments.
9. Culture changes either by the addition or by the loss (rarely) of traits.
10. Culture changes at unequal rates at various times, in various areas, and in its various parts.
11. Culture history is not marked by regular sequences of stages; the concept of stage is an artificial "construct" of the student of cultural history created only for purposes of study.
12. "Progress" is a cultural definition subject to the same content variations in time and space as are other cultural ideologies.
13. Man in all cultures is parasitic on culture; he could not now survive biologically without it.
14. The biological being ("The individual") is not "human" and can become so only by association with other humans.
15. Behavior regarded as "natural" and "human" is an intercultural variable subject to the same time, place, and content variation as other cultural definitions.

[9] Cuber, John F., "Are There Principles of Sociology?", *American Sociological Review,* Vol. VI, No. 3, June, 1941; pp. 371-372.

16. Abilities and capabilities (as distinct from potentialities there-fore) are culturally defined and acquired.
17. "Society" and "individual" are inseparable except as abstrac-tions; they are the discrete and collective aspects of the unity "human life"; neither exists without the other.
18. As each historical time, different degrees of complexity are found among the cultures of peoples belonging to the same race.

The current emphasis in social thought is further indicated by Robert K. Merton. In a recent publication[10] he presents as a possible classification one developed by Columbia University Bureau of Applied Social Research.

Research Problems Classified According to Practical Purpose
1. *Diagnostic*: Determining whether action is required. Magnitude and extent of problem; changes and trends since last appraisal of situation (e.g. changes in level of race tensions); differentials in affected groups, areas, institutions.
2. *Prognostic*: Forecasting trends to plan for future needs. Predict-ing behavior of individuals and groups from stated intentions (post-war plans of demobilized soldiers; people's disposition of liquid assets); predicting needs by trend analysis and other hypothetical means (unemployment, wage, price trends from business-cycle analysis; predicting housing needs by analysis of birth and marriage rates and trends in size of family).
3. *Differential Prognosis*: Determining choice between alternative policies, (e.g. public reaction to rent control or rationing.)
4. *Evaluative*: Appraising effectiveness of action program (assessing effectiveness of information and propaganda campaigns; of Emergency Maternal and Infant Care program in reducing infant and maternal mortality).
5. *General Background Data*: Of general utility or serving diverse purposes (e.g., censuses of population, housing, business, manu-facturing.)
6. *"Educative" Research*: Informing publics upon pertinent data and particularly countering misconceptions.

"Strategic Fact-Finding": This involves the systematic assembling of descriptive data pertinent for popular conceptions and controversial beliefs. Thus, facts pertinet to stereotypes: "labor-leaders-are-foreign" stereotype confronted with facts on place of birth of labor leaders; "United States-remains-the-land-of-increasing-personal-opportunity" con-ception confronted with data on correlations between education and income, occupation, etc."

Robert Merton presents certain gaps between scientific research

[10] *Philosophy of Social Science,* Vol. 16, No. 3, July, 1949.

and policy. "To assess the current and potential role of applied social science, it is necessary to note the scope and scale of the practical problems with which it has dealt. With the excessively large problem only failure can presently be reported and with the excessively limited problem, the results are often trivial. It would be important to identify the *stragetic, intermediate range of problems,* namely, those which have generalized theoretical and practical significance, but which are not too large in scope to be subjected to disciplined research.[11]

* * *

"*The Research is Not Adequately Focused on the Practical Problem. Concrete Forecasts are Contingent upon Uncontrolled Conditions.* Many if not most, applied researches involve forecasts. *These concrete forecasts in applied science differ significantly from abstract predictions in basic science.*

"Basic research typically deals with 'abstract predictions,' i.e. with predictions in which a large number of "other factors" are, conveniently enough, assumed to remain constant. The prediction will of course include a statement of the conditions under which the predicted consequences will probably occur, *Ceteris paribus* is an indispensable concept in basic research.

"In short, applied research requires the greatly complicated study of the interaction of many interrelated factors comprising the *concrete situation.* The research cannot be confined entirely to the interplay of a severely limited number of variables under severely limited conditions.

This requirement of applied research has several consequences:

(a) Every applied research must include some speculative inquiry into the role of diverse factors which can only be roughly assessed, not meticulously studied.

(b) The validity of the concrete forecast depends upon the degree of (non-compensated) error in *any* phase of the total inquiry. The weakest links in the chain of applied research may typically consist of the *estimates* of contingent conditions under which the investigated variables will *in fact* operate.

(c) To this degree, the recommendations for policy do not flow directly and exclusively from the *research.* Recommendations are the product of the research *and* the estimates of contingent conditions, these estimates not being of the same order of probability or precision as the more abstract interrelations examined in the research itself.

(d) Such contingencies make for indeterminacy of the recommen-

---

[11] Further observations on this point are presented by S. A. Stouffer, "The Strategy of the Social Sciences," address before the Harvard Graduate Forum, April 20, 1948 and by R. K. Merton, "Discussion of 'The Position of Sociological Theory,'" *American Sociological Review,* April 1948, pp. 13, 164-168.

FORMATION OF CONCEPTS 173

dations derived from the research and thus create a gap between research and policy.

"*Theory and Applied Social Science*—Basic theory embraces key
concepts (variables and constants), postulates, theorems and laws. Applied science consists simply in ascertaining (a) the variables relevant
to the problem in hand, (b) the values of the variables and (c) in
accordance with previous knowledge, setting forth the uniform relationships between those variables."

Another expression in the development of sociological concepts is
found in the discussion of F. Stuart Chapin and American Sociology
by Don Martindale and Exis D. Monchasi. The following excerpt indicates the trends in this area.[12]

"Experimental Designs in Sociological Research appears as a very
genuine synthesis of Chapin's early methodological explorations. One
no longer hears of "historical," "field," and "statistical methods," re-
peatedly referred to in *Field Work and Social Research,*" "experiment
is simply observation under controlled conditions . . . The fundamental
rule of the experimental method is to vary only one condition at a time
and to maintain all other conditions rigidly constant. There are two
good reasons for this procedure: In the first place, if two conditions are
varied at one time and an effect is produced, it is not possible to tell
which condition is responsible or whether both have acted jointly; in
the second place, when no effect ensues, how can we tell which condition is responsible, or whether one has neutralized the other.

"One of the many ways in which the Experimental Designs in
Sociological Research represents the synthesis of Chapin's methodological
work is found in the fact that prior work on measurement and scaling
is put to the service of making precise the factors to be studied in their
causal interrelation via the experimental design."

Chapin's Substantive Contributions

Granting a hard core of theoretical ideas and a methodology to
serve as the ground rules of investigation and proof, the results could
hardly be other than fertile in concrete research. In his conception of
unit individual and interhuman behavior having unplanned large-scale
consequences, Chapin surmounted the dichotomy of individual versus
society. The probability that interhuman behaviors are patterned and
recurrent establishes the conception of social relationship as an analytical
tool. It is possible with these ideas to take account of human purposes
without personalizing the group.

Thus, while Cooley had treated institutions as little more than a

[12] F. Stuart Chapin and *American Sociology,* Don Martindale and Exis D. Monachesi, University of Minnesota. Presented to Midwest Sociological Society,
April 24, 1953, pp. 6, 7, 8.

state of mind, while Sumner had treated them as a combination of idea and structure with little concrete characterization, and while others had turned institution into tradition (anything established), Chapin advanced the ideas of nucleated and diffused institutions and conducted concrete investigation of their variations. "The institutions of the local community are definite and recognizable. They possess more tangible aspects than the general social institutions, for example, as art, mythology, language, law, ethics, science, etc. The reason is that they possess definite locus and are specific in an area . . . It will be useful, therefore, to differentiate local government, local political organization, local business enterprise, the family, the school, the church and welfare agencies as specific or nucleated institutions.

"The analysis of nucleated institutions into four type parts—(a) common reciprocating attitudes, such as loyalty, cooperativeness, domination and subordination: (b) symbolic cultural objects or traits, such as seals, emblems, flags; (c) utilitarian cultural objects or traits, such as buildings, equipment; and (d) oral or written language, such as charters, ordinances, constitutions—had been made as early as *Cultural Change.*"

"One branch of criticism directed at Chapin's concept of nucleated institutions boils down to the accusation that they are "really" groups. Such criticism is purely terminological, and if accepted, would merely mean that the work was a major step in the empirical investigation of groups."

"Chapin's analysis of institutions led him to a re-evaluation of the interrelations of individual and group. The symbolic elements of institutions are located only in the experience of people. But any given individual functions in more than a single group. The individual thus is at once more and less than an institution. The personality of any given individual may consist, for example, "of the integrated system of his attitudes and behaviors as a Baptist, as a Democrat, as a Mason, as a Banker." Personality is a fusion of institutional segments. The analysis, having begun in surmounting the old-fashioned conception of individual versus society, more precisely locates the lines of possible cleavage between individual and group."

"At the time this was formulated the best available concept of personality was found in Cooley's brilliantly imaginative "looking-glass self" which, while demonstrating the effects of the attitudes of others on the self, left most of the details of influence unspecified. The meaning of Chapin's analysis for personality study is clear. Convergent individual behaviors and attitudes of nucleated institutions constitute core elements of personality. This is a major step in the general direction of a concept of roles which should aid in rounding out the sociological theory of personality."

Recently the head of a department of engineering stated that if, in the first two years of training a student learned a few of the basic techniques, developed a sound attitude toward engineering work and learned basic concepts and vocabulary, it is felt that he had accomplished the maximum for which they may hope. We might summarize the work of this chapter by a somewhat similar statement that an understanding of the major concepts and vocabulary in sociology is of chief importance before any specific research or progress can be made, and we may present as a suggestion the following:[13]

accommodation
adaptation
adjustment
amalgamation
assimilation
association
attitude
behavior pattern
caste
collective behavior
competition
community
communication
conditioned response
conflict
contact
cooperation
crowd
cultural change
cultural lag
culture
culture area
culture complex
culture pattern
culture trait
custom
diffusion
disorganization
ethnocentrism
folkways
geographic or physical
    or natural environment

geographic determinism
group
human nature
imitation
instinct
invention
institution
isolation
leadership
mores
personality
primary group
progress
race
secondary group
society
social class
social control
social distance
social or psychic or
    cultural environment
social evolution
social heritage or
    inheritance
social interaction
social organization
social process
socialization
status
stratification
values

[13] *The Journal of Educational Sociology*, September 1933, "Recommendations of of the Committee," pp. 81-82.

The development of basic concepts is a slow and continuous struggle. Intolerance by the advocates of a new concept for their immediate predecessors is frequently petty, while the evaluation and defense by contemporaries or followers of the old school of thought is often intolerant of anything new. A new idea may be lost through its failure to be accepted. If it is accepted, its origin and author may be forgotten. The pioneer of social thought passes out of the picture either because his message is rejected or because it is so completely accepted that any mention of the struggle required for such acceptance is greeted with a yawn of boredom a decade later.

XI

Re-evaluation and Wider Application

BY 1930 the need for a re-evaluation of sociology became apparent. The major areas were established. Explorations began to take place into sub-branches of the main stream of inquiry and frequently gave promise of leading the investigators, if not to the actual mother-lode, at least to rich fields which added the necessary contributions needed for a more accurate analysis of human relations. Until about 1925 much of the sociologist's concern dealt with major principles of group activity and their interrelationship and with attempts to unravel the tangles resulting from the sudden ad-mixture of various population elements. In the years following the Civil War thousands of Americans from the Eastern part of the United States and many more thousands of persons from wide and diverse European countries poured into different sections of the Middle West and West. Literally millions of people were added to our cities and the problem of adjustment and integration seemed almost insurmountable. The seething mass had hardly become settled when World War I agitated our country again. The germ of world expansion and contacts, which began in 1898, was given new impetus and on the horizon there began to appear signs that the future of America was tied up with all the world. This was not recognized generally. Even the efforts of General "Billy" Mitchell to get our country to recognize the future of rapid aerial transportation were rather harshly slapped down. However, individuals were beginning to call attention to the fact that a new era was ahead of us. The changes occurring were coming with greater speed than in any previous period of history. As a matter of fact, even in the last quarter of the nineteenth century, attention was being called to the destruction of our abundant natural resources with particular emphasis upon re-forestation and depletion of our productive soil. In 1921, under the chairmanship of Herbert Hoover, a report was made on "Waste in Industry" and William Fielding Ogburn brought out *Social Change* calling our attention to the relationship between the performance of men and their basic culture. During the next fifteen years, much thought was given to this field. Among those who attempted to explain the philosophical overall were such well-known works as Oswald Spengler's *The Decline of the West*. Within this same area are Pitirim A. Sorokin's extensive four volumes *Social and Cultural Dynamics*. Works of this nature represented a philosophical approach which in some circles were considered to lack objective data.

In September, 1929 a committee was called together by the President of the United States. It was this committee's obligation to secure the cooperation of eminent scientists for the purpose of making a national survey of social trends in the United States. The survey was to be the work of the committee and its experts and to consist of a complete impartial examination of the facts.[1] The final report reflected the collective judgment of the material and set forth the matters of opinion as well as of strict scientific determination. This was presented to President Herbert Hoover in the autumn of 1932 and was published in 1933 by the McGraw-Hill Book Company.

The first thirty years in the development of sociology in the United States (roughly from 1890-1920) was concerned with establishing and agreement on the concepts. This period also marked the first steps in approval of the general content of basic textbooks. These textbooks dealt chiefly with the logic and standardization of the concepts which determined and outlined the field of sociology.

The second period again seemed to be in a state of confusion. In some respects this confusion was comparable to the period at the end of the nineteenth century when the leaders of social thought were attempting to outline the organization and structure of society and to determine the factors involved. A place had now been reached where it was no longer necessary to justify the conceptual factors, but rather to begin to explain social structures and social functions within these conceptualized areas by an analysis of the existing functional and resultant phenomena.

Social institutions were recognized as social patterns that established the organized behavior of human beings in the performance of basic social functions. This understanding reached into many and diverse fields. We find Ernest W. Burgess considering "The Value of Sociological Community Studies for the Work of Social Agencies"; Carle Zimmerman and John Z. Carson calling attention to "The Migration to Towns and Cities"; Jesse F. Steiner's "Myth or Reality of Community Organization"; specific studies like Jennings Q. Rhyme's "Community Organization in an Indian Settlement"; Frederick A. Bushee's analysis of "Social Organization" and the effective presentation of the scope and function of Social Institutions by Hertzler, which had been preceded by Charles H. Judd's "Psychology of Social Institutions." The trend toward

[1] President's Research Committee on Social Trends: Wesley C. Mitchell, chairman; Charles E. Merriam, vice-chairman; Shelby M. Harrison, secretary-treasurer, Alice Hamilton; Howard W. Odum; William F. Ogburn. Executive Staff: William F. Ogburn, Director of Research; Howard W. Odum, Assistant Director of Research; Edward Eyre Hunt, Executive Secretary.

an analysis of social institutions increased. C. R. Hoffer applied this toward an understanding of the community life, relating it to the neces- sary number of people for any given type of community activity, the changes affecting the stability of the community, what cultural interests the people have, and the interrelation of the various community activ- ities. C. C. North examined some of the trends of the organization movement as applied to the social work of American cities. The evolutionary basis of the science of society was made by Albert G. Keller while H. L. Smith brought together various findings relative to the psychological aspects of human relationships and their part in the structure of human society.

Confusion in understanding is frequently due to the changes oc- curring so rapidly that the results are confused with the concept of basic institutions. This is shown in an analysis of L. V. Ballard's Social Institutions in the development of sociological thinking, and as was stated by Chapin "Although cultural change moves at a swiftly acceler- ating pace, all that is new is merely by way of addition to the existing cultural base of fundamental institutions, and many innovations in socio-economic relations that at first glance look so startling are really but swirling eddies on the deep and placid current of persistent social institutions."

Early in the twentieth century Edward Cary Hayes developed the idea touched upon by earlier social philosophers regarding the distinctive place of conditioning, problem and resultant phenomena. The most obvious changes deal with the status of conditioning phenomena, and problem activities brought about by the growth of population, shifts in population, development of new occupations, and change in the form of social organizations. The resultant phenomena, however, which follows conditioning and problem phenomena is the real crux of the situation. Hence, changing social attitudes and interests are of basic significance to students of sociology. It is within this area where changes and trends reach into all different types of group activities.

A study of the interests and opinions as reflected in public sources from the beginning of the century until 1930 indicated that "religious sanctions have been largely displaced by scientific sanctions and that discussions of education increased to about twice as much proportionate space in general periodicals in 1928 as in 1912," was shown by Hornell Hart in discussing Changing Social Attitudes and Interests. Unfavorable discussion reached its maximum in 1925 to 1928 and while favorable discussion of religious matters and spiritual life reached a high point at the same time as antagonistic criticism, the volume was much less. A study of trends indicated that periodicals read by the masses reflect a growing lack of interest rather than aggressive criticism of religion.

Similarily, a maximum point was reached from 1925 to 1928 regarding sexual irregularities, easy divorce, and sex freedom in general. The rise of these topics "appears to have been closely associated with the decline of religious sanctions for sex conduct." A third point brought out was that opposition to prohibition has increased by 1931 to five times the amount expressed in 1914 and that, "drinking by moving picture heros and heroines is from two to seven times as frequent as for approved characters in short stories of various types." Attention was directed to the increasing interests in social uplift and reform which developed in the first two decades of the century. Following World War I there was "a wave of discussion of socialism and communism, but the opposition expressed was overwhelming. Scientific management, industrial good will, low prices and high wages, service to the customer, and the like became favorite slogans." This was superceded by unemployment and discussion of business conditions. From this point on for the next ten years, from 1930 to 1940, was a period in which an emphasis upon changing attitudes and the measurement of attitudes and public opinion reached unusual high levels of interest. It gave rise to the development of new techniques, not only for measuring and determining attitudes and beliefs, but of many specialized efforts to improve our methods of determining and measuring attitudes and the effects of attitudes upon conditioning phenomena. We entered a period of "polls" to show attitudes and change in approvals and disapprovals. Like any new emphasis, for a short period there was a tendency to substitute mass opinion of a situation or the character of a situation for actual research and measurement and evaluation. There is a place for opinion and atti-tude measurement in the study of social phenomena, but it is not a substitute for critical analysis of a situation.

A committee on social trends headed by Lawrence K. Frank called attention to the lag in the application of available knowledge, not merely among laymen, but even professionally. Attention was called in particu-lar to this need in dealing with children, stating both "it is evident that the major problem is to direct social change toward the conditions requisite for wholesome child life and to test all organizations and activities by the quality of the children they helped to produce." During the decade from 1920 to 1930, this approach was quite general, but with the unsettled conditions in the early '30's it was overshadowed by more temporary dealings and by the pressing need of some sort of immediate action. The evaluation of group activities as suggested by Hayes was gradually becoming incorporated in sociological thinking, and in diversi-fied areas began to take form again after World War II as will be seen in a later chapter. During the '20's, a need for interpreting data and coordinating various types of analysis.

Numerous efforts were made to score community life. The failure to devise an effective scheme has been due largely to the fact that too much stress has been laid upon conditioning factors, and that there has been no adequate measure of the functioning of group activities. The efforts have been confined largely to "the enumeration of conditioning phenomena such as natural physical conditions, artificial physical conditions, density and distribution of population, and similar data. This has made up the bulk of data in most surveys, community studies, and specific studies of social activities in which the enumeration of statistical data played the major part. While it is true that there is usually a high correlation between such concrete conditioning phenomena and the part the related activity plays in the life of the group concerned, the weakness of this type of data as a basis for evaluation is due to the fact that it does not give any actual information concerning the functioning of agencies and activities within the group. The seating capacity of organizations, 'units of attendance interests' of churches, sanitary equipment of homes, the number of books in a library, or the 'per capita investment of time and money' in an organization does not measure health, culture, educational or religious activities, or the actual group functioning along the lines indicated by the agencies or organizations under consideration, although these phenomena may bear a high correlation to the objective evidence."

Institutions which give permanence and stability to the group may be roughly designated as political, economic, educational, recreational, religious, ameliorative, and corrective. Furthermore, the score of the community must be based on three general lines; first, an intimate study of the population and the concrete objective factors related to the life of the people—that is, the usual community survey data; second, a concrete and objective study of the institutions which give permanence and stability to the group. In this division should be included the objective data such as equipment, expenditures in units of time and money, membership, program, and the nature of activities carried on by the organizations; third, the functioning of the institutions and activities within the social group under consideration. That is, the measure of the extent to which the community reacts to the principles of the agency or organization under consideration.

The social processes are intangible and consist of the interaction of the ideas, sentiments, and practices of social groups. You cannot count a process, or measure it with a foot rule. Because of that fact, it is assumed by many that it cannot be interpreted in objective terms. The 'spiritual values' of the boys' clubs must be measured in terms of their functioning. To what extent, or in what way have the social processes within the group been changed by the injection of that particular

activity? In what specific way and to what extent have the ideas, sentiments, and practices of a group of boys changed, as a result of the boys'
club activities among them? What things are now done in a settlement
neighborhood which were not done before its activities were carried on?
In what specific ways do the ideas, sentiments, and practices of a group
of people change, who have had their 'life processes' influenced by
settlement activities?

There is no single method which can be applied to interpretation of
social processes. Instead it must be a combination of several methods.
It must include an approach such as suggested by the study of Polish
Peasants. It must include a study of attitudes as illustrated by the Race
Relation Survey on the Pacific Coast. It must include a statistical study
of objective factors which can be enumerated for study in order to
obtain the actual changes which have occurred. The presence or absence
of any additional factors will be observed in the resultant phenomena.
These changes can be observed and studied, and constitute the factors
which give us a basis for interpreting the social process. When we
bring together the different techniques and methods which are being
perfected, and apply them to the intensive study of particular group
activities, we can give the settlement worker and the boys' club worker
a definite measuring stick, by which he can determine with a reasonable
degree of accurateness the "spiritual value" and the change in ideas,
sentiments, and practices which make up the social processes within his
field of endeavor.

Most of the social changes which we attribute to the influence of
invention and discovery may be explained by changes in our culture.
Since social institutions, which are the result of long growth and development, do not rapidly adjust themselves to new inventions, we find
cultural lag in the case of families not yet adjusting themselves to factory
culture, "the church slow in adjusting to the city; the law slow in adjusting to dangerous machinery; local governments are slow in adjusting
to the transportation inventions; inter-national relations are slow in
adjusting to the communication inventions; school curricula are slow in
adjusting to the new occupations which machines create. There is in our
social organizations an institutional inertia and in our social philosophies
a tradition of rigidity. Unless there is a speeding up of social invention
or a slowing down of mechanical invention, grave maladjustments are
certain to result."[2]

New waves of prosperity will be terminated by new recessions and
there will be recurrent episodes of prosperity and depression which can
only be answered by continued study and experiment. The need for

---

[2] *Recent Social Trends*, McGraw-Hill Book Co., 1933, p. xxvii.

social and economic planning is now recognized, with more specific application than was indicated by the general principle of social planning, expressed by Lester F. Ward at the end of the nineteenth century. Due to the shift from small business to great corporations, there occurs a period when the small business man, the little truck farmer, and the independent craftsman feels that his initiative is being gradually hemmed in. He is sometimes thrown out of income employment due to factors beyond his immediate control. This gives rise to the need for some over-all joint cooperation or social insurance such as was suggested by Charles R. Henderson before World War I as being effective in some European countries. The work of W. F. Ogburn in the late 1920's helped prepare the field for the growth and development as well as the general recognition of social security, legislation and procedure for the next twenty years. It likewise directed attention to problems of social mobility which, while recognized by individual sociologists, had not become a part of the general thinking of society such as it was to become by 1950. There was only an occasional article or monograph dealing with problems of social mobility and social stratification. The time was not ready for the extensive consideration of those problems until the ideas had germinated for a number of years. In discussing the effect of invention upon society, Ogburn stated: "It is not to be implied that mechanical invention is the source of all change. There are social inventions like the city manager form of government, the chain store, esperanto and basketball which have had great effects upon social customs. While many social inventions are only remotely connected with mechanical inventions, others appear to be precipitated by mechanical inventions. Such is the case with workmen's compensation laws, the trade union and the tourist camp. But just as mechanical inventions furnish an incentive for certain social inventions so social inventions sometimes stimulate the making of mechanical inventions as in the 'safety first' campaigns of a few years ago."

Many social changes occurring are the result of mechanical or social inventions which are not directly associated with the new phenomenon. We cannot determine cause and effect by any immediate relationship. In fact the social change resulting from an invention or a new idea may only become manifested when brought into contact with some other phenomenon or a combination of situations. "It takes time for the social influences of inventions to become fully felt. The quickest effect is on the habits of the persons who come in direct contact with the invention in its use. It takes longer to influence an organization or a social class and perhaps still longer to change social institutions, theories of ethics, or social philosophies."[3]

[3] Ogburn, W. F., *Recent Social Trends in the United States,* McGraw-Hill Book Co., N. Y., 1933, Vol. 1, p. 124-162.

Perhaps the most significant technological changes have occurred in the field of communications. The effect of radio and radio broadcasting was foreseen and, while all aspects of changes in the means of communication and transportation had been making an impact during the first quarter of the nineteenth century, it was recognized that the inter-relation of these developments, the effect upon new industry, the development of new occupations, the shifting of populations resulting from these developments, and above all the cross-fertilizations of ideals, attitudes and practices ahead indicated changes that reached beyond the factual understanding of people generally. In 1932 Malcolm M. Willey and Stuart A. Rice stated in Agencies of Communication that "Agencies of mass impression subject the individual to stimuli of sight and sound that may serve to make him think and act, in some measure, like millions of his fellows. With the concentration of these agencies the control over his behavior is increased. The integration of the agencies of communication becomes more apparent. As old agencies are confronted by newer agencies, functions shifts and adjustments are required. This is a moving equilibrium that is disturbed by changes in the old agencies or the introduction of new ones. Out of this integration emerges an all pervasive system of communication from which it is difficult to escape. Each new device provides one more channel that has its ultimate focus in the individual. The tempo of life is speeded, for agencies that facilitate contacts engender them. Man becomes dependent upon the new instruments and their use becomes a part of routine . . . In short, an interconnecting, interconnected web of communication lines has been woven about the individual. It has transformed his behavior and his attitudes no less than it has transformed social organization itself. The web developed largely without plan or aim. The integration has been in consequence of competitive forces, not social desirability. In this competition the destruction of old and established agencies is threatened."

An immediate observable effect of population changes, of invention, and of new methods and types of communication is reflected most quickly upon occupations. The aftermath of a world war with the national reorganizations which followed added to the culture changes taking place and resulted in a period of readjustment with all of the tragedies of readjustment. This took the form of toppling industrial situations which had developed on a different plane for a century. It marked the passing of old occupations and the slow growth of new types of employment, it meant readjustment of family living, of church organization, school programs, and life in general. Life in general became radically different from the period before World War I and technological unemployment rapidly snow-balled into unemployment supplemented by all of the additional social forces until it reached the proportions of a panic. As stated by Ralph Hurlin and Meredith B. Givens, "Thus the complexity of modern life, the technical requirements of present occupations, changing customs and legal restrictions have combined to retard the entry of potential younger workers into the ranks of available labor."

With the trend towards centralization of many of the functions of group life which were formerly taken care of by individuals, by families, by local groups, and because of the movement of great masses of people from one area to another and the shifting of population from occupations to occupations, government centralization of these functions began. This resulted in an upsurge of government employees to an extent and in a variety of forms that would have seemed fantastic twenty-five years earlier. Public service began to multiply the functions of government. This would have occurred even if the changes referred to had moved with the tempo prevalent before the development of new inventions and rapid communication and transportation, but with these changes occurring, and unprecedented unemployment being catapulted into the social arena together, the number of persons whose life and activities were directly tied up with centralized government control went to unforeseen lengths. Occupational insecurity and unemployment became a national problem instead of a family problem and marked the beginning of an entirely new body of social thinking. This new approach to social planning and social thinking, while based upon the principles promulgated by the sociologists of the previous generation, was now broken down into more specific areas and the principles of social organization, social control and social integration were developed and applied to new and variegated areas which had arisen and developed as a result of the other social and cultural changes. The new structures were built upon the foundation of principles previously developed although their new application went far beyond the thinking of the earlier generation and frequently the new architects of society failed to recognize and give credit for the ideas they were using to those who had gone before.

With the extensive natural resources and what appeared to be limitless opportunities of all kinds, the millions of peoples who filled this great new world developed their interests and organizations with little understanding of the inter-relationship of group activities. Astounding contrasts appeared everywhere. These contrasts were found in the degrees of divergence in wealth, in education, as well as overtly manifested in buildings and in different living standards within the same community. It was now being recognized by social scientists, in particular, and all types of people in general; but there was need for viewing the situation as a whole rather than by isolated and small areas. The need for social equilibrium was becoming apparent. Among all of the aspects of social change the most obvious need for stabilization was in our cultural values.

There had never been a time when the concentrated cooperation of trained scientists, scholars, and the backing of literally hundreds of educational and research agencies cooperated in such a joint effort as the Study of Social Trends. The list of contributors does not include the hundreds of individuals who contributed their efforts as associates of assistants of the individuals and agencies mentioned. The studies represent the most complete cross-section of the areas covered conceivable and were based upon records that could be substantiated and serve as a basis for social action. There was a minimum of opinion and of recommendation concerning action which should be taken. However, the bringing together of this material, at that particular time, lay the basis for much of the direction taken by social scientists in their thinking and contributions for the next fifteen years. There was no attempt to elaborate upon social ills or to prescribe remedies. It was rather limited to the specific task of recording, as accurately as possible, changes that had taken place or were in the process of occurring and to report findings uncolored by personal likes and dislikes. Most of the monographs presented were expanded during the following years into significant volumes and many trends in social thinking, which were not formally presented in these reports, bore a direct relation to certain aspects of our culture and social change suggested by these reports.

A basic report dealt with the population of the nation and was prepared by Warren S. Thompson and E. K. Whelpton of the Scripps Foundation For Research in Population Problems. This report called attention to the trend in population change and to the variation in the age distribution, as well as changes in the national and culture background, the shift taking place from a rural to a urban population and the trend from concentration in cities toward suburban areas. Thus by 1930 our attention was called to shifts in service occupations, retail and department stores reaching into trade centers removed from the older "downtown" type of concentration.

The "rapid transportation" of the early 1900's consisting of commuter trains and inter-urban trains were now being supplemented by the automobile, improved arterial highways, and changing the location of the suburban dweller from concentration in small cities centering around a railroad or inter-urban stop to formerly inaccessible areas, filling in the sector between railroads and streetcar lines. Likewise, the shift in population due to varying birthrates at different age levels and affected by economic, occupational, racial, and religious factors was resulting in changes of all related social agencies and activities including practically all of our social interests and manifested in everything from recreation to public schools.

The growth of population by the end of the first quarter of the nineteenth century was taking place chiefly in or near large cities. Three-fourths of the national increase of the population in the ten years from 1920 to 1930 took place in large city areas. In fact, over half of the population of the United States lived within an hour's automobile ride from cities of 100,000 or more. The older census reports classified the population as being rural in communities under 2500 and urban in communities over 2500. Since World War II, such classification began to lose its significance and the more important problem was whether or not the population was located near the influence of the metropolitan center.

It has been estimated that the rapid transportation resulting from the use of the automobile has extended the practical radius of a city to at least 50 miles. Time has become the determiner of city boundaries rather than space. This newer type of community is made up of the old core city and the addition of separate local communities. For a time there was a tendency to concentrate most of the cities, including the larger metropolitan areas, business activities, in the old core center but the increase in population as well as the vehicles of transportation has given rise to a generally found choking up of activities. The result has been the development of new trade centers which are not merely the rebuilding of the little, local stores of the old communities but have actually become metropolitan-type areas which in most cases are actually improvement and modernization of the old core business districts. The new business areas have taken into consideration modern transportation needs and modern merchandising methods which differ from the older type as much as a modern house differs from the old log cabin.

"While the role of the great city in the nation at large has been growing in importance an changing in nature," stated McKenzie[4], "Even more radical and important changes have taken place within the city itself. They have drawn after them a number of local institutions, business outlets and municipal services, creating a real *rus in urbe* in the suburban territories. Industry likewise has tended to migrate outward, not for the same reasons but because increasing congestion in the more central districts has hampered its activities and added to its production costs. The heavy industries go first and farther; the lighter ones and those which are most dependent on proximity to their metropolitan customers do not go so soon or so far; but the tendency in nearly every case is centrifugal."

"When individuals, businesses and industries move out in this way, at the rate which has recently marked these migrations, they leave a partial vacuum. The general effect of this drift, coupled with the more

[4] McKenzie, R. D., "The Rise of Metropolitan Communities." Taken from *Recent Social Trends*, McGraw-Hill Book Co., 1933, Vol. 1, pp. 443-496.

intensive use of land brought about by large structural units, is to hasten the obsolescence of much of the older pattern of the city. This applies to practically every type of institution and service. Every large city is confronted on the one hand with the problem of increasing congestion in certain areas and, on the other with that of revitalizing its blighted areas."

"While the deteriorated areas are largely allowed to go to waste there is an intensive exploitation of certain other areas within the city and toward its periphery. There result problems of transportation and traffic which are among the gravest that confront any modern city. In some cities the growth of private transportation by motor car has tended to disorganize the mass transportation facilities originally existing and has at the same time created a new traffic problem."

"To sum up, the past decade has definitely witnessed the emergence of a new population and functional entity—the metropolitan community or super-city. So far as can be seen this new entity will characterize our national urban life for an indefinite time to come. The next decade may be expected to bring about further efforts to digest it into the economic, governmental and cultural pattern of the nation."

There was first a period from 1900 to 1907 during which time there was some selection on the basis of literacy and physical condition. A second period from 1907 to 1914 in which the attitude toward restriction of certain groups began to appear and attention was focused upon Americanization of aliens in order to present a unified front against the enemy. 1918-1924 was the first real attempt at a restrictive policy with an increase in anti-alien attitude in the laws of 1921 and 1924. From 1924 until 1930 interest began to be directed toward the immigration of newer groups from Mexico and Canada which included not only citizens of those countries, but persons who had acquired a residential status there and who had previously been restricted from coming to the United States through American quota systems. The earlier waves of migration included many who settled on the land. The newer movement, stated the report, was predominately urban and the foreign born from 1910 to 1930 tended to concentrate in urban regions. The report indicated that "In recent years the most spectacular movement of the population within the United States has been the shift of hundreds of thousands of negroes from south to north, introducing into industry a new type of labor and changing the environment of the migrants from the most rural to the most metropolitan." Problems of adjustment were brought to the social agencies and to all types of social and religious, as well as governmental agencies as a result of these tremendous migrations.

Herman Feldman summarizes these difficulties: "(1) Most of these groups have to live down a tradition of disparagement. (2) Regardless of skill most of them have to begin at the bottom. For instance in the northward migration of Negroes many who were skilled as carpenters, masons or even mechanics, began in common labor in the north. (3) Even on this lower level there is sometimes friction, particularly in periods of unemployment or strike, between the newcomer and those who have not risen far."

The increase in intermarriage may be traced to several factors:[5]

"1. The proportion of the older people among the foreign born has grown, especially in communities which do not receive new immigrants. This means that the foreign born of the older group are more likely to find mates of their own age in the native American population than in their own group or the second generation of their own stock.

"2. The proportion of females in the foreign stock has become more nearly equal to the proportion of males so that the practice of sending back for brides is not so frequent.

"3. The growth of a large stable group of the second generation of a number of nationalities has made it possible for both grooms and brides of foreign stock to mate with American born descendants of their own stock without recourse to fresh arrivals from Europe.

"4. The slackening of immigration during the World War and since the application of quotas has reduced the proportionate number of foreign born so that the chances of their mating with American born consorts have been increased.

"Economic and educational progress has meant the emergence of a middle class. No longer are all foreigners or colored people merely laborers. Some are skilled workmen, small business proprietors and professional men."

Rural life as a distinctive area of social thinking was recognized by a considerable number of individual sociologists during the first quarter of the nineteenth century. However, by 1930 it began to take generally recognized form. This was due, not only to the spread of ideals, but to the changes that were taking place which were causing classifica- tions rural and urban to lose much of their distinguishing elements. As stated earlier, the Institute of Social and Religious Research in 1921 carried on some extensive researches in widely distributed areas while preceding and following World War I there were intensive community surveys, while an additional 140 selected agricultural villages were studied in 1924 and restudied in 1930-1931. The universities of Cornell, Kansas, Minnesota, Iowa, Missouri, Wisconsin covered similar aspects of the rural problem. It was on the basis of these and many other studies,

[5] Woofter, T. J., Jr., Brinton, Hugh P. and Johnson, Guy B., "Racial and Ethnic Groups." Taken from *Recent Social Trends,* McGraw-Hill Book Co., 1933, Vol. I, pp. 600, 601.

as well as a comparison of the years 1910, 1920, and 1930 which later also included population distribution that the results of these studies are included in the monograph "World Social Trends" by Kolb and Brunner. Most significant is the increased importance of rural-urban relations. This was directly related to the improved means of communication, specially rural mail delivery, telephone, hard surface roads, and automobiles. The concentric zones of influence shown in studies before and immediately following World War I became extended and intensified in their contact with the urban; the smaller towns and cities merging into the great metropolitan centers and their tributaries. This resulted in more extended regional social planning; in the equalization of educational and other opportunities throughout the rural-urban areas, and the areas of influence of government, education, health, administration of justice, protection of life and property no longer conforms rigidly with the boundaries of the village, township, school district or county. Rural and urban become only relative matters. If there has been urbanization of the country there has also been ruralization of the city by the urbanward migration of millions of rural people. In local, as well as national issues, the twentieth century is spinning a web in which city, village and country, no longer separate entities, are being brought together.

Sometimes the branch of an apple tree grows and develops until it puts forth more fruit than the main parent tree. Rural sociology, a twig on the sociology tree has developed to the extent that it not only has taken care of its particular area, but has contributed much to the development of the general field of sociology. In fact, there have been instances when rural sociologists appear to have contributed more to the field of sociology than was being done in the general field.

Howard W. Beers demonstrated by a study of various polls that on no issue of national interest do farmers present a solid front of opinion, that unanimity is not found on any topic, while Nathan A. Whelpton emphasized the sociological research in the suburban field.

The relationship between sociology and particularly the effect that rural sociology has had in influencing other areas in this country and in the world since rural sociologists probably have been concentrating more on areas outside of the United States than have general sociologists within the past two decades. Polson has summarized ways to improve training of our foreign students:[6]

"(1) Give more consideration to language facility and living conditions so that they will support rather than detract from the student's training program, (2) use more intercultural comparative data in classroom pre-

[6] Polson, Robert A., "Sociological Training, *Rural Sociology*, Vol. 17, No. 1, March 1952, p. 8.

sentations, (3) get the students off the campus for more systematic observation and contact with American family and community life, (4) experiment with doing more of the training work in the field, and (5) provide more training opportunities in the application of social science to problem-solving."

A trend that is definitely taking form is further research in that fringe between strictly rural and urban society. This area seems to indicate a fertile field for research in problems of social adjustment and may indicate a line of social integration which foresees the elimination in the future of distinctive rural and distinctly urban society.[7]

Rural sociological research in its early stages consisted very largely of the collection of informative data. This was a necessary first step. Sometimes members of the older branches of sociology minimized the value of these studies. However, they were very essential first steps which have proven their worth. C. J. Galpin early emphasized some further developments in the objectives of research which Carl C. Taylor further emphasized, and T. Lynn Smith presents five points which should be uppermost in sociological research. These are pertinent even though they were developed in regard to a specific topic.

"(1) The need for local self-direction in planning and conducting research; (2) greater continuity of projects to enable workers to dig more deeply into the problems on which they have started; (3) the development of a more adequate body of social theory; (4) the perfection of a more sharply critical scientific attitude; and (5) more attention to the importance of sociological studies of small areas."

In the study of rural society the recognition of the various types of association, the social processes, the structure and function of social organization, social interaction and integration is based upon the same basic concepts found in sociology generally. The fact that rural sociology is studied as a distinctive area merely is recognition of the need for a thorough understanding of the particularized aspects of social life to which sociological principles may be applied. This is necessary in order that we may determine the expected behavior of groups under special situations. The need for this specific and detailed information gave rise to extensive factual and descriptive study. While the processes of accommodation, assimilation, stratification, and institutionalization may form a basis for our study of the social processes in rural society, the future trends in rural society as summarized by Lindstrom and Edgar included

---

[7] "The Rural-Urban Fringe"—A Special Feature, Articles, Discussion, and Bibliography by Stuart A. Queen and David B. Carpenter, Walter C. McKain, Jr. and Robert G. Burnight, Paul K. Hatt, Samuel W. Blizzard, and Robert C. Angell; Introduction by Charles E. Lively; Rural Sociology, Vol. 18, No. 2, June 1953, pp. 108-120.

"(a) greater emphasis on group and intergroup cooperation, (b) greater emphasis on rural community and country life planning and action largely on the initiative of and by the rural people themselves, (c) greater unity in country life movements, (d) greater national and international concern for the welfare and security of people on the land, and (e) more inclusive social security.

"These rural life trends should result in (a) using, protecting and conserving our land resources as a social trust, (b) the protection and nuture of the family as the basic and most essential social group and economic unit, (c) the fullest possible *continuing* educational development of both those who remain on the land and those who go into other fields of activity, (d) the use of all possible public and cooperative means for the protection and care of health, (e) the development of professional, as well as humanitarian, treatment of rural social welfare conditions, and (f) the organization of the rural community for carrying on essential democratic policy-making processes, and to provide for direct action in solving rural problems."[8]

The direction of change in forty years may be best shown by a comparison of the suggested content of a basic course in sociology in 1933 with the suggestions thirty-four years earlier. The American Sociological Society recommended that in an introductory course in sociology at least 70 percent of the attention be given to the following topics, the particular organization of the topics to be determined by the instructor.

"I. *Groups and group life*
    Social bonds, their nature and variety
    The principal types of social groupings, as community, class, nation, state, voluntary associations, crowds, the primary group, in-group, out-group, etc.
    Collective behavior
"II. *The fundamental social processes*
    The nature of isolation, of contact, and interaction; communication; conflict and competition; accommodation; assimilation; cooperation; differentiation, etc.
"III. *Man's cultural heritage*
    The nature of culture
    Its origin in adjustment to environment
    Geographic environment and culture
    Invention, diffusion, accumulation, culture borrowing, or fusion
    The elements of culture and their significance for social life, such as language, folkways, mores or codes or standards, religion, science, material elements

[8] See Lindstrom, David Edgar, *American Rural Life*, Ronald Press Co., New York, 1948, pp. 370-371.

"IV. *Social organization and structure*
The nature of social institutions
The principal institutions, such as the family, the economic organ-
ization, the state, the school, the church, recreational organiza-
tions
The functions of these institutions and their significance for human
behavior
" V. *Social change*
Society as an evolving process
The nature and causes of social change
Social lag and its significance
Problems of readjustment created by change
Social disorganization
"VI. *Society and the individual*
The biological-psychological equipment of the individual
Wishes, attitudes, instincts
The role of the environment
The development of the human personality through social life
The reciprocal relation of social and individual
Social control and guidance
Personal disorganization"[9]

The twenty year period from 1920-1940 gave rise to many new
groupings of sociologists and individuals interested in social thought.
Many of these represented revivals of interest in already well-established
concepts. Some of them grew out of the desire for recognition by able
young men who chaffed at being considered as part of a marching
column with no specific identity. All of these contributions to a special
aspect of sociology contributed to a better understanding of the whole
problem of the development of social thought and must be considered
a part of the general forward direction. The end results contributed to
a better understanding of the whole instead of becoming a major trend.

Many terms get into our written vocabulary as a result of a specialized analysis. In order to save extensive explanations it is sometimes
found expedient to use a general term as one might use a formula. For
example, in 1877 Lewis H. Morgan classified the peoples of the world as
lower, middle, and upper savages; lower, middle, and upper barbarians,
etc., up to upper enlightened. He made his classification chiefly on the
materials used for dwellings and certain artifacts and mechanical devices.
An article in *Harpers Magazine,* February 1949 by Russell Lynes and
the page of illustrations in *Life,* April 1949 dealing with high-brows,
low-brows and middle-brows present an approach which has become

[9] *The Journal of Educational Sociology,* September, 1933; "Recommendations
of the Committee, pp. 80-81.

very widely used, and which, if not carried to extremes, or made too rigidly stratified, is useful. Sometimes an apt illustration has given rise to a series of applications of the principle involved to a wide range of topics. This is illustrated by the wide use of the little study made of the "Hen pecking propensity."[10] Many of these efforts are revivals of established concepts, with a new application made necessary by some major change in our social organizations. Until the new interpretation has become a part of general thinking, it will seem to be given over-emphasis by the persons concerned. This may be seen by the periodic concentration on such terms as the following, all of which are of significance, and all of them contributing to the reformulations of the whole;—culture, demography, ecology, geo-politics, group-dynamics, industrial sociology, power structure, political sociology, psycho-drama, semantics, situational analysis, sociology of knowledge, social stratification, symbolism, value judgment, verstehen, and many others. Sometimes a new emphasis on the scope, analysis, modification, and application of a concept will dominate the trend of writing and thinking for a time. This is of direct value in the progressive development of a subject, and when the divergent and exploratory efforts have once been settled, the main stream will be found to have benefited by these efforts.

[10] See Schjelderup-Ebbe, T., "Beitrage zur Sozialpsychologie der Haushuhns," Zsch. f. Psychol., 1922, Vol. 88, pp. 225-262.

XII

Reaction and Emphasis in 1942

THE TASK of establishing and arriving at an agreement of concepts marked the first basic era of the development of sociology in the twentieth century. This also marked the fruition of an established period of textbooks. These books, dealing chiefly with the logic and the standardization of the concepts which determine and outline the field of sociology, were read by millions of persons and fixed basic sociological concepts in the thinking and writing by persons in all areas from writers of fiction to analysts of political, economic, psychological, and philosophical thought.

The second major period again seemed to be in a state of confusion. In some respects this was comparable to the period at the end of the nineteenth century when leaders of sociological thought were attempting to outline the organization and structure of society and to determine the factors involved. By the thirties we had reached a point where there was no longer need to justify the conceptual factors, but rather to begin to explain social structure and social functions within these conceptualized areas by explanation of the existing functional and resultant phenomena. Beyond the scope of the general content of sociology, there began to be recognized functional objectives. These were summarized:

"a) To inform and instruct the student concerning the nature of society. This includes such objectives as: to acquaint the student with the nature of the social life going on about him; to develop an understanding of social institutions and social processes; to give the student a technique for analyzing and classifying social phenomena, and for studying communities and other social groups.

"b) To develop scientific attitudes. These attitudes are described as objective attitudes; freedom from biases and prejudices; ability to suspended judgment until facts are available.

"c) To prepare the student for advanced sociological study. This is to be done through (1) stimulating his interest in the subject, and (2) laying intellectual foundations through the acquisition of terminology and fundamental concepts.

"d) To prepare the student for more effective social living. This includes the development of a sympathetic interest in the social life about him; the development of a desire to participate usefully in social life; better adjustment of personal problems and social relations.

"e) To prepare the student for vocational training. The two voca-tional fields in the minds of those instructors who hold to this objective are teaching and social work."[1]

These principles were a part of the accepted thought of sociologists. However, almost before the process of transferring ideas into practical programs could take place, the new era was upon us. The scars of World War I had not been obliterated. Industrial changes, transportation, types of communication and tremendous increase in production of raw materials was occurring, with a general lag in social organization in line with the changing world. The depression of the '30's forced the adoption of agencies and organizations to meet the occurring needs. The general application of principles which had been thought of by a few sociologists, now were being put into practice throughout the country with the con-sequent errors, mismanagement and lack of understanding which natur-ally follows a sudden crisis. However, the end result was good. Millions of people began to be concerned with sociological aspects of social rela-tion and social action. This paved the way for increased effort to evalu-ate and understand social phenomena.

The decade of the '30's marked a period of major social changes in the life of America. The old agricultural life which carried over from pioneer days was ended. A new industrial era, revolution in methods of communication and transportation, food processing, and education re-sulted in a period of actual disorganization during efforts to readjust our social life. Before this was accomplished, World War II was upon us. How was this all going to effect sociology? The Second World War was well underway. Pressure began to be applied to educational groups to modify what they were doing and concentrate more specifically on "war effort." It seemed well to get the opinion of sociologists concerning their direction and emphasis.

Contact was made in 1942 with nearly two hundred sociologists in the United States in order to determine what sociologists at that time considered the major points of emphasis in sociology. Many of those who responded had more than one interest. The responses may be summarized under the following general headings:

General Principles	37	Juvenile Delinquency & Crime	18
Race Relations and Population	30	Personal Adjustment	16
Local Community Problems	26	Social Processes	16
The Family	21	Social Control	15
Sociology of War and Peace	21	Culture & Adjustment	14
Research Methods	20	Collective Behavior	13

[1] *The Journal of Educational Sociology,* September, 1933; "Summary of Findings on the Present Status of the Introductory Course in Sociology, and Conclu-sions" by Cecil C. North; p. 70.

Organization & Disorganization	10	Social Work	5
Latin American Sociology	10	Occupational Sociology	4
Applied Sociology	10	Rural Sociology	4
Far East and Pacific	7	Regional Sociology	4
Sociology of Education	5	Political Sociology	3

There were several other minor and highly specialized fields in which three or less were indicated as the future place of emphasis.

The first group of reactions included here are from the sociologists who responded with reactions as to the direction of emphasis in the area of General Sociology. These are significant in showing the emphasis of the following leaders in social thought at the end of the long depression and the beginning of the Second World War, coming out of a period of extensive trial and error to meet social needs and already a part of the intense situation of being catapulted into another World War.

General Principles Clarence M. Case stated—'In general sociology the keynote of my work is to lay special emphasis upon the basic social processes so as to clearly define and amply elucidate them. In so doing, I try to treat them in their relationships one to the other.' Frank Hankins—'Basic emphasis will be as here-to-fore on realistic, objective analysis in the spirit of science. There is need to stress the shift in ideology from individualism toward collectivism in consequence of changing situation and structure of social relationship.' George Lundberg—'The keynote in general sociology will continue to be precisely what it has been in the past: (a) the principles of sociology as they have been developed to date; and, (b) the methods by which these principles were arrived at and by which further scientific knowledge regarding human society is to be achieved. Illustrative material may be drawn from contemporary events in order to show how the present situation is what it is because of failure to apply indisputable scientific sociological knowledge beyond that. The sociologist need not alter the content of his courses any more than a physicist alters his courses because a hurricane sweeps the country.' E. B. Reuter—'So far as we remain sociologists we will continue to do what we have been doing in the past,—attempt to analyze social relations, define the social processes and attempt to make intelligible the mechanism and nature of social integration and unity. So far as we depart from the above we cease for the time being to be sociologists. Some of us will be engaged in certain types of war work, but so far as we do we are no longer sociologists.' Pitirim A. Sorokin—'No drastic change in general sociology, only somewhat greater emphasis on war and other urgent problems.' Howard B. Woolston—'I do not know of any re-orientation in general sociology. We should cultivate our garden with some attention to the threatening weather. Re-naming courses does not make them more valuable.' Howard Becker—'We need to develop and utilize more historic data for sociological analysis than hitherto has been popular, particularly from the standpoint of the sociology of knowledge and systematic sociology. We have chattered too much about the Kwokiut, on the one hand, and Yankee Town on the other, with virtu-ally nothing in between. I don't wonder that the historians have many laughs at our expense, for where their field is concerned, we are only semi-literate.' Read Bain—'Same as usual. Main emphasis should be on sociology as a natural science, on methods of getting reliable and valid knowledge, and making application to solution of practical problems. However, the war furnishes fine illustrative material—mostly negative— what not to do. Fortunately, the usual line of sociologists can be con-tinued to show what is necessary for world organization and why it is difficult. I suspect that sociologists as a class will find it less necessary to change their line than almost any other academic gang. We have always emphasized what the war is an illustration of, and, also, what is necessary to find a better way than war to settle disputes. Nothing that has happened in the last ten years has made it necessary for me to change. They are just catching up with me!' Paul F. Cressey—'Our major task is to train young people to understand the world they live in, to think more clearly, to be better citizens; in other words, the general aims of a truly liberal education. This is a long range view. I am not neglecting the current crisis when its issues are pertinent to any class material. To use these issues to make sociology more real and vital but not to abandon social science or social propaganda.' DeGrange—'Stress the reality and importance of sociology as an indispensable contribution to understanding, correcting, and organizing the present and the future. It is simply impossible to comprehend what is going on without a soci-ological background. We live in a sociological age.' A. S. Emig—'Empha-sis needed on the problems and processes of adjustment and accommoda-tion.' Charles R. Hoffer—'Continue in the main to teach the principles of sociology but draw illustrations when opportunity arises from current situations.' Elizabeth Nottingham—'Main emphasis on the functioning of social institutions rather than "pathology emphasis".' George P. Mur-dock—'Research in social structure.' Walter C. Reckless—'Deflate the cultural emphasis, emphasize class, social structure, experimental studies of group formation, attitude formation.' Walter Watson—'Give students a clear understanding of the social implications of the world and the place in which they live; help students find a specific place in the world recognizing always that there are short run accommodations as well as long run plans that need to be made.' W. A. Anderson—'A knowledge of the principles of social structure and function are fundamentally the same war or no war. In fact, a knowledge of these things are now more essential than ever.' James H. S. Bossard—'In regard to general sociology I must confess to a feeling of profound uncertainty. I think that this is not the time for expansion but rather for general consolidation of gains made in the last two decades. If the shift of emphasis upon the natural science continues, than the more solid our sociological foundation the more ably may we face the future.' Edmund de S. Brunner—'Funda-mental principles of sociology and their contribution to the understand-ing of the present and post war situation.' Frederick E. Detwiller—'Application of principles more directed to the present state of the U. S. A. attempting to appraise it better.' Jerome Davis—'Study to bring out fundamental principles.' Norman S. Hayner—'It seems to me that this is a time when the fundamental ideas in our field should be stressed more than ever. We have a body of ideas that will help students to understand the world in which they live. It is up to us to get these ideas across.' J. L. Hypes—'The essential unitary and interdependent nature of human society should be stressed.' C. E. Lively—'Emphasis on the population shifts now going on and their implications; the growing interclass conflicts; better nutrition and socialized medicine (not state medicine) are fundamental reforms. Education for democratic living that will get us back to hard work and less entertainment.' Earl E. Muntz —'Principles do not change, but the war provides valuable illustrative material to make current applications.' James Woodward—'Relative emphasis in a developed science are determined not by personal prefer-ence or current events but by the contained logic of the given science. Since sociology is not that fully developed, there is a greater tendency for content and emphasis to change with the current scene—carry out analyses along the lines of their contained appropriateness with nothing but the choice of illustrations influenced by current events.'

It is evident that the reaction of this group was that the established sociological principles should continue to be emphasized with such changes as new trends and research would indicate to be significant. The general feeling was that knowledge of the basic sociological princi-ples were more than ever necessary to understand and meet changing world social situations and world crises.

Population and Race There has probably been no subject within the field of sociology which has been as persistently studied as popula-tion. However, the approach to the study has been usually influenced by local considerations and by current attitudes. Even in the decade follow-ing the Civil War General F. A. Walker, at that time a popular economist, became highly concerned over the subject of population and immigration, and he contended that instead of population increasing as the result of immigration that it merely tended to change its general character and make-up. His point of view, which was generally accepted, was that for every increase in immigration there was a comparable decrease in the native population when any area began reaching the saturation point. While Franz Boas during the last decade of the 19th century began to direct interest to the subject of population, and Richard Mayo-Smith wrote *Emigration and Immigration,* and in some cases present hypotheses concerning the effect of change in conditions upon the character of population, no extensive new points of view were formulated. Carroll D. Wright who as director of the United States Census was concerned with population growth and the problems of migration and immigration presented some interesting material in his *Practical Sociology.* The tremendous immigration during the first decade of the 20th century gave rise to various types of studies many of them based upon a minimum of fact and a maximum of emotion. Typical of which was *The Passing of the Great Race* by Madison Grant and from another approach Edward A. Steiner *On the Trail of the Immigrant.* More scientific studies began to appear such as *The Old World in the New.* Attention was directed to some of the immediate results of population movement by such popular studies as *How the Other Half Lives* by Jacob Riis. From the year 1910 to the beginning of World War II the amount of material published which dealt with immigration reached colossal proportion. Much of it, however, was extremely controversial. A change was being made from the old natural theories concerning population as presented in the publications beginning about the middle of the 18th century with Johann Peter Sussmilch and reaching their culmination with Thomas Malthus. These natural theories of population were tossed back and forth for several decades following Malthus until a series of social theories began to appear which did not try to determine a basic law of population but rather the recognition that population, its growth and character, is determined by a wide variety of circumstances and conditions under which men live. A. M. Carr-Saunders while accepting the theories of Malthus feels that man's growth is quite within man's control and that the optimum population will constantly vary with the nature "of the environment, the degree of skilled employed, the habits and customs of the people concerned, and all other relevant facts" which would give the greatest average return per capita.

Next to general sociology or social theory the groups of persons responding in 1942 who were interested in population and race relations was numerically the largest. It was rather interesting, however, that in spite of the fact that we were already in the war in 1942 the emphasis which it was felt should be placed on this aspect of sociology maintained an even keel. Frank Hankins emphasized the structure of social relations and indicated that emphasis on the eugenic aspects of population was fading out. Similarly, Paul E. Cressey stated that the

need was to give more attention to class structure and the relationship
of classes and races in a democracy. While Maurice Davie felt that
there was need to expand our study of race and nationality to include
post war planning, and Kingsley Davis stated that population seemed
to have more immediate and obvious practicability than many other
aspects of sociology. Constantine Panunzio emphasized democracy, culture, and race with greater clarification of the concept "social."

A somewhat different approach was keynoted by Howard Odum as
a continuation of social theory which focuses upon folk psychology
systematized from empirical studies of the folk—regional society and
applied to realistic understanding of contemporary society as it is reflected in civilization. Lloyd Allan Cook emphasized the structure,
process, and unity of American "community" life at local, regional, and
national levels with particular application to minority peoples, and unity
of thought and action in all phases of life. Guy B. Johnson considered,
in general, race and culture and democracy in the world conflict with
special consideration of racial tensions, race adjustment, morale, and
defense work. Thomas McCormick stated that we are planning to
emphasize social control and social organization with particular emphasis
on race relations, race problems, and methods of research. J. P. Shalloo
felt that emphasis should be placed on the general processes of opposition and assimilation as they affect minority groups in the United States
since such concrete application of sociological principles to specific
minority problems are more useful than general principles as such.
Andrew W. Lind wrote from Hawaii—'Events thus far in the war
indicate the increasing significance of race in the local situation, and
we are inclined to think that the same is true in the larger world outside.' Bernhard Stern focussed on the problems of race and culture
contacts arising out of the war as the framework of the book he was
preparing with Alain Locke—*When the Peoples Meet: A Study of
Race and Cultural Contacts*. Rupert Vance in general sociology placed
emphasis on investigation of the theory of regionalism and its cultural
objectives, and placed particular emphasis on regional and clan differentials as related to fertility, socio-economic status, and so forth. William
C. Smith—'Minority groups in the United States and race problems
seem to be coming to the fore in considerable measure.'

Typical of a somewhat different trend relating to population and
race relations was indicated in 1942. As expressed by W. A. Anderson—
'In our field of rural sociology we are paying some attention to migration, its effect on population, and the effects of war upon rural life and
rural employment. The need to focus our research on migration from
rural areas was emphasized also by Paul H. Landis. Everett Hughes—'The
study of racial and cultural minorities—it seems to me that the condi-

tions under which people under diverse race and culture can be got to participate in a common effort, in war and in peace, present an even greater problem now and for the future than ever before. Especially so since it has become evident that the principles of self-determination cannot safely be interpreted to mean indefinite multiplication of completely sovereign nations.' Likewise, N. B. Bodenhafer considered the field of race relations and population to be of increased importance now and in years to come. This was also the opinion of Frederick E. Detwiller and Carl A. Nissen. They felt that such significant changes are now being made in race relations that they need to be noted and studied. S. C. Ratcliff expected emphasis on social relations, class structure, and similar aspects of population problems with the recognition of a need for a policy. L. P. Edwards spoke of the need to emphasize the unity of the human race and the breakdown of racial, national, and religious prejudices and stereotypes. Also more time to the study of eastern people and their cultures.

Warren Thompson[2] has summarized most effectively the proceeding half-century of development in our understanding and our attitude toward the social aspects of population.

"It seems to the writer that the direction of population study in this country during the last half-century has been determined largely by the problems of more or less general social interest which were emerging and to an understanding of which a larger knowledge of population movements would contribute. It has not followed any "logical" plan of development, it has not had any *field* allotted to it within which it was expected to work. To many this may seem a shortcoming, an acknowledgment of opportunism which is unworthy of a discipline striving to be scientific. To the writer, however, it appears as evidence of a vital adaptability which should help to secure for social science as a whole a more essential place in planning a more satisfactory social organization in the future. Indeed, the writer wonders whether some of the older social disciplines would not do well to be less concerned with preservation of their fields and with their logical growth and to devote more effort to the study of emerging problems with the best scientific tools available, even though they spill over into other fields in doing so. In any event, he does not feel that any apology is needed for the opportunism of population study during the last half-century, and hopes that it will remain opportunistic both as to field and as to methods of operation.

"In the second place, another general aspect of the growth of population study in the United States should be noted, not because it

[2] Thompson, Warren, *The American Journal of Sociology*, May 1945, p. 442.

is peculiar to this field of work but because it represents a trend which is both of interest and of importance. More and more our governments —federal, state, and local—are supporting various aspects of population study because they are finding population data of value in their administrative work. This need is certain to grow, and there is good reason to suppose that larger and larger public support will be forthcoming for many types of population work. This is as it should be. The fact that population study is useful and that much of it is undertaken for its usefulness does not condemn it as unscientific. It will become unscientific only when it becomes untruthful, when the public authorities suppress findings which are unpalatable, or when they compel interpretations which are not based on all the evidence available. We should not ignore the possibility that bureaucracy may stifle advance in population research, but neither should we assume that this will surely happen. The increased support of population study by public money should be all to the good as long as we have a vital democratic system. If that goes, then population study by public authorities will be perverted to class purposes; but so will similar study by private individuals and agencies. It would seem inevitable that, as larger and more varied bodies of fact are needed for population study, these fact must be gathered by public agencies and the early stages of their processing must be carried out there. It would be unfortunate, however, if all interpretations of these facts were to be confined to these public agencies and if they were to allow their work to become so routine that they did not constantly explore the possibilities of the measurement of new aspects of collective behavior."

The interest in poulation has always taken very concrete form and was influenced and determined by current circumstances to which attention was directed. In 1909 President Theodore Roosevelt sponsored the first Child Welfare Conference. Here the emphasis was placed primarily on the care and feeding of children, children's diseases, infant mortality and similar topics. By 1930 conditions had changed to such an extent that the entire emphasis of the conference was shifted. A nation-wide survey was summarized in the following statement: 'It may be said that our studies on the life of the child in the home reveal a higher standard of practice, when details of care are considered, than was anticipated.' The result of the study indicated that there were many siginificant social adjustments which took place in accordance with social change effectively but almost unobserved. The acceptance of standards worked out by experts and incorporated in the life of the people were found to exist and were in line with professionally recognized methods of procedure. Hence, twenty years after this first Child Welfare Conference emphasis was placed upon the psychic relations of parent and children. It has been evident that the study of population and race has been effected by current events and trends of thought more than some other aspects of sociology.

The Family. The study of the family has presented three rather distinct trends: (1) chiefly historical, including the changes and develop- ment in laws and customs relating to the family; (2) the institutional approach viewing the family as a unit of the social structure with par- ticular concern regarding its role in the greater structure, its mode of functioning and changing, and adjusting to all conditions of society; (3) a trend which has received the greatest emphasis during the second quarter of the twentieth century has been an associational approach concentrating on the various aspects of inter-relationship of the com- ponent members of the family. The direction toward which all are pointed, however, is the recognition of the family as a focal point where all of the social sciences bear on the activities and adjustments of a unit which is a functioning part of society and where the impact of changing values and changing environment are first felt.

In somewhat the same stages of development as was found in social research we find in the development of a particular field of inquiry, such as the family, that the approach to the subject since 1895 repre- sents three major stages of development with the manifestations of new trends since 1945. Waller and Komarovsky[3] classified the three principal interests in the sociological writings of the family, 1895-1914, as dealing with (1) the origin and evolution of the family, in its forms, and in primitive and historic societies; (2) appraisal of the institutional changes in the family since the industrial evolution (Did these changes constitute progress?); (3) contemporary social problems and their control. They state that "of the thirty-four articles on the family in the *American Journal of Sociology* between 1895-1914 thirteen were on the changing status of women: women in industry, their wages, higher education, suffrage, sex differences. Of the thirty-three books in the field of the family reviewed in the same journal during this period nineteen were books on women." It is further stated that child labor, divorce, eugenics, prostitution, and illegitimacy were other frequent subjects of books and articles. A dominant theme was the plea for social legislation in these areas; child labor laws, minimum wages, protection of women workers, reforms in marriage and divorce laws. In the early writings of the family there was practically nothing within the area which is generally desig- nated as social psychology. Even the writings of W. I. Thomas in that period were largely of an economic, historical, or narrative type. The writers, in general, frankly stated what they considered to be their

[3] Waller, Willard and Komarovsky, Mirra, "Studies of the Family," *The Ameri- can Journal of Sociology,* May 1945.

moral objectives and were not inhibited from expressing value judg-ments. In fact, much of the writing dealing with the family in that period came within the general category of preachments rather than scientific evaluations.

There were some exceptions to the general rule as well as certain monumental studies which formed a basis for later analysis and dis-cussion. For example, Edward Westermarck's monumental work *History of Human Marriage,* 1891; George Elliott Howard, *History of Matri-monial Institutions,* 1904; John M. Gillette, *The Family,* 1906; C. R. Henderson, courses on the family, early 1900's; J. Q. Dealey, *The Family in Its Sociological Aspects,* 1902; Helen Bosanquet, 1906; A. J. Todd, *The Child in Primitive Society,* 1913; William G. Sumner, *Folkways,* 1906; Willystine Goodsell, *The History of the Family as Educational Institution,* 1915; Arthur Calhoun, *The American Family,* 1919; Sophonisba Breckinridge and Grace Abbot, *Child in the City Streets,* 1909. These represent some of the excellent earlier studies.

Opinion in 1942 regarding the place of the sociology of the family in the coming years was strongly expressed by a wide distribution of sociologists. The need for more emphasis was strongly expressed by Jesse Bernard, J. Stewart Burgess, and Raymond L. Hightower who stated that while sociology lost some of its "punch" with the passing of applied sociology, the recognition of the need for studying family prob-lems will continue for many years. Joseph K. Folsom felt that more attention would be placed on child care, while Alvin Good looked for continued discovery and spread of knowledge for successful living in the family, both from the point of view of husband and wife and from the point of parents and children. James H. S. Bossard stated—"Since 1938, when I came to the Carter Foundation, I have been trying to develop a Sociology of Childhood and of Child Problems. Manifestly I am proceeding with this since Pearl Harbor. We are laying some emphasis upon the impact of war upon childhood, both as a part of the family group and as a separate personality. We are planning to carry this quest forward." Hornell Hart was seeking to develop operational answers to some of the major problems involved in social ethics in rela-tion to the family—work in problems of courtship and of predicting this quest forward." Hornell Hart was seeking to develop operational success in marriage. John F. Cuber stated—"It appears that the major emphasis in my work will be 'practical'—distasteful as the term is to me and to other 'purified' sociologists. Greater demand for marriage, pre-marriage, and more general consultant services." W. H. Heinmiller felt that major emphasis in sociology during the next few years should be upon social institutions in view of the far reaching social changes which are taking place and which leave us without adequate institutionalized behavior patterns. "This should be the keynote of work on the family." C. R. Hoffer—"For the next few years emphasis will be placed on adjustment of rural families in the war situations." Stuart A. Queen stressed the changing nature of "social problems in war time"; the effect of war on cities and family life; "realism" vs. "escapism." Leonard Broom—"The investigation of the evacuation of the Japanese and its influence on family organization which implements theory and the method of acculturation." Clifford Kirkpatrick stressed whatever seems timely, which in practice is not so simple, but we need to stress the influence of war on the family life. A. G. Truxel likewise felt that attention would be directed on the impact of the war and the family. A. J. Todd stated—"I'll be retiring before long or pulled into war work, so my opinion may not be worth much. If I were to continue in my special field, I should emphasize the need for off-setting the present pre-occupation with bodily pleasure and romance in marriage, and the need for recognizing stability, good sportmanship, and spirituality as objectives in teaching the Family." Willard Waller stated—"I expect to see in sociology during and after the war relatively little abstract theory and methodology (Parsons, Lundberg, Doob), relatively heavy emphasis on things that can be applied, such as Social Problems, Morale Work, Community Organization. Am turning my own attention largely to the concept of morale and the study of ways in which it may be maintained. Work with families and entire field of family study will in the end be strengthened by the war. Sociology of conflict also very important, but will have to change emphasis. I guess that's batting out the predictions." Oscar Wesley—"No great change in general sociology, but in the family I shall try to adjust according to new conditions. Many of my girl students are asking whether to go on and get married now or wait. Many standards are gone." Bessie B. Wessel—"The problems posed by the need of reconstruction in the field of the family, community, and ethnic relations seem to me to be foremost." W. C. Waterman—"The study of the family will be revamped somewhat in view of present conditions." R. M. MacIver stated—"There are broadly two ways of approaching the study of the family. We may regard it as constituting a little unity in itself, the system of interacting personalities composed of parents and children. We shall then concentrate on the manifold aspects and types of inter-relationship between the component members—husband with wife, fathers and mothers, with sons and daughters. The other approach views the family as a unit of the social structure, and is concerned particularly with its role within that greater structure, its mode of functioning through the succession of the generations, changing with and responsive to all the conditions of society. The former approach we may perhaps term the 'associational';

the latter, the 'institutional.' Each has without doubt its own importance. The former deals primarily with the social psychology of the
family; the latter, more strictly, with its sociology. On the whole American textbooks on the family, unlike those of other countries, have been
more concerned with the associational aspects. It may be fairly said
that they have given less than due attention to the profoundly important
institutional aspects."

The comments included above are significant since they are the
reaction of a wide range of sociologists, many of whom had not published anything relating to the family in the years of our entry into
World War II. Some persons well known in the literature of the field
did not respond, or if they did, indicated that their point of view was
expressed in a paper which they had read and which would probably
be published. However, among the approximately two hundred sociologists who expressed their opinion regarding probable trends in various
fields of sociology which they consider of major importance, we had a
most impressive and reliable indicator of what sociologists in the United
States believe would be the trend in the relatively near future.

War and Sociology Since the war in Europe had been proceeding
for some time, and the United States had been actively engaged in the
World War for several months, it is interesting to note the direct effect
it had on the work of sociologists.

About ten per cent of the answers indicated that the major emphasis would be placed on war, peace, and post war planning. Dr.
Jessie Bernard stated—"Our college has asked us to tie our subject up
with the war, therefore, the keynote of my work both in general sociology and in marriage and family will be keynoted to the impact of war
on our society. I think this can be overdone, and so I shall try to maintain a perspective, but it is difficult to sidetract an issue that touches
the girls' lives so closely." M. F. Nimkoff stated—"At Bucknell we have
readjusted our program in sociology because of the war conditions as
follows: (1) introduced a pre-professional orientation course in 'Fields
of Social Work' in response to the felt need for more vocational guidance for our students; (2) stepped up our training in social research for
the same reason; (3) added a couple of seminars on the problems of
war and peace." Seba Eldridge said—"It looks as if much of our work
will be oriented toward the war time problem and also problems of post
war reconstruction." Raymond V. Bowers—"The work I had planned
to do on my own research program will have to wait until the war is
over at least." Kathrine Jocher—"It seems to me that the emphasis of
sociology today should be directed toward what sociologists can contribute to the present situation in a realistic way and the place of sociology
in post war planning." Similarly, Clifford Kirkpatrick said—"Sociological

material relevant to post war reconstruction." E. B. Harper—"Emphasis on the effects of war in public welfare administration, on the new developments in defense, health and welfare services, civilian defense, and reorganization of public and private welfare in general to meet the emergency." Neumeyer states—"There is hardly a course that does not involve a consideration of the relation to the war effort. Examples: In my courses on *leisure and recreation* the problems of recreation in and near military camps, war industries, and community morals are im-portant. Radio as a *social institution* includes a consideration of radio in war time. The family and the war is a part of the general family course. Urban and rural sociology both involve a consideration of the effects of war. The key to sociology during the next few years is the emphasis on the importance of research of group life, social processes, and social change as effected by the war and as a basis for post war reconstruction." Walter A. Terpenning emphasized in both general and special fields the problems growing out of the war and especially the problems of post war social planning. A. G. Truxel—"As much stress must be laid not only on present war issues but on post war reconstruc-tion from an institutional point of view." Louis Worth—"How to win the war, how to win the peace, world reconstruction, ideological and institutional and social planning with special reference to urbanism and race relations." W. C. Waterman—"Sociology for the next few years must be hooked up with war and reconstruction." Wilson Gee—"Con-sideration of the current national situation. Of course, this becomes still more the case under present world conditions. I do not like the idea of lecturing on military happenings in connection with class work because we have so little information on the basis of which to do so. Even if we could be military experts there are dozens of connections in which the causes of the present war, its implications, and planning for peace come up. I think the situation is accommodated just as well this way— even better than by setting up special courses." Joyce O. Hertzler—"The sociological aspects of the peace ahead and of peace organization of the world." R. P. Holden—"Succinctly stated social planning and social reconstruction." Cecil C. North also stated the problem of social planning after the war internationally and at home; institutional reorganizations that will be necessary; reexamination of the concept of democracy. R. A. Polson—"First, assisting with the organization of all communities for the war effort; second, keeping an eye on the farm labor problems and the rural youth migration situation; third, being prepared to assist in the post war migration adjustment; fourth, to do some exploratory work in post war planning; fifth, assist with 'spot' jobs that appear from time to time, such as, prevention of juvenile delinquency, housing war project workers, etc." W. F. Ogburn stated the major work is to see what is happening under the war economy to our total society, its economic and political organization, and to try to see what will take place after the war. In short, the impact of war on society. James M. Reinhardt—"Emphasis on cultural and institutional change as effected by global war and the problems of writing a global peace." Dwight Sanderson stressed the study of rural attitudes on war and peace problems. Shankweiller—"Social change implying cultural lag in social institutions and bearing of this factor on war causation and the place of social planning for post war development." Fred R. Yoder—"The sociology of war in all its phases and also propaganda as it relates to war." L. L. Bernard—"The sociology of war and peace, social control with emphasis on war, the use of force and fraud should have increased emphasis, likewise more consideration of psychological warfare."

It is evident, even when specific consideration was taken of the war, that sociologists felt their work should be effected by somewhat greater emphasis of what they had been doing rather than setting up a new specialized program. Several sociologists mentioned the requests by their administrative officers to do something specifically for the war effort. The reaction quite generally was "We are directing our entire program toward the problem of learning to live together; the war may interrupt our program, but when the fighting has ended, and even before, the work of the sociologist will be of major importance. Readjustment of social controls and social behavior and winning and maintaining the peace.

Sociology of Conflict   The conflict theory of social processes was apparently somewhat revived in 1942 after a decade of unprecedented government control and concentration of effort to the development of cooperative society under government domination. The reaction of individuals expressing themselves on the subject are indicated by some of the following: John M. Gillette—"I am going to emphasize a course in the sociology of conflict." A significant statement Gillette made at this time was—"Our enrollment is so shot that some of our courses are going out, I doubt if rural sociology gets any enrollment next semester." This in one of the leading agricultural areas and from one of the founders of rural sociology. T. L. Harris—"Emphasis would be placed upon competition and conflict"; while Lindesmith said—"Research in the sociology of war." Charles E. Lively—"Growing interclass conflicts"; and Gerald W. McMinn stated—"Stress particularly the nature processes and difficulties of social adjustment and social adaptation with the view of cutting down the frequency of national as well as international conflict." Donald R. Taft stated—"While I do not think that every course should drag in the war topic unnecessarily, I believe, it would be appropriate to show implications of the various aspects of

the field of sociology for the understanding of war." Stuart A. Queen—
"Stress cultural differences and similarities, conflict and accommodation
in relation to very concrete happenings of our world today, cultural
change, lags and resistances, and their practical significance, propaganda
and moral."

The Community   The decade ending about 1940 had seen us
through the throes of a long depression, in which the local community
problems had become merged into a nation-wide recognition and
nation-wide procedures for meeting local needs. In this major process
the individual was largely submerged, and the localized neighborhood
and community had lost much of its former effectiveness. The situation
was not unlike the diminishing recognition of primary groups due to
the enlarged effectiveness of the secondary group. Similarly, some of
the distinctive contribution of the "near" group or community were
neutralized or forgotten in the shadow of the greater outside force. By
1952 there was a positive return to recognition of the part of the community, and it began taking an added importance in the studies of the
day. But in 1942 when this check was made the significance of the
community was at a low ebb, and only a few of the sociologists expressed themselves as considering it as one of the major fields where
emphasis should be placed.

Joseph K. Folsom—"Focalize interest on the local community, its
organization in war time, and its organization in general." J. Stewart
Burgess said—"Of particular urgency for sociologists are the questions
of race relations, the problem of family organization and disorganization, and those questions related to life of the local community."
Maurice Davie—"Stressed modern community studies, such studies as
housing and community organization with reference not only to war
but to post war planning." N. P. Gist—"Concentrate mainly on the following: (1) the community, with greater emphasis than before on planning; (2) collective behavior, particularly social movements, public
opinion, etc.; (3) occupational sociology, a neglected field." Walter
Watson—"I view the community and urban sociology as a continued
attempt to give students a clearer understanding of the social implications of the world and to accumulate information about our own area
that will be of basic usefulness." Earl E. Muntz—"Increasing interest in
the urban community, particularly as a result of new dislocations due
to migration and concentration and dispersion of industries. Housing,
health, and recreation bid fair to be more serious problems than ever
before." Carl Nissen—"There are such significant changes occurring in
the rural and urban community that they need to be noted and studied."
Lowry Nelson—"Can speak only for rural sociology where we are
placing considerable emphasis upon changes brought about by the war,

including farmer response to changing conditions. New organizations being introduced, such as neighborhood committees. War Board: problems incident to increased production goals, like farm labor changes, cropping systems and the like. Some of these changes in rural organization are apparently superficial, others have possibility of being more lasting. Rural schools will be compelled to consolidate, for instance, and this may be permanent." Lee M. Brooks—"Dynamics of cooperation as an international, national, regional, and subregional process, and programs with special work on the community."

Regionalism   As was indicated earlier, the study of communities showed the need for reaching out into adjoining communities and for certain aspects including a region. The responses in 1942 were typified by Howard Odum—"Specialization in scientific delineation of regions and in regional planning." D. B. Rogers stated—"More concentration on the various community influences which extend with different degrees of effectiveness into areas within natural regions." Rupert E. Vance— "The investigation of the theory of regionalism and its cultural objects in the special field of population."

Research Methods   Perhaps more than in any other field the status of sociology and the direction it was going in 1942 is indicated by the responses regarding research. We had just ended a decade of social reorganization in which the depression and the resultant emphases on social control had played a major part. We were on the verge of a world catastrophe whose beginning had been gaining momentum in Europe. We were being pulled in from the Atlantic side and propelled in from the Pacific.

Much of the reaction to research is incorporated in the emphasis put upon specific fields of concentration. It is of interest that responding to the inquiry, the group, for the most part, place emphasis upon research and research methods rather than research within any particular field of study.

For example, Herbert Blumer stated that he expected to concentrate on an analysis of the art of observing human behavior as likely to provide the answer to the methodological problem of scientific procedure in sociology. While Lee M. Brooks said that sociology has reached a point where there is virtual agreement as to content and objectives. A start has been made in the problem of testing. Tests should be developed particularly for the material covered in general courses. L. J. Carr— "Interested in developing an adequate frame of reference in search methodology for the study of collective readjustments with particular reference to the problem of how collective learning occurs." J. M. Cooper felt that the big task ahead is the gathering of its own basic core of sociological data. Edwin L. Clark succinctly stated—"Thinking scientifically—without prejudice and according to rule of evidence and logic." Lundberg expressed himself (see "Can Science Save Us"). McCormick emphasized the need for increasing effort to improve methods particularly designed for social research. R. F. Sletto—"The development of a more adequate theoretical frame of reference into which the findings of sociological research can be integrated. Improvement of techniques of measurement and prediction. This in turn is contingent on advances in theory of social measurement."

More specifically emphasis was placed by some on particular problems. As W. Rex Crawford indicated—"Whether we want to or not we shall be forced to ask ourselves to what urgent problems are techniques and special knowledge pertinent." F. Stuart Chapin replied—"The emphasis for the next few years in my own work will be on divisions of my special field: statistical research, war and post war housing, organization of institutions in war and post war period. To devote any time to so-called 'general sociology' would be an unjustified waste of anybody's time." While John F. Cuber stated—"Research, in so far as there will be time for any, must be short run and oriented to current practical problems." C. R. Hoffer said that his research will be focused on special problems or adjustments arising from the war. George P. Murdock emphasized research in social structure, and M. F. Nimkoff said step up teaching research methods to help students meet vocational needs. Odum planned to devote time on specialization in scientific alienation of regions and in regional planning. Eldridge and Raymond Bowers were drawn into government research and thus were typical of many other who for a time left the field of sociology as such but devoted their time to the sociological interpretation of governmental problems. The situation was expressed by Calvin F. Schmid whose work had already been effected by the war situation. He stated—"Our colleges and universities are experiencing many fundamental changes, and it is impossible to predict what the ultimate outcome will be. Many institutions will go out of existence while others will be transformed into something that resembles both a military camp and a university. Sociology along with other social sciences (not so much economics), law, and certain of the humanities probably will not be considered very essential in the new curricula which will be developed. Engineering, physics, mathematics, chemistry, and certain professional subjects will be greatly emphasized. The need for trained technicians especially in the field of statistics, as well as the draft law itself will determine what many of the younger sociologists will do for the duration. The draft law or the manpower mobilization program may force some of us into other fields."

"There exist," according to Burgess, "certain serious handicaps to the further development of research commensurate with the maturity which sociology has now achieved as a science. These may be briefly listed: the inadequate, uneven, and often fragmentary training of graduate students in research methods; the great excess of subject-matter over research courses in the graduate curriculum; the existence among many sociologists of a cultist rather than a catholic attitude toward research methods; the relatively small number of trained sociologists and of graduate students in proportion to the vast area of problems for sociological investigation, and as compared with the larger personnel in psychology, economics, political science, or history; the absorption of sociologists in teaching to the disadvantage of research undertakings; and the small amount of funds available for sociological research."[4]

Juvenile Delinquency and Crime. This field is always of much interest to the general public. Persons who have taken little or no interest in these problems become very vocal on occasion. In 1942 throughout the country there were lay groups who suddenly become concerned and often made positive demands upon colleges and universities to "do something about juvenile crime." A few typical responses of sociologists give us the emphasis and trends in this area.

Mabel A. Elliott—"In my special fields, which are social pathology and criminology, there is abundant opportunity to discuss the problems of war. War itself is a result of other disruptive factors but in turn produces further disorganization by its impact upon institutions, lives, and social structures. In criminology, what would otherwise be a crime becomes the highest good in the case of an act which is the defense of one's country. At the same time, war seems to promote juvenile delinquency, whereas adult crime rates tend to go down." Walter Reckless—"Criminology dealing with a comparative behavior approach is concerned with violation of rules, the problem becomes one of who are conformists and who are violators, of a comparative definition of violation according to various value scales what makes a recidivist and a professional criminal and what happens to first offenders (why don't they continue on); a problem confronting us is prediction of factors on violators of code, of criminal code, first offenders, recidivists, professionals." Fredrick M. Thrasher—"While in general we may emphasize the control of conflict, in my special field I expect to emphasize crime prevention and community reorganization with special attention to research in these fields particularly to determine the early causes of white collar crime." Nathaniel Canter—"Felt the continued emphases would be on the psycho-sociological approach to the general field of delinquency." Walter Bodenhafer stated—"Criminology may be pushed more to the front; to those in other fields this may seem trivial, but

[4] *The American Journal of Sociology,* Vol. L, No. 6, May 1945, p. 482.

even so I feel it important." Similarly, Lloyd V. Ballard, Lee M. Brooks, D. R. Taft, and Carl A. Nissen listed as a major field needing emphases to be crime and delinquency. David B. Rogers stated—"Crime prevention. It should include helping the near delinquent to keep out of trouble."—and George B. Vold added—"While I give practically full time to what I suppose you would call 'my special field' criminology, what the organization of sociology teaching in the emergency should be is only part of the larger problem of what the whole social science problem should be, which in turn is related to the whole question of desirable changes in the structure of education."

Social Control   Since Lester F. Ward emphasized the function of social telesis, the concept of social control has grown. Taking definite form in the epoch making book on social control by E. A. Ross, it has been a fundamental concept in sociology. Swinging from the extremes of an abstract ideal to very concrete manifestations in the form of a particular movement as found in national socialism of Germany, facism in Italy, or communism in Russia, social control has taken many forms. After a decade of increasing national government control in America far beyond any previous governmental attempts in this country and with the aid of new forms of communication—the radio, talking movie, and already beginning in the late 30's highly developed forms of television—, we have new forms of applied propaganda which is more than the beginning of a new social order. Alfred McClung Lee reacted to what is before us as follows: "Continuing our general courses in sociology and pre-professional Social Work, but we are adding some emphasis on the application of social psychology and sociology to practical situations in the various departments of American Life. We are strengthening our offerings in public opinion, public relations, and collective behavior. It strikes us that sociology has a great contribution to make now and after the war, but this contribution must not be left to the imagination of non-sociologists. Sociologists must make clear the kinds of problems they can help to solve and to what extent they are likely to offer sound guidance." Similarly, Paul Landis emphasizes the crying need for sociologists to offer guidance. T. L. Harris spoke of the need for understanding new techniques of propaganda and trends in social control, while Frank Goodwin said that the keynote in sociology is to stress ability for man to achieve control of men as well as physical environment if knowledge in sociology is sought and applied. L. S. Garwood included the importance of the sociological attitude toward world problems. Robert Faris stated—"I advise the students to master their subjects better than ever before, if that is a 'keynote'." T. D. Elliott said—"Illustrate sociological principles from current events and situation processes. Now it's the war, that's all. I suppose there will be more emphasis on principles of conflict and accommodation and on post war planning and social controls." L. L. Bernard stated that social con- trol will take form through education, recognized as the chief instru- ment of training in employment and incompetency. Contemporary men and women require that they learn three important things in their school: (1) vocational competency; (2) efficiency in performing func- tions of citizenship including self-government; (3) a general cultural adaptation to modern life on the social moral and intellectual sides.

There were some who emphasized social control in terms of specific procedures relating to a particular interest. This point of view is well expressed by Frederick M. Thrasher—"My own special interest is juvenile delinquency and crime prevention, and I am particularly desirous of developing a machinery for community reorganization which will make effective crime prevention possible by attacking it at the point where juveniles first become delinquents. I believe we need considerable research in this field particularly on the early careers of white collar criminals in order to round out our knowledge of the etiology of crime." Some of the reaction to the part government was beginning to play was emphasized. Paul H. Furfey—"It seems to me that by far the most vital question facing sociologists is academic freedom from governmental control. All our work will be conditioned by this issue." While Charles C. Peters said—"After dealing with a definition of education in terms of practiced behaviors, and with the technique of the democratized school and other educational features, I make an analysis of the meaning of democracy, the lag between our ideals of democracy and present at- tainment, the nature of the social revolution that is going on, the prob- lem of social control in a democratic society, the problem of demagogy and of constructive leadership, and the possibility of telic progress. I think these are the most important issues of the present day so far as my area of activity is concerned." C. E. Lively felt government cooperation must receive more attention. T. E. McCormick said emphasize social control and social reorganization. F. E. Lumley summarizes his point of view as follows: "As far as investigators can discover, there is no ultimate and predestined *plan for man* in this universe; there is no particular destiny that he *must* fulfill willy-nilly. Consequently, his destiny is *more in his own hands*—more than any previous generation has supposed. There is no place to which he *must go,* no kind of creature that he *must be,* no kind of social system that he *must* have—except as blind, stumbling individualism *or* large-scale cooperative effort makes it so. If man is his own worst enemy, as has been so often asserted, it is also true that man is his own best friend. In the last analysis it is man himself, with his pooled energies, who must determine which he will be. The two billion people on this earth possess incalculable resources, both natural and human, to help them go where they want to go and be what they want to be. Where do they want to go and what *do* they want to be? 'That,' as Hamlet put it, 'is the question.' "

Social Psychology When the term psychology was first used it may have meant the study of groups or collective behavior to some and to others the resultant of the interaction of human beings. At present there is little attempt to make these distinctions considering it more as the analysis of human interaction. Up until the end of the 19th century social influences held little interest for psychologists. Psychology more nearly fell within the older category of moral and intellectual philosophy. Even as late as 1890 William James was concerned with judgments and reasoning.

The doctrine of instinct resulted from an attempt to explain emotion, and while sociologists had long since started the instinct theory of William McDougall for many years his point of view remained unchallenged.

A new approach to social psychology appeared when G. Stanley Hall began to emphasize genetic psychology with particular focalization on the child. Treatises on social origin began to appear (see Thomas et al) tracing the development of some of the major social institutions. Group concepts began to take form and the influence of William Graham Sumner in his *Folkways* can hardly be over estimated. Ellsworth Faris has stated—"What Sumner demonstrated in definite manner was the variety of customs and the almost infinite variability of human nature. Since Sumner it has been impossible to deny the priority of the group or primacy of culture."[5]

While the first book published under the title of *Social Psychology* was published in 1908 and written by E. A. Ross, the following twenty years brought forth a flood of material which would fall within that designation. With it came a definite shift from speculation of social philosophers to individuals seeking verifiable data. By the end of a period, twenty-eight years after the writing of Ross' book, social psychology had reached a stage when many of its earlier concepts had been found unfruitful, but its main position had been clearly enough established that the way was opened for a refinement of research such as the early students of the field could not have conceived as possible.

Some of the most important problems of present day world depend on the developments in social psychology. Recognition of this occurs as a rule in connection with some disaster or a war. It is found all the way from the reaction of a small group, like a family, at a time of crisis to the social psychological effects and attitudes of masses of new popula-

[5] Faris, Ellsworth, "The Beginning of Social Psychology," *American Journal of Sociology*, Vol. L, No. 6, p. 424.

tion who are participants or observers in a hot or cold war. The early attempts of social psychologists were to find and establish certain basic principles in collective behavior. Soon, however, there appeared in myriad of attempts to apply more or less established principles to all types of situations in which the resultant activity of group behavior became the object of study. Instead of philosophical speculation based upon current activity. The over-emphasis of the application of exact measurement to studies, surveys, and evaluations actually contained an element of progress. As elsewhere stated by Small, even though a research project proves to be a blind alley, if it is done so thoroughly that no one needs to repeat the research, it has added to the sum total of human knowledge by eliminating it as a factor to be considered.

Collective Behavior and Social Relations. N. P. Gist stated—"I expect to concentrate mainly on the following in the future: (1) the community, with greater emphasis than before on planning; (2) collec- tive behavior, particularly social movements, public opinion, etc.; (3) occupational sociology, a neglected field." Alfred McClung Lee— "Sociology has great contributions to make but this contribution in relation to collective behavior must not be left to the imagination of non-sociologists. Sociologists must make clear the kind of problems which they can help to solve and to what extent they are likely to offer sound guidance." Andrew W. Lind stated—"A more specialized interest in collective behavior and more particularly in civilian morale grows naturally out of the war situation. We hope to follow as closely as possible the developments here in the Islands, and we feel that this is a legitimate point of emphasis for our students. Local defense agencies have come to look to us for assistance in this area." Lowry Nelson— "Considerable changes in the way of collective behavior are being brought about. New organizations are being introduced such as neigh- borhood committees, problems incident to increase production roles, farm labor changes, cropping systems and the like. Some of these changes in rural organization are apparently superficial, others, have possibility of being more elastic, rural schools are being compelled to consolidate and this may be permanent." Carl Nissen—"Emphasized changes in collective behavior and social relations being brought about in community life." And S. C. Ratcliff—"Felt the need to emphasize social relations, class structure, and a need for policy in population problems." Sarvis—"Increasing interest in systems of interaction, especially on different levels." Howard B. Woolston—"In my special field, group behavior, we continue to discuss attitudes and opinions as expressed in cities, nations, and in social classes with some attention to their manifestation in war time including some application in lecture on panic prevention."

Clear Thinking—Emotional Adjustment   Edwin L. Clark, one of
the chief exponents of "clear thinking" among sociologists from 1830
to 1840, stated what he considered the basic emphasis among sociologists
as follows: "(1) thinking scientifically, without prejudice, and according
to rules of evidence and logic; (2) necessity of increased cooperation
between nations, some kind of world organization; (3) necessity of
increased cooperation within a nation, with social security for all; (4) a
fraternal spirit will lead toward a happy future, gross individualism
will drag the world down." Robert Faris in view of the impeding war
stated that in time of emergency "advice students to master their subjects better than ever before." While Paul F. Cressey warned—"Not
abandon social science for propaganda." Gerald M. McMinn stated—
"Stress the nature, processes, and difficulties of social adjustment and
social adaptation with the view of cutting down national and international strife." While A. J. Todd felt that emphasis needs to be put
upon the seeking of tests to determine how far social planning is workable and desirable. F. J. Freidel stated—"Emphasis will be with students
on making suitable social adjustments and help them maintain social
equilibrium." Carle C. Zimmerman—"When it is over I am going to be
almost purely a population theorist and family specialist, I have gradually been evolving that way over a number of years." Howard B.
Woolston summarizes an attitude expressed throughout in his succinct
statement—"Cultivate our garden with some attention to the threatening weather."

Culture and Adjustment   Some attention was directed in 1942 to
the particularized field of sociology which we might designate as culture
and adjustment. Leonard Bloom stated—"The studies which will claim
the bulk of my time in the next few years are—(1) the theory and
method of acculturation; (2) an investigation of the evacuation of the
Japanese and its influences on family organization which implements 1
above; (3) an investigation of American sociologists and the institutional
features of American sociology." While Elizabeth K. Nottingham stated
—"Problems especially connected with the individual and culture—a
psychosociological emphasis." Stuart A. Queen—"Stress cultural differences and similarities, conflict and accommodation in relation to very
concrete happenings of our world today. Cultural change, lags, and
resistances and their practical significance; propaganda and morale."
M. Wesley Roper—"Emphasize the significance of culture and social
relations in producing human nature with more than usual on the rights
and contributions of minority groups globally." Bernhard Stern—"Focus-
ing on problems on race and cultural contacts arising out of the war."

Social Processes   Clarence M. Case stated—"I stress the two concepts of social progress and social age or maturity, including their rela-

tionship one to the other. I lay considerable stress upon the idea of social age, social growth, social infantility, all of which apply to persons and social imbecility which represents the kind of behavior which groups attain in consequent of the social infantility of their members." J. Stewart Burgess—"Stress the meaning of the democratic process." While Emory S. Bogardus stated—"A further analysis of the processes of social life, what they are, how they are interrelated, and what does a comprehension of them mean for social improvement and for the solving of social problems." C. E. Gehlke—"Social change,—how slow it is." L. L. S. Garwood—"The acceleration of social trends which led to the present turmoil, an awareness of our ethnocentric judgments, and the importance of the sociological attitude toward world problems." W. H. Heinmiller and Gerald M. McMinn seem to agree with Edgar Schuler who stated—"I think sociologists need to be concerned with the problem of social processes, how to develop an international structure which will arouse emotional identification changes other than national feelings and loyalty, it is a big order."

Organization and Disorganization. While there is considerable overlapping in some of the fields in which sociologists felt emphasis would be placed, some distinctions are clear. Ruth S. Cavan—"I am not teaching sociology at present, but if I were I think I would emphasize social organization and disorganization with a view to giving an understanding of present problems and a grasp of the social reorganization that must follow the war." F. E. Detweiller, Ernest B. Harper, Lloyd B. Ballard and T. C. McCormick agreed on emphasizing social control and social reorganization. While N. L. Sims particularly felt that sociological knowledge should be focalized on world post war reorganization. This was likewise agreed to by Sanford Winston.

In 1945 Edwin H. Sutherland summarized the established principles in this field[6] by stating: (1) social pathology has come to be defined in relativistic rather than in absolustic terms; (2) it is being explained in abstract principles rather than by heterogeneous multiple factors; (3) it is being studied principally as a condition of society, characterized by conflicts of values, rather than as classes of personal behavior. He felt that approximate consensus had been reached regarding the following points: (a) the social scientist makes the appraisal of any social unit, (b) the criteria used by the social scientist in appraising a social unit are the internal inconsistencies in that unit, as a result of which common objectives are relatively lacking, (c) these internal inconsistencies may be of two kinds, namely, anomie, or lack of internal organization, and conflicting social organizations within the unit, (d) it is

[6] *The American Journal of Sociology,* Vol. L, No. 6, pp. 429-435.

further agreed that relativity of social pathology has been recognized from the beginning and that persons engaged in these fields are not interested in every inconsistency or conflict of values in society, but have used in general practice a criteria based on the number of persons involved or the intensity of the conflict.

Far East and the Pacific. While extensive studies had been made for a long time of Asiatic and Pacific areas, at this particular period the sociological problems of the Far East, which needed emphasis, were particularly found in the writings of Jesse Steiner in his 1942 book *Behind the Japanese Mask,* the writings of George P. Murdock, W. C. Smith, and the studies of Carle C. Zimmerman. While many sociologists indicated this interest, the attitude was shown in a carping criticism made about me to the university authorities because I had stated that by 1952 the Far Eastern situation would loom up as important as the problems of Europe.

Latin American Sociology A new approach began to be shown in some of our universities by the introduction of sociology courses dealing with Latin America. L. L. Bernard set the pace for this interest. Others who either emphasized Latin America or gave courses dealing with Latin American life and living conditions included J. H. S. Bossard, Clarence Case, Maurice Davie, Hornell Hart, Guy B. Johnson, and M. C. Elmer. Maurice Davie felt the need particularly for stressing his particular area and Latin America.

The Sociology of Education This field had reached a rather high point in the 20's, but now twenty years later, 1942, the outstanding exponents of the field were Charles C. Peters who said—"After dealing with a definition of education in terms of practiced behaviors, and with the technique of the democratized school and other educational features, I made an analysis of the meaning of democracy, the lag between our ideals of democracy and present attainment, the nature of the social revolution that is going on, the problem of social control in a democratic society, the problem of demogogy and of constructive leadership, and the possibility of telic progress. I think these are the most important issues of the present day so far as my area of activity is concerned." Lloyd Allan Cook felt that radical changes are now underway in school program with particular attention being given to local community needs and services. Nathaniel Cantor—"The interest of a dynamic sociology of education and the dynamics of learning which is an attempt to integrate the fields of social theory, mental hygiene, and social case work techniques."

Applied Sociology Kimball Young keynoted this grouping by stating—"(1) there will likely be a far greater demand on the practical and applied aspects of sociology. Much of our research will arise out of direct questions asked of us by policy-makers and program-makers. I look for a continued expansion of governmental controls. And we face some danger that the objectivity we now have—which is not too great—may be considerably reduced. It is important to keep general sociology as 'free' in the sense of systematic formulation as possible; (2) as to social psychology, the same thing applies so far as applied work is concerned. There will be more work on public opinion and leadership especially." Raymond Hightower—"We must explain social organization so that it can be understood by the people. Sociologists must help plan society not just describe who does what. Very probably we shall have to make some unpleasant reports of post war democracy." Alvin Good—"Felt we needed to attempt to find methods of applying sociological principles of living in groups to the type of social living that will exist after the war. He further stated that it would be interesting to compare what may be of special interest in the new future and note how the outcome of the war may change our interests."

Social Work which had been a dominant emphasis in many departments of sociology after World War I had by 1942 become recognized to a large extent as a professional field requiring considerable understanding of sociology but not an immediate goal of sociology. On the other hand, occupational sociology and the beginnings of industrial sociology began to be emphasized by A. J. Todd, Frank D. Watson, and N. P. Gist who felt that here was a field that had been unduly neglected by sociologists. Political sociology which had received some enthusiastic interests during the 30's was almost unobserved as the echoes of the first battle of the war began to reach the university campus. Similarly, other fields of emphasis in the field of sociology which at time had reached rather large proportions were mentioned by only a few individuals such as, Rural Employment by W. A. Anderson, and T. L. Harris. Change of values and problems of personality by J. H. Barnett, Howard Becker, John Dollard, Emory Bogardus, and John F. Cuber and some discouragement regarding sociology by Seba Eldridge and Hines.

The period covered in this chapter is of particular significance. Sociology had had fifty years of extensive acceptance and trial. The general area had been established and its many facets had received consideration. We had just passed through a world war, the resulting period of adjustment. This was followed by a major period of economic depression, and the introduction of many aspects of sociological thinking into our social life and structure. On all fronts of the world a second great war had burst forth. Every type of suggestion and proposal was being advocated by persons in political power, by educators and leaders of all kinds. The question arose,—"What proposals and plans do sociologists have in this major crisis?" The answers indicated that instead of becoming panicky, the general consensus was to work harder and more diligently along the lines that had been developing in the past. There was no feeling that the emphasis of the past had been incorrect, but rather that the past efforts had indicated the direction of future work; that the concepts and the application of sociological principles of the past had pointed the direction in which there must be greater concentration and research in the period ahead.

The actual statements cited in this summary are of greater significance than any analysis of a few especially selected articles would be in giving an actual picture of the direction of thinking in this period of our history. It gives us the wide coverage which includes not only the most articulate and best known sociologists, but in addition those who, while they may not have written anything on the subject concerned, were actually by their extensive contacts helping to formulate the ideas and practices of many thousands of persons.

The first apparent effects of World War II appeared in a greater intensification of effort and more careful attempts to measure each phase of sociological inquiry and of the general understanding of social life. Probably the most significant result, however, was that World War II prepared the way for a degree of social understanding never before reached among so widely distributed peoples. Sociological concepts which were formerly thought of as applying to relatively local areas were now recognized as having world-wide application. Social motivations, social controls, and social processes were being recognized as basic phenomena among all human beings by thousands of persons who had never heard of sociology.

XIII

A Period of Readjustment

THE development of social thought cannot be blocked off chronically by any sharp lines of demarcation. The best that can be done is call attention to increased concentration of emphasis on certain aspects at different periods of time. After a rather extensive development and acceptance of concepts, there began to be increased analysis and wide understanding of the application of specific concepts within new areas. During the second quarter of the twentieth century, and particularly after 1940 much was done along this line. It was sometimes mistaken for a mere repetition of principles already established. Actually, however, what was occuring was further development and clarification of sociological theory, and the apparent emphasis on side lines and on specific concepts was pushing a frontal action by concentration on areas which general social change made ready for study. The status of sociological theory was much advanced during this period, and its use in further understanding and analysis of the social structure and organization increased.

When a system of thought has been accepted for some time, facts, opinions, wishes, and usage become more or less confused. Because of general social progress or social change, there are additional facets added to the social structure which modify the interactions and consequent functioning of society. Social theory thus needs to be re-evaluated from time to time. This is accomplished by the concentration upon particular aspects which are brought into focus by a new combination of circumstances. It represents a process which is going on continually. In the succeeding pages attention will be called to a few such trends in order to indicate what is occuring in the development of social thought.

In summarizing fifty years of sociological theory, Robert K. Merton stated, "The phrase 'sociological theory' has been used to refer to at least six types of analyses which differ significantly in their bearings on empirical research. These are methodology, general orientations, conceptual analysis, post factum interpretations, empirical generalizations, and sociological theory."[1]

Herbert Blumer has called attention to three types of social theory of which he has particularly emphasized the third form "which stands or

---

[1] *The American Journal of Sociology*, Vol. L, No. 6, May 1945, p. 462.

presumes to stand as a part of empirical science,"[2] The first kind of social theory mentioned is one that "seeks to develop a meaningful interpretation of the social world or of some significant part of it." The aim of this kind of social theory being to help people have a clearer understanding of their world, of its possibilities of development, and directions along which it may move. "There is a need for meaningful clarification of basic social values, social institutions, modes of living and social relations." "Most social theory," says Blumer, "of the past and a great deal in the present is wittingly or unwittingly of this interpretative type." The second kind of social theory mentioned was termed "policy" theory. "It is concerned with analyzing a given social situation, or social structure, or social action as a basis for policy or action." The third, in which the aim of theory is to develop analytical schemes of the empirical world, with which the given science is concerned . . . theoretical schemes are essentially proposals as to the nature of such classes and of their relations where this nature is problematic or unknown." "Such proposals become guides to the investigation to see whether they or their implications are true . . . Theory, inquiry, and empirical fact are interwoven in a texture of operation with theory guiding inquiry, inquiry seeking and isolating facts, and facts affecting theory."

Viewed as an empirical science, "social theory in general shows grave shortcomings. Its divorcement from the empirical world is glaring. To a preponderant extent it is compartmentalized into a world of its own, inside of which it feeds on itself. We usually localize it in separate courses and separate fields. For the most part it has its own literature. Its lifeline is primarily exegesis—a critical examination of prior theoretical schemes, the compounding of portions of them into new arrangements, the translation of old ideas into a new vocabulary, and the occasional addition of a new notion as a result of reflection on other theories. It is remarkably susceptible to the importation of schemes from outside its own empirical field, as in the case of the organic analogy, the evolutionary doctrine, physicalism, the instinct doctrine, behaviorism, psychoanalysis, and the doctrine of the conditioned reflex. Further, when applied to the empirical world social theory is primarily an interpretation which orders the world into its mold, not a studious cultivation of empirical facts to see if the theory fits. In terms of both origin and use social theory seems in general not to be geared into its empirical world."

He further stated that, "Social theory is conspicuously defective in its guidance of research inquiry. It is rarely couched in such form

[2] Blumer, Herbert, "What is Wrong With Social Theory," *American Sociological Review,* February 1954, Vol. 19, No. 1, pp. 1-10. Paper read at the annual meeting of the American Sociological Society, August, 1953.

as to facilitate or allow directed investigation to see whether it or its implications are true. Thus, it is gravely restricted in setting research problems, in suggesting kinds of empirical data to be sought, and in connecting these data to one another. Its divorcement from research is as great as its divorcement from its empirical world."

The relation between applied research and social theory and the bearing of empirical research upon the development of social theory was presented by Merton.[3] "Ideally constructed relations between scientific theory and applied research. Basic theory embraces key concepts (Variables and constants), postulates, theorems and laws. Applied science consists simply in ascertaining (a) the variables relevant to the problem in hand, (b) the values of the variables and (c) in accordance with previous knowledge, setting forth the uniform relationships between these variables."

"Perhaps the most striking role of conceptualization in applied social research is its transformation of practical problems by introducing concepts which refer to variables overlooked in the common-sense view of the policy-maker. At times, the concept leads to a statement of the problem diametrically opposed to that of the policy-maker.

The work of systematization should always parallel first-level research. The more facts the field researcher turns up, the more material is available for the systematizer to weave into his system; and the more the system is developed, the more significant and crucial are the problems that the systematizer can turn over to the researcher for empirical investigation. Systematization and first-hand research should proceed together and the relations between them should be mutually advantageous.[4]

The development of sociology implies the building of all its aspects and propositions into an effective system. This is a necessary phase of scientific procedure. "A system of sociology," states Furfey,[5] "is not merely to be conceived mentally; it has also to be presented to others, and presented in such a form that its logical structure will be recognizable." The latter result is attained through formalization. When the science is properly formalized it becomes relatively easy to detect and remedy weaknesses. Therefore, the process can be extremely helpful in perfecting systematic sociology. Indeed, a greater degree of intelligent formalization is perhaps the most pressing current need of the science.[6]

[3] Merton, Robert K., *American Sociological Review,* Oct. 1948, pp. 505-515, and *Philosophy of Science,* Vol. 16, No. 3, 1949, p. 178.

[4] *The Scope and Method of Sociology,* Furfey, Paul Hanley; Harper Brothers, New York, 1953, p. 499.

[5] Furfey, Paul Hanley, *The Scope and Method of Sociology,* Harper Brothers, New York ,1953, p. 509.

[6] See also Phelps and Stafford, "Criteria of a Systematic Society, *American Sociological Review,* 1939, p. 388.

There have been a number of areas which have received particular attention. This was in part due to the tremendous growth in the means of communication and transportation. New contacts were made at a rate which would have confused the imagination at the beginning of the twentieth century. Social processes which occurred over an extended period of time and permitted gradual growth and integration occurred in a fraction of time formerly required. Decisions had to be made on a few minutes notice. New social contacts were made which demanded a backlog of experience and understanding. This significance of many of the established concepts required new interpretation, new application, and re-integration. The significance of social integration, of social stratification, public opinion, propaganda, and the concepts of social adjustment, social needs and social control required re-interpretation. The activity in social thinking which took place could be likened to the movement of a big wagon wheel—concentration on one part of it seemed to indicate movement in one direction. Concentration on another part indicated the opposite direction. Actually, the movement was forward, on dead-center, or along the ground. The re-emphasis on social integration is an example of consideration which, since World War II has played an important part in revamping our thinking in many aspects of sociological thought. This, however, is not a new concept. Hsun Tzu, a Confucian scholar in the third century B.C., in his Essay on the Princely Institution stated:

> Man cannot live apart from the group. In a group, absence of assigned status will lead to struggle. Struggle will lead to chaos. Chaos will lead to separation between the individuals. Separation will lead to the weakening of society, which in turn will cause the failure to conquer nature, there will not be even houses to live in or food to sustain us. Hence not for a moment can we abandon rituals and righteousness to define social status.

Integration

Sociological thinking has long recognized the designation of concerted interests in any particular line as a group interest. The concepts group, social group, and interest group were established early in sociological analysis. The interrelation of group and group activities, whether expressed as group consciousness or even as the social processes, was somewhat slower in becoming an established concept. Charles H. Cooley, Clarence Case and others did much to clarify thinking along this line in the decade following World War I. Before the advent of extensive communication and rapid transportation, the social order tended to be relatively stable. The established groups met most of the interest needs. But with the rapid increase of population and the extensive intermingling of large numbers of people with diverse cultural backgrounds, new interest groups were formed. The rapid expansion into different forms of industrialization, such as expansion of the local blacksmith-wagon shop to a gigantic automotive assembly plant, gave rise to numerous other groups. The resulting cultural lag, gave rise to fear of social disintegration as the fearful ghost foreshadowing the future. But, the addition of these new group interests to the old forms of the family, the church, the school, and the shop did not mean disintegration. It did give rise to the need for a new understanding and a greater necessity for social integration. The old type small community with its localized control based upon tradition and stimulated by gossip did begin to disintegrate. More extended lines of communication reached out and pulled together widely separated elements into new interest groups. The temporary confusion caused by these new lines of interest tended, for a time, to confuse the picture until the integrated pattern of influence began to take form like a completed spiderweb. Thus the need for not only a recognition of integration but of the effective functioning of integrated forces began to take form. "Sociology is concerned with social organization and disorganization, the social structure and the social processes involved in social relationships. This relationship is not limited to mere dependence of individuals and groups upon each other. Social relationships which consist of business relations, professional services, and meeting each other's educational and religious needs may not include a further social phenomenon which consists of the various degrees and processes of persons becoming identified with a group. This identification may take various forms. Until the processes involved reach the stage where actual welding into a cohesive whole begins to take place there is merely association or adjustment. The stage in the social process where diverse units begin to harmonize and unify into a new homogeneous culture is the keynote in a sociological structure. This is the beginning of social integration."[7]

Integration which involves the welding together of the persons identified as a group must have certain common values recognized and accepted. Integration may take many forms. Sorokin calls attention to four types: (a) spatial or mechanical adjacency, (b) association due to an external factor, (c) causal or functional integration, and (d) internal or logico-meaningful unity.

"An integrated society, as we have been discussing it, is in some respects a moral community. Its members have at least a few ultimate values in common. No matter how many individualized ends, whether like or unlike, are being pursued, there must be some qualities of life

[7] *Social Integration: A Study of 275 Families and 172 Individuals in the Pittsburgh Area in an Attempt to Determine Some Basic Factors Which Contribute to Social Integration* by Strong, Anne E.

that all respect and wish to have maintained. One cannot specify the number of strands of moral community there must be to produce a society that is satisfactorily integrated, but it is obvious that it need not be many. So long as there are a few broad objectives, which all unite in seeking, the rest of the social structure may be adapted to them in some organized way. Most of the ends and values of individuals may be divergent, and still the society will hang together, if there is a common core with which these divergent ends and values are not inconsistent."[8]

Even in a highly integrated society there exist different values and conflicting emphasis on what is of most significance. This is a basis for social change and is essential to the life of society to avoid deterioration.

As shown by Sims, the development of the concept of social change and fear of deterioration was found even in primitive man and his fearful attitude of change, making him unduly cautious and fearful, and that among the ancient writings generally found was the conclusion that social change tended to lead from 'good to bad and from bad to worse.' Sims calls attention to the lost paradise doctrine which had held vogue in the Orient. The hopelessness of continued deterioration was relieved somewhat by the belief of ultimate intervention of the gods, which gave rise to a reversal of the process and the beginning of another cycle. The elaboration of the early ideas and the development in a concept of indefinite progress which could be viewed as an upward climb to civilization was not clearly formulated until relatively modern times.[9] "Change is today viewed as continuous and inevitable, but not as general progress, nor certain advancement along any line. Neither is it held to be certain deterioration. There is a growing belief that much movement is cyclical. On the whole it is seen as constant alteration with the direction partially determined by man himself and partially under control of forces within the social situation that have not yet been subjugated to conscious social purpose."

Charles S. Johnson has thus expressed certain aspects of the ideas of integration and disintegration:

"When peoples of different cultures come together, there is acculturation, in which there is a constant struggle between integration and disintegration. Basically this is education. Education, thus, is more than the transmission of culture from one generation to another. It is this transmission and it is also transformation of peoples who are more or less in conflict. Under these circumstances the whole process may

[8] Angell, Robert Cooley, *The Integration of American Society, A Study of Groups and Institutions;* McGraw-Hill Book Co., New York and London, 1941, p. 19.
[9] Sims, Newell LeRoy, *The Problem of Social Change,* Thomas Y. Crowell Co., 1939, Ch. 1, pp. 3-27.

become painful, because it may lead to the disintegration of the culture of one or more of the groups in contact. Technical knowledge can be transmitted with relative ease. Ideas are more difficult to communicate. Implicit in the process of acculturation is solidarity of the society. In times of change, as in the present, the moral solidarity of the society may be undermined. One aspect of acculturation appears in the con-stant struggle to get a new society and a new solidarity."[10] And finally as a vehicle for integration, Angell calls attention to institutions. "Of great importance for the integration of a large society are institutions. Common values are much strengthened if they are implemented by structures. Common orientation is likely to be ineffective if it remains merely a state of mind; it gains power in proportion as it is precipitated in institutions. If our democratic values are to integrate our society, for instance, it is necessary to have them expressed in forms to which the people can feel loyal and toward which they can behave with respect."

"Institutions are systems of social relationship to which people feel loyal because these systems are judged to embody the ultimate values that these people have in common. They are therefore expressive of moral community. Their acceptance need not be rational or conscious; it is often traditional or emotional. This is obviously true of such long-established institutions as the family."[11]

Social Control and Public Opinion

The subject of social control of public opinion has played an important part in sociological thinking since the beginning of the cen-tury. In fact, since Ward's *Psychic Aspects of Civilization* and the contributions of Schaeffle, LeBon, Tarde and the early writings of E. A. Ross and Cooley, various aspects of social control have been important strands in the warp of social thinking. During the late '20's and '30's, increased emphasis was being placed upon the part played by conscious social control by propaganda and the resultant public opinion. Illustra-tive of such writings as previously mentioned have been such special books as Lumley's *The Means of Social Control and Propaganda Menace*, L. L. Bernard's *Social Control*, and John Albig's work on *Public Opinion*. The use of polls for the measure of public opinion appeared with increasing frequency. At first chiefly for the purpose of molding public opinion, but gradually improved to the point where effective standards were established for the securing of reliable samples.

[10] Johnson, Charles S., Editor, *Education and the Cultural Process*, reprinted from *The American Journal of Sociology*, Vol. XLVIII, No. 6, May, 1943. "Education and the Cultural Process: Introduction to Symposium."

[11] Angell, Robert Cooley, *The Integration of American Society, A Study of Groups and Institutions*, McGraw-Hill Book Co., Inc., New York and London, 1941, pp. 24-25.

230 CONTEMPORARY SOCIAL THOUGHT

Richard T. LaPiere presented in an effective manner characteristics of particular types of groups, crowds, and sections of our population and in 1954 has brought the whole subject up to date, bringing together the theories of sociology and social psychology and reacting from a frequently expressed idea that man's determined course of action is by the effect of mass communication and propaganda.

Professor R. L. Finney raised the question whether that proportion of the population represented by the average man and the considerable proportion less than average can be taught to think fruitfully about social issues. He indicates in his book that when the average man does state worthwhile truths, he is repeating statements. "The truth seems to be that a mere echo is the best which can ever be expected from the duller half of the population," and he further states, "It is not enough that we teach children to think, we must actually force feed them with the concentrated results of expert thinking." This is a point over which considerable controversy arose but it is a significant trend in the area of propaganda of material. Albig in his very effective volume on *Public Opinion* states that "If the common man can achieve enough insight into the propaganda process, he can thwart the special pleader who is advocating causes not in the general interest . . . the propagandist is himself ruled and limited by his social miliu, and a part of that environment is the alertness, intelligence and critical ability of the publics with which he operates. Although propaganda is pervasive and will be persistent, it need not be fatal to intelligent public decisions."

Kingsley Davis[12] has clearly stated the scope and meaning of the term "the public." "Unlike the crowd, the public is a dispersed group. Except in the case of small isolated communities, it never meets together. Its interaction must take place through indirect media—through long chains of private conversations, through rumor, gossip, news, via press, radio, newsreel, and television. Such indirect media enable the public to have a far larger membership than any crowd could have. In fact, one can imagine a great world public comparable in breadth of information and strength of cohesion to the public of a single nation today. Yet, as a result of its size and dispersion the public cannot exhibit the milling process, the sharp focus, the emotional intensity, and the impulsive unanimity of the crowd. It is hardly an acting group at all but more of a feeling and thinking group—hence the linkage of "public" with "opinion." Any action by the public is done through representatives or through separate individual acts such as voting."

The term public opinion, while extensively used for a long time, is an example of how a general concept may be established, but which

[12] Davis, Kingsley, Human Society, The MacMillan Company, 1949, pp. 356-361.

gradually grows as well as comes into clearer focus. The over-all mass communication makes possible a mass culture which rises above the sub-culture which is found in a hetergeneous population and which is fur-ther complicated by a wide diversification of interests and activities. Bennet and Tumin state that "As these culture differences intersect and influence one another, a great deal of change occurs. This creates a tendency in the direction of one general, overall mass culture exampli-fied by such patterns as are found in advertising, the movies, public lectures and the like."[13] Thus, public opinion represents broad zones of attitude similarity. Informed propaganda in the form of the expression of values which are generally accepted as a part of American life is found not only in the editorials, sermons, and literature, of our times, but also in advertising of anything from a breakfast food to a vacation trip or from a house to a can of beer.

Lee calls attention to the fact that both scientific conclusions and purely imaginative ideas may be woven into propaganda. He defines propaganda: "Propaganda is thus the expression of a contention overtly set forth or covertly implied in order to influence the attitudes and, through attitudes, the opinions and actions of a public. It is one of the key instruments of power seekers."[14] Progress is the social control of propaganda and its effect upon public opinion is definitely moving forward. In one of his last books, Edward A. Ross made the following statement: "Resentment of any manipulative or tampering with the truth and stern demand for strict fidelity to fact in all declarations and utterances addressed to the public are, no doubt, more general to-day than ever before."[15]

Industrial Sociology

Another example of recent attempts to make a re-application of sociological concepts and to attempt new social evaluations is industrial sociology. When the industrialization of society reached the point where a major shift began to take place in the established social order, the need for adjustment and correction became evident. This reached a high point by the end of the first quarter of the nineteenth century when Robert Owen at New Lanark, in addition to modifying the hours and conditions of labor, particularly of young children, became con-cerned with the problem of unemployment, of establishing schools and encouraging a system of cooperation. In fact, Parliament influenced by

[13] Bennet, John W. and Tumin, Melvin M., *Social Life,* Alfred A. Knopf, 1948 p. 230.
[14] Lee, Alfred McClung, *How to Understand Propaganda,* Rinehart and Com-pany, Inc., New York and Toronto, 1952, p. 18.
[15] Ross, E. A., *New-Age Sociology,* D. Appleton and Company, 1940, pp. 488-489.

CONTEMPORARY SOCIAL THOUGHT

the agitation of Owen and others passed some of the first significant factory legislation in 1818. Welfare work for employees was found in individual cases throughout the nineteenth and the first quarter of the twentieth century. Boettiger defined 'employee welfare work' as "Voluntary effort of the employer, in excess of the requirements of law, of the market, or of custom, directed toward the improvement of employment practices."

Labor groups and labor organizations began to concentrate on the improvement of industrial organization, both within particular areas or occupations and within inter-group processes. Sometimes such efforts were more or less concerted, but frequently occurred only where disagreement or irritation had reached a point of conflict. This in a more general way has been extensively supported and supplemented by legislation prohibiting gross maladjustments and by various types of social security legislation such as unemployment, sickness, and old age insurance. This was first introduced in individual states, but eventually was made a national policy.

To a very large extent meeting particular situations is still the case and as a consequence much of the efforts to stabilize our industrial organizations is still carried on by groups and individuals whether labor or management or by the government in spot-patching within specific settings. Thus, in spite of the increased inter-relationship of all group activities, the even tenor of the functioning of industrial society is still disrupted by hundreds of small units seeking a personal advantage. We are still largely at the primitive stage suggested by two neighbors who disagree over a line fence and establish a seige over each other which will prevent either of them from using his ranch equipment until one gives in. One of them may have a herd of cattle that need to be fed or watered and is forced to give up. The settlement of the line fence controversy is not based upon any sociological principles or upon any other facts. If one protests against that method of settling a disagreement, one is still answered by the statement, 'But the system followed gets results.' Industrial sociology carries with it the germ of a new and broader approach. "Industrial sociology[16] as a field of study may be considered as being an inclusive whole which contains all industrial relationships, each of which consists of a complex of work situations." ". . . A sociological study of industry in order to have practical value must give us the basic principles underlying adjustment as well as causes of conflict. There has been a tendency to confine research activities of industrial sociology to the provision of remedial machinery for eruptions, conflict, and class antagonism. Industrial sociology must go farther than

[16] Elmer, Glaister A., "Industrial Sociology," *The Journal of Educational Sociology*, November 1950, pp. 144-146.

"repairing plaster which continues to fall within the structure." It must attempt to find basic, underlying causes rather than specific factors found in isolated instances or circumstances which apply to special lines of work. In short, industrial sociology is concerned with the process of association and adjustment which is necessary in the formation of the group. It is, however, likewise concerned with the "consciousness," identification, co-hesiveness and harmony of the factors of any phenomenon. It is this latter concern of sociology which seems to be of significant value when studying industrial research and experimental projects."

It was not until the late 1940's that there was much concentrated effort to develop a sociological approach to this field. Within the last ten years there has been a very extensive amount of careful study made of the subject, and the indications are that industrial sociology will add to the core substance of sociology much basic interpretation even as rural sociology has done in the past thirty years. While not in any way all inclusive, the following persons are representative of the contributors within this recent development: Elton Mayo, W. L. Warner and J. O. Low, W. F. Cottrell, Paul Meadows, Herbert Blumer, D. C. Miller and W. H. Form, W. H. Whyte, Jr., W. E. Moore, and many others.

Social Stratification

In a rapidly changing society almost unlimited variations among men appear. The differences which are most obvious relate to material wealth, occupations, and social, political or other roles played by individuals. The status of individuals placed on less easily observed values are sometimes too far removed from immediate considerations and sometimes it would be embarrassing to call attention to them. The study of social stratification has become an area of extended interest because of the expectation that it will reveal the basis for group action and the growth of an awareness of group interrelationship.

"Research on social stratification in American sociology has tended to deal primarily with the relations between the position of individuals in the social hierarchy and their behavior in various areas of life such as crime, religion, family relations, politics . . . it has accumulated a wealth of data on the differences between various social strata. . . . Much of this research is interesting and important, but it is not . . . cumulative either theoretically or methodologically."[17] A typical example of the reason for increased interest in stratification is illustrated by changes in population status. Lewis Corey states that while the working class multiplied six times from 1870-1940, the middle class as a whole multiplied eight times and the *new middle class* sixteen times. This new

---

[17] Reinhard Bendix and Seymour Martin Lipset, *Class, Status and Power*, The Free Press, Glencoe, Illinois, 1953. p. 15.

middle class growth is based upon increasing demand for technical employees for greater number of clerical employees and managerial personnel. The old middle class, which was largely based upon a widespread
ownership of small independent holdings has been pushed aside by the
development of modern industrialism, but the middle class status is now
composed of the above mentioned types. The basis for determining
class varies in different areas. For example, in Venezuela, the difference
between the middle class and the lower class is determined not so much
by the economic standard as by the cultural standard. The economic
change is more rapid than the cultural change; consequently there are
many individuals who on the basis of property and income may be rated
as middle class but who still are held down by the cultural lag. In the
Venezuelan middle class the cultural factor more than the economic
factor determines the social strata. The cultural factor moves an individual of the lower to the middle class even though the economic factor
is significant in placing an educated person of the middle class to the
upper class. In short, a "cultural" individual can be in the middle class
or in the "elite," whereas an "uncultured" individual could not be
accepted by the middle class even though his economic status was adequate. There is still the carry over in Venezula of the old empirical
classes called "well-bred" and "common."

In the development of a system of sociology or in fact of any field
of study, it is first necessary to establish a logical overall relationship
of the various concepts involved. The first major struggle of sociologists
included a variety of concepts in explaining general social organization,
disorganization, and the social processes concerned. Thus, while there
was a considerable amount of discussion of the general concepts in the
early years running through the works of Ward, Ratzenhofer, Gumplowicz, Small, Sumner, Giddings, and Cooley, relatively little appeared
for a considerable period of the major concepts as a system. However, in
the period from 1930 interest began to develop and Kingsley Davis
recognized the need to clarify the concept of stratification and restate
some basic principles.[18] Particularized concepts such as social control,
social forces, social contract, social conflict, and many others dominated
the field of discussion for certain periods. Each of those in their particular heyday were discussed from such a wide range of approaches that
on the one hand it gave the impression of confusion and on the other
reached a point of far-fetched attempts to use the concept in order to
attract attention. However, out of this apparently chaotic state there
usually has emerged a relatively clear-cut understanding of the concept

[18] "Conceptional Analysis of Stratification," *American Sociological Review*, June
1942, Ch. 7, pp. 309-321; "Some Principles of Stratification," *American
Sociological Review*, April 1945, Ch. 10, pp. 242-249.

and its use has become of great value in understanding social relationships. We need not be disturbed over the statement which may have
much truth in it, as made by Harold W. Pfautz[19] regarding stratification. "Probably no area of current sociological interest suffers so much
from the disease of over conceptualization." Pfautz has classified the
333 articles and books which have appeared under the subjection of
social stratification under the following headings.

I. Conceptualization and Theory
    A. Social Stratification
    B. Status and Class

II. Methodology
    A. Class Delineation and Placement
    B. Socioeconomic Status, etc.
    C. Methodological Studies
    D. Mobility

III. Empirically Oriented Studies
    A. Types of Units Stratified
    B. Dimensions of Class Analysis

He states that: "Finally, however, it can be fairly stated that, in
spite of the lack of consensus which has been reported regarding the
theories, methods, and results of empirical studies (in addition to the
barrage of criticisms which have been leveled at these materials,) at least
two promising notes are struck. On the one hand, the period 1945-52
can perhaps be interpreted as experimental from the perspective of both
methods and concepts. And, on the other, the tendency in the most
recent contributions has been precisely to clarify the theoretical and
methodological issues which have been precipitated by the materials. It
is to be hoped that these two trends will converge to provide designs for
productive research."

Paul K. Hatt attempted to show that the apparent "chaotic state"
in the study of social stratification was less extensive than might be
superficially assumed. He claimed that if the varying theoretical and
empirical materials are placed in any sort of sensible order, the materials
tend to converge. He listed the chief sources of difficulty as follows:[20]
"(1) terms, (2) whether the determinants of stratification are subjective or objective, (3) whether class is classificatory or substantive,
(4) the variety of institutional matrices within which stratification occurs, and (5) the question as to the extent to which stratification is to

[19] "The Current Literature on Social Stratification: Critique and Bibliography,"
The American Journal of Sociology, Vol. LVIII, No. 4, January 1953, pp.
391-418.
[20] Hatt, Paul K., "Stratification in the Mass Society," *American Sociological
Review,* Vol. XV, No. 2, April 1950, p. 216, 218.

be regarded as occuring on the local community level and the extent to which it is to be seen on the level of the mass society."

"If, then, the problem of nomenclature is temporarily ignored and the questions of subjective-objective and classificatory-substantive conceptualizations are deferred for subsequent consideration, it is possible to summarize the problems in stratification theory in a sentence or two. There are six (or perhaps more, if institutional contexts in addition to those listed by Weber are chosen) possible orders within which stratification develops. These may be seen as a paradigm containing Weber's three orders of stratification, each one of which in turn may be viewed as existing on either the level of the local group or the level of the secondary society. This paradigm can serve as a frame of reference within which to examine alternative formulations."

Hatt has suggested as procedures for determining stratification in mass society: (1) solution by correlation which takes note of single factor indexes and multiple factor indexes, (2) solution by summation dealing with analysis by role and status and by community reputational analysis. In connection with this may be listed W. Lloyd Warner who has called attention to six methods for obtaining information in the classification.[21] (1) Rating by matched agreements, (2) rating by symbolic placement, (3) rating by status reputation, (4) rating by comparison, (5) rating by simple assignment to a class and, (6) rating by institutional membership; and a third approach, the relationship between community reputational analysis and solution by correlation.

"In short," states Hatt, "Warner's recent work has opened up the possibilities of greater agreement in the field of stratification through its indication of the validity of a multiple factor or even a single factor index based upon values which can be applied both within the local community and the mass society."

It is the general feeling that change in the system of stratification is slow and usually are resisted long after the functional requisites for a new order have been demonstrated. Cuber contends that stratification systems because they are deeply entrenched in the habit structure of people and in the codifications of law and government change, for the most part, slowly and undramatically.[22]

Cuber considers the following list of questions as basic when considering social stratification in the United States during the 1950's.

1. Is there a single American stratification system?

2. Does every person and/or family have a more or less clear position in the stratification system?

[21] Social Class in America, p. 37-38, 222.
[22] Cuber, John F. and Kenkel, William F., Social Stratification in the United States, Appleton-Century-Crofts, Inc., 1954, pp. 4, 12, 22-30.

3. Can we reach a conclusion relative to the truth or falsity of the American Dream as an explanation of social mobility in the United States?

4. Do the facts of stratification in the United States warrent the use of the term *social class* in the sense that the persons in each "class" are *objectively* "set off from" the persons in the other "classes"?

5. Is the American stratification system "functional" and, if so, in what sense?

6. What are some of the larger implications of the structure of power in American society? What attending issues have formed? How, and to what extent, are they being resolved?

7. What about class consciousness and class conflict in the United States? Do they exist? How are they manifest? What is their significance?

8. What negative judgments of the American stratification system can be made, using as a base for evaluation the *stated objectives* of American society?

9. What favorable factors in the system can be found, using the same criteria as in Question 8?

10. What imminent developments in the stratification system in the United States can we anticipate?

A statement regarding an interpretation and the variation in its usage of the term social class is presented by Cuber and Kenkel. They state, "Radical differences, to be sure, do exist in wealth, privilege, and possessions; but the differences seem to range along a continuum with imperceptible graduation from one person to another, so that no one can objectively draw 'the line' between the 'haves' and the 'have nots', the 'privileged' and 'underprivileged', or for that matter, say who is in 'the working class', who is 'the common man', or who is a 'capitalist'. The differences are not categorical, but continuous."

The point of view that the differences between individuals, groups and even classes are continuous, and in reality, and particularly that the concepts relative to stratification are not independent, but rather a part of general sociological theory, is further emphasized by Parsons.[23]

Talcott Parsons summarized the trend of thinking in social stratification: "The major point of reference both for the judgment of the generality of the importance of stratification, and for its analysis as a phenomenon, is to be found in the nature of the frame of reference in terms of which we analyze social action. We conceive action to be oriented to the attainment of goals, and hence to involve selective processes relative to goals. Seen in their relations to goals, then, all the

[23] Parsons, Talcott, "A Revised Analytical Approach to the Theory of Social Stratification," *Class, Status and Power*, Free Press, p. 93, 1953.

components of systems of action and of the situations in which action takes place, are subject to the process of evaluation, as desirable or un-desirable, as useful or useless, as gratifying or noxious. Evaluation in turn has, when it operates in the setting of social systems of action, two fundamental implications. First the units of systems, whether they be elementary unit acts or roles, collectivities, or personalities, must in the nature of the case be subject to evaluation."

"The second implication is the well-known one that it is a condition of the stability of social systems that there should be an integration of the value-standards of the component units to constitute a "common value-system."

Parson states further: "From the point of view of American society as a social system this problem leads us into the areas of "microscopic" variability of the social structure, since we have good evidence that the differences in which we are interested are only partly a function of the broad differences of class status of families. But in no way does this circumstance make it any less a sociological problem area than if we were attempting to explain only the broadest differences between mobility (or its lack) in the American system of stratification and in the caste system of India."

Identification of Social Classes. Richard Centers[24] states that social classes in their essential nature can be characterized as psychologically or subjectively based groupings defined by the allegiance of their mem-bers. The structure of the class is expressed by a common understanding of the members of the class of factors characteristics and attitudes com-mon to the individuals who compose the group. These constituent ten-dencies in the formation of social classes are the response of individuals to the whole complex situation of their lives, but are determined to a very large extent by their statuses and roles in getting a living.

The study of identification has been largely within the field of psychology, although identification as a social concept is becoming increasingly a problem of sociologists; the study of social phenomena has frequently been inadequate because of the attempt to deal with such phenomena from the viewpoint of individuals who make up the group. The recognition that identification is regulated by complex social factors is indicated by the statement of Sherif and Cantril, ". . . it is surprising that most psychologists investigating group problems have not often bothered to go out of their little worlds and examine the wealth of material already collected by sociologists.[25]

---

[24] Centers, Richard, The Psychology of Social Classes, Princeton University Press, Princeton, 1949.
[25] Sherif, Muzafer and Cantril, Hadley; The Psychology of Ego-Involvements, Wiley and Sons, New York, 1947, p. 283.

The import of identification as a social concept is summarized by G. A. Elmer:[26] "The social forces of group membership identification are dependent upon the social values and interest groups found within each situation. The psychologists have evidence to demonstrate an individual's identification with factors of his environment. The anthropologists have associated this identification with cultural phenomena. The sociologists have demonstrated that social identification is directed toward the social values of interest groups. These interest groups and their subsequent values cannot be dealt with apart from the total situation. Consequently, identification of persons with a particular situation is relative to their identification with all interest groups related to such a situation." The tendency toward increased stratification is directly effected by the intensity of identification of individuals with the class, role or status with which they are associated. Its relation to general sociological theory as stated by Parsons:[27] ". . . . the theory of stratification is not an independent body of concepts and generalizations which are only loosely connected with other parts of general sociological theory; it is general sociological theory pulled together with reference to a certain fundamental aspect of social systems. Such merits as the present analysis may possess are therefore overwhelmingly the product of advances in general theory which have made it possible to state and treat the problems of stratification in such a way as to bring to bear the major tools of general analysis upon them. It is above all the fact that we have much better general theory than a generation ago which makes a better understanding of stratification on a theoretical level possible, though of course in turn study of the problems of stratification has made a major contribution to the development of general theory."

In flying over a forested area one sees many things never known to be there: depressions, hills, variations in the density, vegetation, and in types of trees as effected by soil and drainage. Other things are seen only by walking through the area among the trees and through the underbrush. Two persons either flying or walking along somewhat different routes may report particular trends which vary. As time passes and the trails indicated by the pioneers, it may be found that while each was correct within its limitations, that continued observation, analysis and evaluations will eliminate many of the apparent, but minor differences and the actual phenomena will be obvious to all. New problems and the capacity to make more detailed analyses will appear and

[26] Elmer, Glaister A., "Identification as a Social Concept," *Sociology and Social Status and Power,* The Free Press, Glencoe, Illinois, 1953.
[27] Parsons, Talcott, "A Revised Analytical Approach to the Theory of Social Stratification," p. 127, Reinhard Bendix and Seymour Martin Lipset, *Class, Research,* Vol. 39, No. 2, 1954, pp. 101-109.

be met because of the preliminary surveys and the development of techniques of analysis and understanding of procedures which today are beyond the reach of our imagination.

XIV

Looking Ahead

THE SOCIOLOGIST of the second half of the twentieth century may look forward to an era as different from what has gone before as the production, manufacturing, and industrial activities of the future vary from those in the first half of this century. The future may be approached by a hopeful, forward looking attitude not based on a dream, but upon nearly a century of trial and error, of confusion, struggle, and success. The trend indicates the need for a further restatement of basic principles, which through the efforts, the experience, and growth of the past have become recognized generally as significant. We have moved from the area of controversy over basic and now generally accepted aspects of social action to the analysis of social interrelations and their resultant phenomena. The rapidity of change in social thinking is shown by the relocation of emphasis in less than two decades.

There will be little attempt to evaluate the current reactions, even though the actual recording of them is significant for later interpretation. There will be important articles and books which will later be used to show what were the trends of thought, but these will not take the place of actual statements by the people engaged in directing social thinking of this time.

In 1941 a poll was taken of about 200 sociologists throughout the country. They were asked what they considered to be the area of sociology upon which emphasis should be placed during the next decade. The results of this poll-taking which followed ten years of general depression and marked the beginning of World War II has been summarized in a previous chapter. After a decade and one-half another similar poll was taken. Most of the people who responded at an earlier date and were still living responded again. In addition there were many younger men included who had entered the field since World War II. The statements sent in were not meant to be comprehensive or even reasonably inclusive of their ideas. A number specifically indicated the difficulty of making a statement which would be at all fair. Two or three in answer to the question, "What should be the main emphasis of sociologists during the next decade?" wrote a letter of several pages. We have tried to summarize their statements, very probably, inadequately. One person answered, "I give up on this one," and another stated, "The only thing I long for is more wisdom, but that's like being in favor of virtue." However, there has been a very definite trend indicated which is decidedly different from the trend indicated before World War II.

The general emphasis was decidedly in preference of basic theory. In their own words we include here their opinions expressed in a succinct phrase, which is in most cases an exact quotation of their answers. W. A. Anderson—development of sound theoretical framework. Alvin H. Scaff—foundation of theory. Gordon W. Blackwell—working toward more basic general theories. William Peterson—development of basic theory. Jack H. Curtis—small groups and "low-middle range" theory—build theory from the ground up. Peter A. Munch—theory, not a special branch of sociology but in terms of a consistent body of theoretical knowledge. Harold W. Pfautz—test empirically propositions related to a systematic general sociology. Donald E. Walker—if the goal is to deepen the field, theory. If the aim is to attract favorable public attention and support, quantification and prediction.

The general trend suggested above is somewhat elaborated by the addition of a further explanatory statement when J. H. S. Bossard states—we must go back to basic principles of scientific method instead of checking hypotheses. C. H. Hamilton—better and more scientific methodology. Emphasis on service and application. Eugene V. Schneider—combining theory and research; elaborating a body of theory for its own sake as an end in itself, which will incorporate valid empirical findings. Burton W. Taylor—integration of theory and research. Kimball Young—systematic integration of theory and empirical research findings. Integration of work in sociology, psychology, and cultural anthropology. Wellman J. Warner—close articulation of research and theory. Emphasis upon further theoretical clarification. Closer tie-up between the academic and investigational interests of sociology and the development of applied areas. Ernest H. Schiedler—dynamics of group interaction, theory and research. Irwin Sanders—replication of research testing some of the "contending" theories. Carle C. Zimmerman—search for integration of theory and empiricism. Arthur L. Wood—the real integration of theory and empirical research. J. H. Kolb—tie together theory, research and service. Maurice R. Davie—emphasis by theorists on less philosophic and more realistic problems; emphasis by methodologists on problems of larger scope and greater significance. Alfred McClung Lee—development of more adequate sociological theory in forms usable by both liberal arts students and research technicians. H. Warren Dunham—testing predictions from theoretical models constructed in relation to aspects of social systems and behavioral systems. Edward W. Pohlman—refining concepts and meaning of terms and discovering the theoretical limits of scientific methods. Melvin

J. Williams—developing a sound methodology free from the neo-positivism that results in fads, in statistics, and research for research's sake. Lloyd E. Ohlin—the development and refinement of general sociological theories and concepts by research in specific problem areas. Adolph S. Tomars—consolidation of concepts and basic systematization of social theory. Fred R. Crawford—re-examination of theories of organization and disorganization in view of increasing body of empirical data. E. T. Hiller—emphasis should be upon the substantative content that has been crowded out by dogmas about interaction, positivism, quantification, abstractions, reduction, scientism, subjectivism, with all their cumulative and current inanimities. H. Ashley Weeks—testing empirically some of the basic theories. Improve research techniques and designs. Arthur Ely Prell—development of testable theory of society. A. B. Hollingshead—application of theory to practical problems of society, industry, business, medicine, laws. Charles P. Loomis—more functional theoretical framework. Stuart C. Dodd—model testing using hypotheses and control experiments to develop sociological laws. R. A. Polson—develop more testable theory. Ira L. Reiss—develop substantative theory and techniques. Frank L. Parks—getting together on fundamental concepts. Bring some sociology back from the trend to go off the "deep end" statistically. Edward A. Suchman—bring together theory and research. T. M. Newcomb—better and closer interdependence of theory and research. George E. Simpson—continue to bring sociological theories and empirical studies into closer relationship. Floyd M. House—integration of concepts, methods, theories; more use of research to determine validity and usefulness of concepts and theories. Calvin F. Schmid—more rigorous, systematic and empirically oriented theory. Leonard Z. Breen—codification of theory. Arnold M. Rose—closer integration of theory and research. Linton C. Freeman—systematically integrate sociological theory and research findings. James F. Short—the integration of theory and research, probably through development of "middle-range" theory and its testing. P. M. Houser—development and testing of theory of "middle-range." Quantification of variables and attributes with which we deal. Herbert Blumer—a development of a clearer and better analytical scheme rather than on research techniques. Howard Becker—more attention to value systems and social control. More attention to the use of history as data for sociology. F. F. Stephan—strengthening all fields particularly by scientific unification and clarification. Lewis Diana—emphasis on theory of social organization. John J. Cuber—formulating some adequate concept of the total field. We have fragmentized so much there is confusion. Francis R. Duffy—the production of usable principles. Martin H. Newmeyer—integration of theory and research. G. E.

Swanson—the development of social theory tied to empirical observa' tion. R. K. Merton summarizes the main emphasis which should be placed in sociology as technically oriented empirical researches in sociology.

The general uniformity of emphasis on clarifying and standardizing theory is more clearly evident than at any period in the past seventy-five years—a definite sign of approaching maturity in sociological thinking.

A large group placed more emphasis on research. In this area we likewise find a great clarification of objectives among those who answered. Stuart E. Queen—integration of results of separate empirical studies; information of major problems, retesting by experimental and other research procedures. Otis Dudly Duncan—more hard-headed quanta' tive research, and less yakety-yak about the several properties of social systems. Melvin Seman—doing significant research uncluttered by preoccupation with the technique or with "sociologese." William F. Kenkel—rigid empirical studies involving general populations. Leonard Broom—the raising and maintenance of professional standards and rigor in research and teaching. Russel R. Dynes—research within the context of larger theoretical schemes. James W. Wiggins—cross-cul' tural data in testing hypotheses. J. M. Simons—further efforts toward objectivity, attention to placement . . . use of sociological training and methodology. Sociologists are being squeezed out of some logical areas. Peter P. Lejins—research and stress in strict adherence to the rules of scientific method. W. A. Lunden—more meaningful research in impor' tant areas. Calvin F. Schmid—development of more rigorous and systematic theory, techniques and experimental methodology. Richard DeWors—development of all forms of research, not quantitative only, integration of empirical fact and theory. Thomas E. Lasswell—empirical research findings emerging sociological theory. James D. Tarver—con' centrate on basic research. Austin Vander Slice—more integration of research and principles and to their application related fields. A. R. Mangus—main emphasis should be on empirical research to establish general principles and to bridge the gaps between sociological theory and the fields of social procedure. Harold W. Saunders—continued or cumulated, rigorous empirical research informed by integrated middle' range theory; with constant application to constant vital areas. Llewelyn Grass—the methodology of theory construction, integration of theory and empirical research. Milton J. Yinger—theoretically guided and oriented research. Not random research or unchecked theory. Albert Reiss—codification and design of research in accord with axiomatic theory. Robert E. L. Faris—no main emphasis, but continuation of research, toolmaking and relating the findings. Experimental methods will probably be somewhat emphasized where possible. Ernest Mowrer

—more precise development of technique for obtaining data. F. Stuart Chapin—improvement in the scientific character of (1) collection of observations of social behavior, (2) the valid analyses and interpretation of such sociological data. Joseph K. Balogh—scientific objectivity toward sociology as a science. George Lundberg—continuance of present trend (1) empirical, quantitative, experimental methods; (2) intensive study rather than world surveys; (3) the natural scientific attitude. Howard Rowland—better quality, less quantity and a better integration of theory and research. Guy Johnson—advance on a broad front toward becoming a science of society, not putting all methodological eggs in one basket. However, says William T. Goode, "Each man ought to stick to one subject long enough to create a genuine break-through." He says, "The sociology of . . . is interested as a preliminary but after that we have to get to work and begin finding out something that is not known to everyone."

In all these we see a marked growth toward clarifying the direction and centralization of research toward the building of a science of sociology, which has resulted from over half a century of pioneering in specific areas, and which has resulted in the development of concepts and techniques necessary for its growth toward a more effective and useful phase of life.

A third group has emphasized the place of sociology by illustrating the wide scope of applied sociology. Bruce Melvin—take its place in international situations. Newhill N. Puckett—the sociology of international relations. T. Lynn Smith—develop a genuine natural history of society with emphasis on basic units of observation and recognition types and classes of social phenomenon. William C. Bradbury—we should escape the provincialism of almost purely American studies and look for sociological principles applicable to other complex societies. Florian Znaneicki—a world-wide comparative study of the various types of international cooperation which has been going on since the end of the nineteenth century. W. B. Brookover—intergroup and international relations; cross-cultural studies and the function of education in both domestic and international change. Wayne C. Neely—sociology of international relations. John F. Schmitt—social psychology of the interaction of human beings. Charles R. Hoffer—increased emphasis on the sociology of social action. Charles B. Spalding—social evaluation. Fred L. Strodtbeck—we must teach sociology as a scientific discipline, tendency now to confuse sociology with an ideal position. Our main objective is to sell sociology over a wide front and no delimited emphasis will serve this purpose. Milton W. Gordan—study of important problems such as war, over population, race, mental health, family. Merton D. Oyler—recruit broadly trained graduates for professional training in sociology specialities. Judson Landis—sociology of child development and mental health. Carl A. Nissen—the effect of differential social class origin. Louis M. Killian—dynamics of social control, power structures, political sociology, collective behavior. W. Wallace Weaver—social change and social stability. Arnold W. Green —chart the course of contemporary social trends. Leslie D. Zeleny— the sociology of small groups, regional sociology, sociology of peace. Joel B. Montague—research on society-wide problems, i.e. social institutions, social organization, communication. Arthur Hillmann—closer relation and understanding with other professional groups; and W. M. Banksett —group dynamics in view of Supreme Court ruling on segregation. Rudolf Heberle—changes in the structure of Western society. Morton King—vigorous objectivity, consistent development of basic conceptual and methodological functions of sociological research and analysis. Robert Birstedt—integration of the knowledge we now possess and the application of this knowledge. L. J. Carr—development and verification of systematic concepts for observation and analysis of human association. Millard Jordan—how society may adjust to the frequent and marked changes. F. H. Barnett—training sociologists to work with doctors, lawyers, and in government agencies. Donald Stewart—practical application of the findings of basic research in current social problems—too much of what is being done now is preceding in a social vacuum. Lee M. Brooks—communication, demography, race relations. Lowry Nelson—problem of communication. Arnold M. Rose—research that is more oriented to the solution of social problems. Charles H. Page—the restoration of interest in the study of social change; sharp evaluation of research efforts, many of which I suspect are worth little, sociologically or socially. W. Arthur Shirey—more research and application to the solution of pressing social problems. T. Earle Sweeney—research on social problems with more emphasis on social problems and social adjustment. Leonard Z. Breen—the reorganization and redirection of research. James A. Davisk—emphasis on the range of variation in normal families, groups, institutions, and communities rather than merely exotics and deviates. Inter-disciplinary integration. E. K. Francis—consolidation, evaluation and utilization of the tremendous store of factual knowledge collected in the last two decades.

Finally, the application of sociological theory to other areas and groups. Attention is directed to the shortcomings of sociologists in directing other fields of the contributions of sociology to all fields of human endeavor. William L. Kolb—renewal of the relationship between sociology and humanities, community research and value theory. Donald L. Taylor—sociologists must learn to be clinicians and social engineers. Bernard Stern—adaptation of social change and principles in present structure. C. K. Yang—development of sociological principles—so that sociology can be applied to broader issues of our times. M. F. Nimkoff—search for additional principles of social inter-action. Walter A. Friedlander—contribution of sociology to the related disciplines. J. Howell Atwood—integrative studies with attempts to bridge the gulf between the several social sciences. Verne Wright—methodological improvements, inter-disciplinary activity, influence of applied theory and professional positions in the community. W. Rex Crawford—synthesis, application to various areas of the globe. John P. Gillin—more attention to cross-cultural verifications of generalizations. James W. Gladden—preparation of professional sociologists, more gen-eral theory, better designed research. Atlee L. Stroup—development of a body of integrated knowledge and of making practical applications. Alfred Sheets—being scientific is no excuse for not developing more application for life's problems. We should be more useful to society than in the past. Otis T. Duncan—more application to human relations in industry, urban development, population shifts, conflicts and assimi-lation of heterogeneous groups. J. L. Hypes—seek values upon which informed men will agree, cooperate with other professions and disci-plines. Fred Cottrell—techniques for predicting the emergence of new values and their putative consequences. Further development showing relationship between mergence, science, technology and social conflicts. James Reinhart—human relations, emerging obligations, social control. Fay B. Karpf—research along broad, integrated sociocultural lines. Harry E. Moore—social psychology, better social integration with emphasis on the mechanism of communication. H. A. Phelps—small scale observational research reported in simple English. Edward Schuler—learn to communicate more effectively with the influential segments of our society. Lorren S. Woolston—while research and theory are of great importance, the main emphasis should be placed upon spelling out in lay terms the useful materials and generalizations in daily human relations. Charles E. Lively—definitely moving in the direction of greater application and practical utility. Paul F. Cresse—a better analysis of the very phenomenon of social change—escaping from the cliches "cultural lag" and similar terms. O. Pierce—comparative culture of civilized peoples. S. C. Newman—continued and increased rapport with neighboring fields. N. J. Demerath,—attracting more and better students and increasing vigorous and useful attack on problems of innovation, conformity, culture contact, and world order. H. C. Brearley—the adjustment of individuals to society and his relationship to the changing culture. R. A. Schermerhorn feels that the problem ahead is to inform the public of the findings of sociology in terms that they can understand.

CONCLUSION

Sociological thinking bears a direct relationship to social trends. In turn the individual develops in a specific manner because of the culture within which he lives. When new situations arise, he meets the needs of the times by applying his past experience and knowledge and combining it with such understanding as he may derive from the new situation. This gives rise to new efforts, procedures, and principles which prepare each generation for the next social episode.

During the nineteenth century there arose increased interest in the natural sciences. This began to be combined with two other areas which had already reached a high level of development;—namely, philosophy and statistics. As was true in many areas, even in literature and music, the great interest in the natural sciences was reflected in the social sciences. They were particularly effected by the general inquiry and unrest. Social changes occuring in the first quarter of the nineteenth century developed a new approach to history, as found in the writings of Karl F. Eichhorn, Barthold S. Neibuhr, and Frederich Karl von Savigny, Aldolphe Quetelet Guerry de Champneuf, Aguste Comte, Herbert Spencer, and Albert Shaeffle. These are names we associate with pioneering in the European background of early trends in sociology which in the United States reached a new level in the works of Ward, Giddings, Sumner, Howard, and Small.

Sociology began to emerge as a distinct discipline and a place was made for it in American colleges and universities. Changing conditions and new interests brought a re-alignment of emphasis and often even new fields of study. New activities, general and professional, began to appear. As the social structure of the entire world began to change, the need for a wider application of the principles and concepts of sociology arose. Not only were studies in the general fields of group behavior, particularly rural and urban groups, undertaken; but social work, social reform movements and community surveys, and social psychology with its many variations began to be emphasized.

When the first flush of interest in immediate situations was over, the development of the new trend tended to settle down to tactical consideration of the particular problem, and to a re-consideration and re-evaluation of the underlying principles of human relations which was of a more over-all—may we say strategic nature.

The general scope of sociology and the formation of accepted concepts and vocabulary were becoming established. Text books and all kinds of books, magazines, the newspapers, and public usage began to follow an established pattern of expression and understanding. The further expansion of mass communication and transportation, together with changes in our entire industrial, political and social systems, brought need for re-evaluation and refinement of sociological concepts.

A transitional period always gives rise to some confusion. The introduction of new concepts and the discussion of various conceptual modifications led to confusion among persons who had accepted a previous pattern of explanation as final. It became a hackneyed joke—that "sociology was a subject which dealt with what one knew told in language one could not understand." Sociology is a dynamic subject. Even students of sociology who mistook what they had learned as final, without recognizing the changing scene, became confused by a new evaluation of what they preferred to consider settled. Others following a new trend were sometimes led to believe it was the main course and over-emphasized the significance of their findings. A careful backward look helps us to see the main line of development. A surveyor needs to sight back over the earlier interval markings in order to avoid a wasteful diversion. By what men have done, we learn what man can do.

Long range prophecy is rash, but the sociologists by recognizing and determining the scope and characteristics of social processes and the effect of their inter-relationship may establish principles which will enable persons familiar with these procedures to meet crises and to make social adjustment as the need arises. A physician cannot prophesy the frequency nor the nature of the next epidemic, but his knowledge of basic causes and means of control can enable him to meet an emergency.

INDEX

Collective behavior, 20, 216; effort, 15; mind, 15
Communication and interests, 100
Community, the, 162, 210; organization, 143
Comte, Auguste, 3, 4, 5, 6, 7
Concepts, 156, 175; growth of new, 101; influence on writing, 194
Condorcet, Marie Jean Antoine, 3, 68
Conflict, 9, 209
Confusions, 1
Cook, Lloyd Allan, 201, 220
Cooley, Charles Horton, 27, 35, 36, 37, 38, 173-174, 226
Corey, Lewis, 233
Cort, Stanton, 144
Cottrell, Fred, 247
Cottrell, W. F., 233
Conring, Herman, 66, 69
Craig, J., 67
Crawford, Fred R., 243
Crawford, W. Rex, 212, 247
Cressey, Paul F., 198, 120, 218, 247
Crime, 213
Criminology, 94, 95
Croxton, Fred, 122
Cuber, John F., 169-171, 205, 212, 221, 236, 243
Cumulative change, 91
Culture, 218
Culture and sociology, 92
Curtis, George W., 140
Curtis, Jack H., 242

Davie, Maurice, 201, 210, 220, 242
Davies, George, 97
Davis, James A., 246
Davis, Jerome, 199
Davis, Kingsley, 201, 230, 234
Davis, Michael, 42, 43, 60
De Grange, 197, 198
De Moivre, Abraham, 67
De Montmort, P. Remond, 67
De Witt, Jan, 67, 69
De Wors, Richard, 244
Dealey, James Quayle, 58
Delinquency, 213
Delinquents, 140
Demerath, N. J., 247
Detmiller, Frederich E., 199
Devine, Edward T., 137
Dewey, John, 34, 108
Diana, Lewis, 243
Disorganization, 219
Dodd, Stuart C., 243
Dollard, John, 221
Dow, Grove S., 159
Duffy, Francis J., 243
Dugdale, Richard L., 141
Duncan, Otis D., 244, 247
Dunham, H. Warren, 242

Durkheim, E., 60
Dutton, S. P., 108
Dynes, Russel, R., 244

Early teachers, 44
Education, and sociology, 108-116, 220
Educational sociology, 109
Edwards, Lyford E., 120
Edwards, L. P., 202
Eichhorn, 4
Eldridge, Seba, 207, 221
Eliot, Samuel, 140
Eliot, T. D., 214
Elliott, Mable A., 169, 213
Ellwood, 27, 87
Ellwood, Charles Abram, 34-36, 111
Elmer, Glaister A., 239, 252
Elmer, M. C., 27, 74, 220
Elmore, Andrew E., 140
Elvius, Peter, 67
Emerging sociology, 10
Emig, A. S., 198
Emotional adjustment, 217
Emphasis of sociology, 196
Error in sampling, 132
Ethics and sociology, 57
Eubank, Earle E., 25, 159, 160
European sociologists, 3

Fairchild, Henry Pratt, 105-6
Family, the, 204
Fargo, North Dakota, 97
Faris, Ellsworth, 120, 121, 216
Faris, Robert E. L., 21, 214, 218
Feeble-minded, 140
Feldman, Herman, 188
Ferguson, Adam, 133
Fermat, Pierre de, 67
Finney, Ross L., 110, 230
Fitch, S. A., 74
Folk sociology, 81
Folsom, Joseph K., 205, 210
Form, W. H., 233
Fourier, Jean Baptiste Joseph, 68
Frame, Nat, 96
Francis, E. K., 246
Frank, Laurence, 180
Franklin, Benjamin, 67
Frazier, E. Franklin, 118, 120
Freeman, Linton C., 243
Freund, Ernest, 149
Fridel, F. J., 218
Friedlander, Walter A., 247
Fuller, R. C., 138
Furfey, Paul H., 215, 225
Future of sociology, 117

Galpin, C. J., 91, 96
Garwood, L. S., 214, 219
Geddes, Patrick, 89, 90
Gehlke, C. E., 219
General principles in 1942, 197

Giddings, Franklin H., 2, 16-21, 60, 73, 87, 131, 135, 136; view of sociology, 18-21
Gillette, John M., 46, 47, 112, 209
Gillin, John L., 27, 91-94
Gillin, John P., 247
Gist, N. P., 210, 217, 221
Givins, Meredith B., 185
Gladden, James W., 247
Goddard, Henry H., 141
Goethe, 5
Good, Alvin, 205, 221
Goode, William T., 244
Goodsell, Willystine, 205
Goodwin, Frank, 214
Gordon, Milton W., 245
Gow Jr., James Steele, 126
Grant, Madison, 200
Graunt, John, 66, 69
Grass, Llewelyn, 244
Green, Arnold W., 246
Group concept, 51
Group dynamics, 133
Growth of scientific method, 128
Guerry, Andre Michel, 68, 70
Gumplowicz, Ludwig, 3, 8, 9, 22

Hall, G. Stanley, 216
Halley, Edmond, 67, 69
Hamilton, Alice, 178
Hammurabi, 1
Hankins, Frank H., 21, 101-103, 197, 200
Harper, E. B., 207
Harris, T. L., 209, 214, 221
Harris, William T., 108
Harrison, Shelby, 28, 84, 85, 122, 178
Hart, Hastings H., 141
Hart, Hornell, 125, 179, 205
Hart, Joseph, K., 110
Hatt, Paul K., 191, 235
Hauser, P. M., 243
Hayes, Edward Cary, 16, 55-57, 87, 179
Hayner, Norman S., 199
Heberle, Rudolf, 246
Heinmiller, W. H., 205
Henderson, Charles R., 28, 34, 44, 73, 88-89, 137, 148
Henderson, David, 106
Henderson, L. J., 134
Hertzler, Joyce O., 178, 208
High school sociology, 112, 113-116
Hightower, Raymond L., 205, 221
Hiller, E. T., 120, 243
Hillman, Arthur, 246
Hobhouse, Leonard T., 34, 89
Hoffer, Charles R., 179, 198, 206, 212
Hoffman, Frederick L., 148
Hogg, Margaret, 132
Holden, R. P., 208
Hollingshead, A. B., 243

Hoover, Herbert, 177
Howard, George Elliott, 58, 59, 63, 87
Howe, Samuel Gridley, 141
House, Floyd N., 165, 243
Hsun, Tzu, 226
Hughes, Everett, 201
Human ecology, 76, 77
Human society, 20
Hunt, Edward Eyre, 178
Hunter, Robert, 2
Hurlin, Ralph, 185
Huygens, Christian, 67
Hypes, J. L., 199, 247

Ideals and social control, 59
Institutions, 181
Industrial action, 51; sociology, 221, 231
Insane, 140
Institutionalized exploitation, 31
Integration, 226
International society, 59

Jahoda, Dr., 168
James, William, 216
Jenks, Jerimiah W., 34, 105
Jennings, Helen, 133
Jocher, Kathrine, 207
Johnson, Charles S., 228, 229
Johnson, Guy B., 189, 201, 220, 245
Jones, D. Caradog, 108
Jordan, Willard, 246
Journal Educational Sociology, 175, 193
Judd, Charles H., 178

Kant, Immanuel, 3
Karpf, Kay B., 247
Kawabe, Kisaburo, 120
Keller, Albert G., 158, 179
Kellogg, Paul U., 28, 74
Kelly, Florence, 143
Kenkel, William F., 236, 244
Killian, Louis M., 246
King, Gregory, 67
King, Morton, 246
Kingsley, Charles, 21
Kirkpatrick, Clifford, 206, 207
Kirkpatrick, Edwin A., 109
Kiser, Clyde V., 132
Kline, Phillip, 122
Kolb, J. H., 75, 190, 242
Kolb, William L., 246
Komarovsky, Mirra, 204

Laissez-faire of Spencer, 8
Landis, Judson, 246
Landis, Paul H., 201, 214
Laotze, 1
La Piere, Richard T., 230
Laplace, Pierre Simon, 68
Larrovitch, Feodor Vladimir, 17
Laski, Harold, 134

Lasswell, Thomas E., 244
Lathrop, Julia C., 143
Lavoisier, Antoine Laurent, 68
Lazarus, Moritz, 60
Lee, Alfred McClung, 167-169, 214, 217, 231, 242
Leibnitz, Gottfried Wilhelm, 67
Lejins, Peter P., 244
Letchworth, William Pryor, 141
Lewes, George Henry, 60
Lewin, Kurt, 132, 133
Lichtenberger, J. P., 21
Lieber, Francis, 71
Lend, Andrew W., 201, 217
Lindesmith, H. R., 209
Lindstrom, David E., 192
Linton, Ralph, 167
Lippert, Julius, 8, 22
Lippitt, Ronald, 133
Lipset, Seymour Martin, 233, 239
Lively, Charles E., 191, 199, 209, 215, 247
Locke, Alain, 201
Loomis, Charles, P., 243
Lovejoy, Owen R., 143
Low, J. A., 233
Lulle, Ramon, 66
Lumley, F. E., 215, 229
Lundberg, George, 97, 126-128, 193, 197, 245
Lunden, W. A., 244

MacIver, Robert M., 162, 206
MacLean, Annie Marion, 24
Malthus, Thomas, 200
Mangus, A. R., 244
Margold, Charles W., 120
Mark, Louise, 122
Martindale, Don, 173
Mayo, Elton, 134, 233
Mayo-Smith, Richmond, 2, 72, 73, 87, 200
McClennahan, Bessie A., 122
McCormick, Thomas E., 201, 212, 215
McDougall, William, 60, 216
McKain, Walter C., 191
McKenzie, Roderick D., 25, 28, 75-76, 117, 178, 187
McGraw-Hill Book Company, 178
McMinn, Gerald W., 209
Meade, George H., 34
Meadows, Paul, 233
Mehus, O. Myking, 97
Melvin, Bruce, 245
Merriam, Charles E., 178
Merton, Robert, 171-173, 223, 244
Miller, D. C., 233
Mills, J. S., 21
Mitchell, Wesley C., 178
Monachesi, E., 173
Montague, Joel B., 246

Moore, F. W., 8
Moore, Harry E., 247
Moore, W. E., 233
Morgan, E. L., 96
Morgan, Lewis H., 193
Moreno, J. L., 133
Mowrer, Ernest, 120, 244
"Muckrakers," 87
Muenster, Sebastian, 66, 68
Munch, Peter A., 242
Muntz, Earl E., 199, 210
Murdock, George P., 198, 212
Muret, J. L., 68
Mumford, Louis, 89

Need for interpretation data, 10
Neely, Wayne C., 244
Nelson, Lowry, 210, 217, 246
Neibuhr, 4
Neuman, Kasper, 67, 69
Neumann, Henry, 57
Neumeyer, Martin H., 208
New areas, 87; interests, 100
Newcomb, T. M., 243
Newman, S. C., 247
Newstetter, Wilber I., 134
Nimkoff, M. F., 123, 207, 212, 247
Nissen, Carl A., 202, 210, 214, 246
North, Cecil C., 178, 208
Nottingham, Elizabeth, 198, 218

Objectives being formulated, 195-196
Odum, Howard W., 16, 81-82, 178, 211-212
Ogburn, William Fielding, 44, 117, 123, 124, 177, 178, 183, 208
Ohlin, Lloyd E., 243
Organization, 219
O'Shea, M. V., 109
Owen, Robert, 5, 23
Oyler, Merton D., 245

Page, Charles H., 246
Panunzio, Constantine, 201
Pareto, Vilfredo, 41
Park, Robert E., 27, 119-120
Parks, Frank L., 243
Parmelee, Maurice, 49, 94
Parsons, Talcott, 56, 166-167, 237-239
Pascal, Blaise, 67
Paterson, Donald, 75
Payne, George, 110
Peabody, Francis G., 147
Personal data, the value of, 10
Peters, Charles C., 110, 215, 220
Peterson, William, 242
Petty, Sir William, 67, 158
Pfautz, Harold W., 235, 242
Phelps, Harold A., 106, 165-166, 225, 247
Phenomena, the nature of, 15
Pierce, O., 247

This book was set in Intertype Kenntonian with heads in Goudy Old Style, printed on Warren's Olde Style Antique Book Paper by the Westinghouse Valley Printing Company at Wilmerding, Pennsylvania and bound in Novelex by Russell-Rutter, N. Y., for the University of Pittsburgh Press.